Thinking and
Learning
Together

Thinking and Learning Together

Curriculum and Community in a Primary Classroom

Bobbi Fisher

HEINEMANN
Portsmouth, NH

Heinemann
A division of Reed Elsevier Inc.
361 Hanover Street
Portsmouth, NH 03801-3912
Offices and agents throughout the world

Every effort has been made to contact the copyright holders for permission to reprint borrowed material where necessary. We regret any oversights that may have occurred and would be happy to rectify them in future printings of this work.

The author and publisher wish to thank those who generously gave permission to reprint borrowed material:

"Reading" and "Spelling" from *Getting Parents Involved* (Fall 1991 and 1988). Reprinted by permission of the Whole Language Teachers Association.

Chapters 1, 2, and 6 appeared in different form in the journal *Teaching K–8* (November 1992, November 1993, September 1994, and October 1994).

Appendix A5–2 and Appendix A8–1 were reprinted by permission from *Joyful Learning: A Whole Language Kindergarten* by Bobbi Fisher (Heinemann, A division of Reed Elsevier Inc., Portsmouth, NH, 1991).

Library of Congress Cataloging-in-Publication Data

Fisher, Bobbi.
    Thinking and learning together: curriculum and community in a
primary classroom / Bobbi Fisher.
        p.   cm.
    Includes bibliographical references
    ISBN 0-435-08844-0
    1. Education, Primary.   2. Curriculum planning.   3. Language
experience approach in education.   4. Classroom environment.
I. Title.
LB1511.F57   1995   94-43728
372.24'1–dc20   CIP

Editor: Carolyn Coman
Production: Melissa L. Inglis
Text and cover design: Jenny Jensen Greenleaf
Cover photo by Liz Schreiner

Printed in the United States of America on acid-free paper
99 98 97 96 95 EB   2 3 4 5 6 7 8 9

To Debby Cornwell,
a loyal friend and dedicated teacher

CONTENTS

CONTENTS

CONTENTS

FOREWORD

I visited Bobbi's first grade one day last spring. Picture walking down a quiet corridor before school starts. Teachers go into classrooms, get ready for the day. Occasionally someone calls out a welcome. Copy machines sound out into the halls. Heels click on tiles. Then there is a silence and a detachment. And the children come in. This is a hectic time in any school. Children—especially first graders—have many needs in the morning: slips to be turned in, lunches to be put on the shelf, playground activities to be talked over with the teacher. Bobbi's room was no exception.

It was like other classrooms in the morning that I've visited. Bobbi went outside the door and into the corner to talk to students about incidents that needed to be resolved. Students came in excited, happy, sad, preoccupied, visiting with each other, and Bobbi greeted each of them. They came in carrying books, coats, lunches, notes, treasures, toys, balls, and odds and ends. Friends were holding hands. Joe came in with his new haircut and stopped traffic. They all entered with a burst of energy. The world blasting into the building; energy unleashed in a small space. "A positive caring and learning community generates from our positive ways throughout the day. It matters that we greet everyone as they come in . . . When we are positive, children are positive," Bobbi writes.

There was a difference in this room from all the schools I've ever been in. As soon as children came in, they went off to corners and tables to all sorts of activities. Right away, off to work. If I'd asked them what they were doing, I might have gotten a variety of answers. They might have said that they went to read or write or count, or to activities that they chose, or to finish things left over from yesterday, or to important works that they thought of during the night. The point is they all came in and went off to continue their own business. Independently and competently, they set about generating their own curriculum. Bobbi has called this initiative, "children as curriculum coordinators." Nobody waited for the teacher to tell them what to do. In fact, I think they might have been surprised that I had even thought of that as a possibility. They were all too busy with a multitude of things to have worried about what I expected them to do. I thought of what Michael Armstrong, in his book *Closely Observed Children: The Diary of a Primary Classroom* calls watching "moments of intellectual absorption." That's what I was seeing, school as intellectual absorption.

One little girl beside me spent quite a bit of time setting the science big book open to the page she wanted the class to think about this day on the easel. It seemed to be her self-appointed task. She worked at getting the book to stay open to that page, but it wouldn't, talking away to me the whole time until she hit on the idea of putting paper clips on each corner to keep the book open. I was amazed at the endurance of her effort, the directiveness of her planning, what Michael Armstrong calls her "seriousness of purpose—her high intent." She made me reflect on first graders' very great competence with the stuff of life in school.

When Bobbi wanted to talk to everyone, she simply began to sing. It was a song that everyone seemed to know. Students joined in the singing and gradually everyone drifted over to the rug where there began a group sharing of books, readings, and songs. Children finished what they were doing first, finding a good place to stop. There was a powerful air in the room of honoring the work in progress. No one, including Bobbi, seemed to assume that what the teacher was doing was more important than what anyone else was doing. Everyone's tasks, self-appointed or not, were equally important. I was affected by this feeling, too, and did not go immediately to the group, absorbed as I was in watching the children finish. One boy spent quite a bit of time rearranging chairs around a table. When he finally joined the group, Bobbi thanked him for all his hard work.

Bobbi respects children. It is clear in everything she does that she sees children as individuals with lives, rights, and intentions of their own. In her book, *Joyful Learning: A Whole Language Kindergarten*, Bobbi writes, "I trust children as the authorities of their own learning" (1). During my visit, I saw children engaged in activities they had selected, developed, and assessed. They plainly saw themselves as authorities on a great variety of ideas.

When two kindergartners came to read a student-made book to the class, the first graders welcomed them with respect, listening intently as one read and the other showed the pictures. The warmth and benevolence of the first-grade audience reminded me that the children return what is given to them; and so through mentoring, we present to children a vision of a respectful, coherent, and compatible life in society. Bobbi writes, "Children will rise to our expectations of the kinds of caring and learning that should go on."

In this classroom children served on committees as a way of centralizing and organizing the work and the responsibilities of the classroom. "I start with my teaching goal, which is to help the children in my classroom develop as lifelong learners in a democratic society," Bobbi writes. Establishing procedures that allow children to assume responsibility for various aspects of life in school enables them to establish ownership, choice, and pride in classroom life. Bobbi recognizes that children have minds of their own, that they come to school with many competencies and opinions. Margaret Donaldson, in *Children's Minds*, believes that " . . . teachers need to be clear [about] not only what they would like children to become under their guidance but about what children are actually like when the process is begun" (8). Children under Bobbi's guidance rest assured that she takes their lives outside the classroom into account as she does their lives in the classroom. She recognizes and helps them to strengthen their competencies.

Students in Bobbi's room created tasks for themselves, fulfilling their own purposes, taking it all very seriously. One child engaged in a long episode of counting the pencils available at one center, saying, "But I have to find out how many we have!" I was reminded that left to their own devices, empowered and endowed, children recognize the world of the classroom as an important place with important work to be done and they respond. Teachers don't make school important. In Bobbi's classroom, school *is* important.

When I think of Bobbi's classroom, I see a very special place. Margaret Donaldson visited a similar classroom and observed, " . . . a visitor to the school who knew nothing about our society might have been inclined to think he had found Utopia . . ." (3). That was how I felt, too. Entering Bobbi's classroom was like leaving my own world far behind and entering a world all of its own. I forgot where I was and was taken up by the lives of children, who also seemed to have left everyday life behind and entered into a very special place where everything they did was very special—a place where they could grow.

PAT CORDEIRO

ACKNOWLEDGMENTS

I teach at a school where teachers share with one another, celebrate each other's uniqueness and special contributions, and care deeply about each other. I am grateful for the support that this community has provided me.

Chet Delani, my principal at Haynes School, has created and fostered this environment, which we pass on to the children. He respects us as professionals and has always encouraged us in our educational journeys.

When I moved from kindergarten to first grade, Marcia Fitzgerald, Maria Papetti, and Marge Thurber—the three first-grade teachers in the building—opened their doors to me and helped me as the new kid on the block. Liz Schreiner, my aide for the last three years, unselfishly gave her time, energy, and talent to me and the children. Maureen Silva, graciously read this entire manuscript, and as a teacher new to first grade offered many helpful suggestions.

This book is written from the experiences I had with three first-grade classrooms. Although in some instances I have changed their names, each child holds a special place in my heart. Along with their parents, we created a thinking and learning classroom together.

Throughout the country I have met hundreds of dedicated teachers at conferences and workshops. I thank them all for sharing their ideas and for encouraging me to continue to write about our common goal of providing the very best classroom communities in which children can think and learn together.

There are also many friends to thank: members of the Whole Language Teachers Association steering committee; Pat Broderick, editor of *Teaching K-8;* Carolyn Coman, my editor, who continually contributed helpful suggestions, advice, and encouragement; Melissa Inglis, associate production editor; Nellie Edge, of Nellie Edge Seminars; Diane Hays, the Heinemann and Rigby representative in the Boston area; Philippa Stratton of Stenhouse Publications; and Rebel Williams of the Wright Group.

ACKNOWLEDGMENTS

I am especially grateful to Pat Cordeiro, a colleague and personal friend, who very kindly wrote the Foreword. We are always thinking and learning together.

Finally, many thanks to my family. My children Tim and Emily have always encouraged me to write and my husband Jim, my first editor, has provided steady and positive support throughout the many years that I have been sharing what I do through workshops and writing.

INTRODUCTION

The inspiration for this book's title comes from my first-grade students who over the past three years have eagerly described their classroom communities as "The Thinking Class," "The Learning Class," "The Caring Class," and "The Singing Class."

This book is all about our thinking and learning together in a caring community: how a sense of trust in each other was fostered; how the daily schedule, classroom space, and materials were organized and orderly; how I demonstrated and the children participated in shared literacy; how the children practiced and shared what they learned; how literature, reading, writing, math, science, and social studies topics were explored for authentic purposes, with the children pursuing their own interests and areas of inquiry; and how parents joined in the classroom community.

This book is written in the spirit of sharing what I do and why I do it, as one of many resources for teachers to use as they establish and maintain their own thinking and learning communities with the children. These classrooms are as unique and diverse as the teachers and children who participate in them. They are all, however, places of deep caring that reflect everyone's concern for one another and that fully support and enhance the pursuit of learning.

1

Classroom Community

"I want everyone to know what a great class we are." Erica's remark perhaps best sums up what classroom community is—the feeling of being part of a great class: hard to define, but when you are part of it, you know it.

The ingredients that make up community have been described in different ways. Ralph Peterson, in *Life in a Crowded Place* (1992) talks about the importance of ritual, rites, ceremonies, and celebrations as ways to develop community. In *The Magic of Ritual,* Tom Driver (1991) states that "rituals serve three main purposes: making and preserving order, fostering community, and effecting transformation." For me, community in the classroom is the amalgamation of rigorous learning and caring about one another. Community is built through routines, procedures, and attitudes that evolve over time as the teacher and children develop trust in one another.

Community is the entire orchestra playing in harmony, with each musician contributing his or her best to the piece. Just as the conductor is responsible for the quality of the music, we as teachers are responsible for the quality of community that develops in our classrooms. What we expect, model, and create becomes the reality. Children will rise to our expectations of the kinds of caring and learning that should go on.

This calls for a great deal of commitment and responsibility on our part, but it also allows us, as professionals, to make a positive difference in the lives of the children we teach. It requires that we read widely, talk with colleagues, attend conferences, and continually reflect on our practice because the community we establish reflects who we are as human beings and what we believe about teaching and learning. The community is continually evolving and developing.

LIVING THE LIFE OF THE CLASSROOM

The model for building community life inside the classroom is life outside the classroom. Natural learning starts in the home, as children learn to talk through bonding with their primary caregiver (usually their mother). It extends as they learn from relatives, siblings, and others with whom they come in contact. It continues in the classroom as the children bond with us, their teachers. It deepens as we share what is important in our lives during community circle and is imbedded in all our actions as we learn together and take responsibility for the classroom environment. It is brought to consciousness when we ask the children what kindness they have given and received today. It continues through smiles, thank yous, and the words, "I know how you feel."

When Ben arrived as a new student late in May, he learned most of our classroom rituals and routines by watching what the other children did, not by being told the rules. When I started singing, he followed his classmates to the rug. When his turn came to be the moderator (leader) for the day, he sat in the special chair without being told and knew how to call the groups to line up. He figured out the procedure for silent reading by watching others. He joined the first-grade club in my classroom (Smith 1988).

Cambourne's Conditions of Learning

Community is built through the conditions of natural learning, as described by Brian Cambourne. Throughout the day the teacher and children are *immersed* in an atmosphere of caring. For example, during group time, emphasis is on the *demonstration* of literacy. The teacher simultaneously demonstrates positive attitudes toward learning, which are conveyed through his *expectation* that the children can and will learn and that they will take *responsibility* to become *engaged* as they participate in or *use* literacy. Encouragement and opportunities to take risks and *approximate* are a central part of the group demonstration. *Response* is mostly given to the entire group. On the other hand, during practice time, *response* is individual and emphasis is on individual *use* as the children practice what has been demonstrated (Cambourne 1988).

Holdaway's Natural Learning Classroom Model

Holdaway (1986) applied the conditions of natural learning to the classroom setting, and his model, which includes *demonstration, participation, practice/role-play*, and *performance* helps us cultivate and sustain a positive classroom community. During whole class group times the teacher plays the dominant role as *demonstrator*. In modeling a positive attitude, she engages the children to *participate* in learning. These attitudes are then *practiced/role-played* throughout the day as the children work independently or collaboratively during writing, reading, workshop, and math. We know that learning has occurred when they ask to share or *perform* their work. The children become the *demonstrators* or teachers.

During group time (*demonstration* and *participation*) the teacher's attention is directed primarily toward the group rather than toward the individual. Children are usually not singled out as they participate. Rather, "The unison situation, properly controlled in a lively and meaningful spirit, allows for massive individual practice by every pupil in the teaching context" (Holdaway 1979, p. 129). On the other hand, during work times (*practice/role-play*), the children work on their own and with their peers. The teacher directs her attention toward individual children, and responds specifically to the child's work. Finally, when children are sharing (*performance*) they take the role of the teacher as demonstrator and lead their peers and teacher in a demonstration.

Setting the Tone

The children look to us to set the tone for caring and learning and they copy what we do. If we listen to them, they listen to each other. If we validate them and support, encourage, and celebrate what they do, they will do the same for each other. If we encourage risk taking and accept

3

approximations, they do the same for themselves and for others. If we are learners in the classroom, they become learners, too.

A positive caring and learning community generates from our positive ways throughout the day. It matters that we greet everyone as they come in, help a child pick up the crayons she has dropped, listen carefully to stories from home, read our own book during silent reading, and celebrate the piece of writing that a child has put in the sharing basket. When we are positive, the children are positive. When we demonstrate attitudes of caring along with the skills, strategies, and content of learning, we become the bonded adult (Holdaway 1986) or more expert member of the club (Smith 1988) whom the children emulate and look to for assurance that this classroom is physically, psychologically, and emotionally a safe place in which to take risks.

Getting Started

I start with my teaching goal, which is to help the children in my classroom develop as lifelong learners in a democratic society. I want us to create a democratic classroom community in which we all have responsibilities for the learning and caring environment. Although the children are involved in this process, I am the catalyst for generating this community. It just won't happen if I don't set up routines, develop expectations, and respond to specific situations in accordance with my beliefs about children and how they learn (Fisher 1991). As I do my part, the children take more and more responsibility in generating this continually developing learning and caring community.

Since caring and learning develop simultaneously (as we learn we care, and as we care we learn), I don't spend the first six weeks working on a social curriculum before introducing a content curriculum. Rather, on the first day we begin with both and we begin by doing more than by talking. We plunge into learning through the structures and routines I introduce, and as we do, opportunities for caring and discussion arise.

A week before school begins the children receive a newsletter in the mail from me (see Appendix B1–1), which welcomes them to the class and tells them several things to do when they arrive on the first day. Knowing these tasks ahead of time gives them a context for discussion with their parents about what school will be like and introduces some of the routines and procedures for the year. It eases anxiety about the first day by specifically answering the question, "What should I do when I walk into the room?"

Each task, which carries a *message* about our caring and learning community, can be carried out successfully by every child. My role is to greet everyone and, as necessary, help them get started with their tasks. I find that after a few children get going, they are able to assist the others. Some of the tasks I suggest are:

- Hang up your coat and school bag. Message: Please come in and stay; you have a place for your belongings in this room.
- Sign in. Message: I believe that you can write your name; you are important as an individual; I want to get to know you (see Photo 1-1).
- Find your writing folder at your place at the tables. Message: You are a writer; writing is important in this classroom; you are responsible for your own work.
- Take your favorite book to the student teacher. Message: You are a reader; your choice of books is important; the adults in the room want to know your interests.
- Look around the room. Message: You are free to move about the classroom; there are interesting things going on here.
- Find the note in your mailbox and put it in your bag to take home. Message: I'm interested in what you want to tell me; when you write me, I'll write you back.
- Talk with your classmates. Message: Friends are important; talk is important; we will be thinking and learning together in this class.
- When I start singing, come to the rug area. Message: You are important as a group member; we will be doing a lot of singing.

As much as possible, I try to follow a typical daily schedule on the first day (Fisher 1993). The children are eager to get going and so am I. An authentic learning and caring community can be established only in the normal setting in which the community will flourish. We aren't warming up or practicing. The year has actually begun.

PHOTO 1-1 *Signing in*

LISTENING, TALKING, AND RESPONDING

Community is built by the way we listen and talk to one another. Caring people listen. For me, the essence of listening is being involved with the other person, both verbally and nonverbally. When we listen we usually look at the person, react to what the person has said, and ask questions. We also nod our heads, smile or frown, and perhaps pat someone on the shoulder. There are many combinations of verbal and nonverbal responses and usually they are so natural and automatic that we aren't conscious of them. However, it is important for us to be aware of the different ways that we respond because some of the traditional teacher responses do not support the learners in a classroom.

For example, praising one child's academic success in front of the group can diminish the confidence of the other members and separate the "successful" child from the community. If I tell David that he is a

6

great artist, some may infer that they are not good artists. On the other hand, if I tell all the children that they are great artists, the comment becomes worthless. A more successful approach would be to talk to David about his art work while he is drawing. I might tell him what I notice about his work and ask him to tell me how he drew a particular figure. Teachers support their students' growth when they show interest and encouragement, rather than when they give personal value judgments (Kohn 1993).

Group Time

During shared literacy teacher responses are most effective when directed toward the group rather than the individual because they encourage group participation. I don't praise or evaluate a child's comment or answer to a question, but usually acknowledge the response by nodding my head or by saying, "Yes." Often the children are responding together, and as Holdaway suggests, the shared reading format encourages children to respond individually, "in union." At these times they are not listening to each other but are responding or "talking to themselves."

Knowing when to use these two different kinds of participation can be difficult for children unless there are signals for them indicating which kind of response is appropriate. Usually the signals are subtle. My tone of voice invites everyone to respond or I might use a one word cue such as "Everyone" with an uplifting intonation that opens up conversation rather than closes it down. Nonverbal communication such as nodding my head or moving my hand are also ways I encourage group participation.

When I want one person to talk at a time, I usually put up my hand as a signal, accompanied by the word, "Hands." Occasionally I remind the children that the reason that one person will be talking at a time is so we can *all* hear what that person has to say. For example, when Caroline is speaking, she is speaking to all of us, not just to me.

Individual Time

Most of my responses during settling-in time, when the children first arrive in the classroom, are individualized. I make sure that I briefly acknowledge everyone by name during that first twenty minutes. I might listen to Lynn's story about moving into her new house, talk with Brian about the wasps' nest he has brought and is putting on a display tray, or listen to Jane tell about the robins hatching in her backyard.

When I confer with children during writing, workshop, and reading, I respond by validating, acknowledging, and commenting on the content of their work and what they tell me. I try to refrain from giving any value judgments. There is a big difference between the response, "The way you started your story made me want to keep reading" and "I like the way you started your story." Both responses are positive; but when I say what I like, I convey that what is important is that the child should keep trying to please me and figure out what I want. This takes ownership of the creative process away from the child.

RISK TAKING AND APPROXIMATING

Community is built in an atmosphere in which both the children and teacher understand that risk taking and approximating are essential for growth in learning. When we look at children learning to talk through the conditions of natural learning, we can see the necessity of approximations. We would never expect an eighteen-month-old baby to speak with conventional syntax, pronunciation, and meaning. Similarly, as adults, learning the computer for example, we approximate and try things out as we begin to catch on to the rudiments of word processing, and we continue to approximate as we tackle more complicated programs. Although we may strive for mastery, we will never reach it, because there is always something else to learn and approximating will always be a part of the learning process.

Recently educators have come to understand that in order for learning to occur, children must feel free to approximate and be willing to take risks, have a go, and give something a try. Current teaching and evaluation procedures reflect attitudes, responses, and routines that foster a learning community grounded in risk taking and approximating. We create an atmosphere in which we all know that we learn by making mistakes; in which we won't be laughed at or put down for trying; in which competition is not part of the learning and caring environment.

The following classroom examples illustrate the point:

- When I ask for the children's predictions of what a new story might be about, I receive each response with an acknowledgment. I don't respond to one child with "Yes" and another child with "What a great idea, you are so creative."
- I call on children who want to take a risk and respond, rather than try to catch them so they will pay attention. Taking a risk is a choice that only the learner can make.
- When children answer incorrectly, I try to respond in ways that validate their efforts, give them some accurate information, and encourage them to keep trying. For example, if we are listing animals in the cat family and a child says snake, I might say, "If we were listing reptiles, that would be a good example."
- Throughout the day there are numerous opportunities for the children to work and learn together. There is an expectation that children will help each other and that working together is beneficial to everyone. For example, they read the morning clipboard together to figure out what to do, ask each other how to spell words, share their writing, and practice reading together.

A LEARNER WHO TEACHES

Community develops when we as teachers believe that we are also learners in the classroom and when we let the children see us in this role (Cordeiro 1992b). I tell them about my interests and hobbies and share books and personal stories. I told them about my trip to Colorado Springs and brought them each a piece of fool's gold. As they come in from lunch and get their books for silent reading, they see me reading the current book I have brought from home. When we write in our reading response journals, I share along with the students.

I also want the children to see me as a risk taker, learning from my mistakes and approximations. This gives them permission to give something a try. During shared reading, if I point to the wrong word, I acknowledge my mistake, and then go on with the self-correction. If I make a mistake while writing in front of the class, I cross it out, and go on with the task. I don't dwell on the miscues, but treat them as normal occurrences in learning.

If we want children to be engaged in learning, we must give them the responsibility for managing many of their own classroom routines; and if we expect them to develop as responsible citizens in a democratic society, we must provide opportunities for them to participate in the daily decision making of classroom life. My belief is that democracy isn't first learned from a civics book in high school, but it is learned by living it in our lives from the time we are very young. When children experience it as part of the life of the classroom, they will develop a deeper and more practical understanding of how it works. The democratic principles of inclusivity, equity, and respect for all are supported through the conditions of natural learning.

DEMOCRACY IN THE CLASSROOM

In my classroom we have established some democratic practices and procedures, modeled after our town government, that enable everyone to participate actively in our classroom government. They include active committee work, leadership by a student moderator, and regular class meetings. Everyone is on a committee, the leader for the day is called the moderator, and about twice a month we have a class meeting to discuss classroom issues.

The Committees

The class is divided into five committees or teams: math, reading, science, trips (social studies), and writing, which represent our major disciplines of learning. Membership on a committee lasts for about eight weeks and during that time committee tables serve as the main office or seating for the members. Each table is located near the shelves that hold the supplies for its discipline and a bulletin board, which displays related news and topic projects. A plastic file box holding the children's writing and workshop folders and a committee clipboard listing daily jobs and committee members, are kept on each table.

Committee Jobs

Each day when the children arrive, one of their tasks is to check the committee clipboard and perform any committee work necessary to get ready for the day (see Photo 1–2). For example, the math committee prepares an estimating project for the class, the reading committee checks their list and notifies the class reader for the day, the science committee plans a class observation, the trips committee adds post-cards to our bulletin board, and the writing committee changes the date on the chalkboard and date stamps. I underline the tasks that need to be done and add any other special jobs for the day (see Figure 1–1).

In September

When the children arrive on the first day, they find their name card on the committee table assigned to them. My only requirement at this point is to create a balance of boys and girls. When we subsequently change committees throughout the year, the children have some choice in assignments. Also, although they often work at their committee tables, they have many opportunities to choose other places to sit throughout the day.

A few weeks into the school year, at our first class meeting, we brainstorm a list of different jobs that each committee could perform to help our classroom run smoothly and efficiently. I then meet with each committee to generate a list of specific jobs that the members are willing to perform and print copies of the list to go on the clipboard so the children have a reminder of their various jobs.

Committee Jobs

Math Committee
1. Food Pantry
2. Estimating project
3. Box math
4. Announcing the groups

Reading Committee
1. Organize class reader
2. Put dots on books

PHOTO 1-2 *Checking committee clipboard*

3. Take books back to the library
4. Organize books on book shelf

Science Committee
1. Organize weekly observation
2. Straighten science books
3. Organize displays on science table
4. Water plants

Trips Committee
1. Postcard project
2. Trivia question
3. Pass out passports
4. Straighten the area
5. Recycle the recyclable paper

12

Tuesday
10/26

Science Committee Jobs

1. Observation – Has everyone done the acorn?

2. Straighten science books

3. Organize displays on science table

4. Tana Hoban project. Did someone bring in an apple?

5. Arrange science bulletin board

6. Pick a new observation for tomorrow.

FIGURE 1-1 *Science committee clipboard with underlined tasks*

Writing Committee
1. Change the date on the board
2. Change the date stamp
3. Empty the pencil sharpener
4. Clear sharing board
5. Straighten writing shelves
6. Check floors
7. Clap erasers

At a subsequent class meeting, I introduce the concept of a daily committee monitor. The responsibilities of the monitor are to oversee that the jobs are done, see that the table is cleared at various specified times throughout the day, pass out papers when needed, and perform any special tasks assigned to the committee.

Committees Throughout the Year

One way to keep the work and goals of the committees alive is to change the committee membership from time to time. We do this about

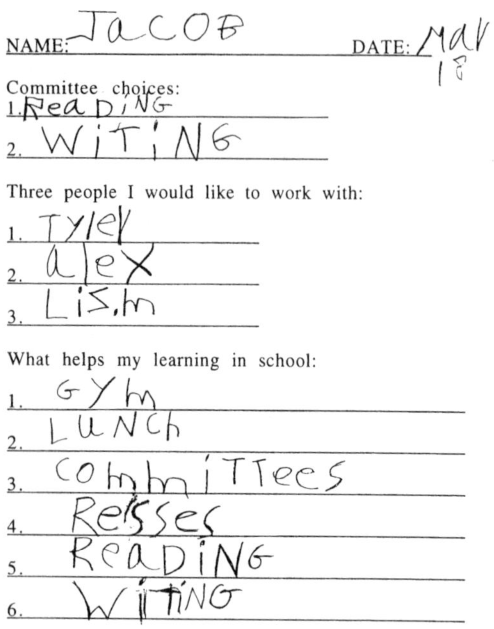

NAME: Jacob   DATE: May 18

Committee choices:
1. Reading
2. Witing

Three people I would like to work with:
1. Tyler
2. alex
3. Lis,m

What helps my learning in school:
1. Gym
2. Lunch
3. Committees
4. Reisses
5. Reading
6. Witing

FIGURE 1-2 *Committee choices form*

five times a year or about every eight weeks. The children write down their first two committee choices and I decide on the final membership, which is usually five children per committee, depending on the size of the class. Sometimes they write their choices on a piece of paper. Other times I ask them to fill out a printed form to give me more information as I make up the committees (see Figure 1-2). This form asks for committee choices, three classmates with whom they would like to work, and what is helping their learning in school at the moment (see Appendix A1-1).

Although I try to honor the children's first choices, I find that our classroom community is more cohesive if, as the adult in the classroom, I have some control over the committee assignments. I don't want children competing for places, excluding classmates, and hurting each other's feelings as they vie for places near close friends. It is important for boys and girls to work together and for children to work with different individuals, groups of children, and committees throughout the year and to know that they have a special place to call their own for an extended length of time.

PHOTO 1-3 *Bulletin board with postcards*

Each time we change committees, the new members meet to re-view the jobs and decide on the order of the monitors. Some of the jobs are standard throughout the year, such as emptying the pencil sharp-ener, watering plants, and recycling paper. Other jobs change with the curriculum. For example, the postcard project (we tried to get postcards from every state and displayed them on a bulletin board), which the trips committee managed, only lasted a few months (see Photo 1–3), while food brought in for the food pantry was tallied by the math com-mittee at the beginning of each month throughout the year (see Photo 1–4). Jobs that weren't necessary or current were taken off the list and new jobs were added.

As the year goes on the children are able to take more and more re-sponsibility for managing their committee meetings, and I assume a less active role. For example, by the third committee change in December

PHOTO 1-4 *Tallying items for the food pantry*

the children were able to meet without me to make the necessary committee changes. They transferred their writing and workshop folders to their new tables and agreed on the seating arrangement they wanted. They met to reevaluate the committee jobs and decided upon the order for the daily monitors, giving me a revised list to print up. For the order of monitors, each committee used some form of alphabetical order; three groups by first name, one used last name, and one used the last letter of the first name.

The Moderator

The job of class moderator rotates alphabetically by first name and changes daily. The moderator performs many of the jobs traditionally assigned to the leader of the day, such as recording the lunch count and attendance and taking it to the office, leading the pledge, feeding any animals we have in the classroom, and getting things for the teacher. But in my class the moderator also has specific leadership responsibilities, such as checking the room after cleanup, calling children to line up before leading them to specialists, leading daily sharing time, and calling on people to speak at class meeting.

During group time the moderator sits in a special chair and acts as the class messenger. She gets me a pencil, piece of paper, or a book if I need it and sometimes calls on children as they volunteer to respond to a text. The moderator also keeps track of the different things we do during shared literacy, by keeping a tally of the number of books and poems we read, songs we sing, phonics, spelling, writing, counting, and math opportunities (see Appendix A1–2). This helps us to be conscious of our different learning opportunities and alerts us when we haven't focused on a specific area during the day. For example, Jane reminded us that we weren't reading enough poems.

Class Meeting

Our class has a weekly class meeting, during which we talk about ways to create and sustain a positive classroom community and discuss problems. I developed many of these procedures through my participation in a year-long social competency program, "Reach Out to Schools: Social Competency Program" (Seigle & Macklem 1993).

We sit on chairs in a circle in order to distinguish the meeting from the other group times when we gather and sit on the rug. I sit by the easel so I can record the important points of the meeting and write any rules we establish, which we post in the room so we can review them throughout the year and refer to them when a problem arises. Someone volunteers to take minutes by copying what I have written and adding their own notes as well. These minutes are then posted in the room. The moderator helps run the meeting by calling on people to speak and asking questions of the group (see Photo 1–5).

Class meeting is divided into two parts, although often the two overlap. First we discuss a topic that focuses on positive ways of working and playing together. Then we concentrate on a specific school-related problem that we need to solve so that our classroom will be a positive living and learning environment for everybody. Some of our most successful topics focused on how to be a good listener, what

PHOTO 1–5 *Class meeting*

makes a good leader, the differences between tattling and reporting something dangerous or destructive, negotiable and nonnegotiable rules, and ways to solve one's own problems.

Specific School Problems

I find that addressing problems formally in a class meeting helps us all to focus on the issue, take ownership of the problem, and be part of the solution. The procedure is just as important for me as for the children, because it enables me to listen to their ideas and solutions.

We choose topics in several ways. We keep a suggestion box in the meeting area and add our written suggestions as issues arise. At the beginning of class meeting we read them over and decide what to discuss. Sometimes I bring up a topic that needs addressing or one of the children raises an area of concern. Other times we brainstorm a list of topics and then pick one to discuss. Topics have included lining up, walking in the halls, sharing colored pencils, following rules for tag at recess, and including classmates during work and play.

Brainstorming List for Class Meeting Topics

1. Fighting outside
2. Pushing outside
3. Arguments with friends
4. Bumping and getting hurt
5. Making teams at recess
6. Playing with people in other classes
7. Pushing inside
8. Sharing books
9. Bumping and running in the hall
10. Kicking
11. Poking
12. Teasing when someone makes a mistake
13. Moving chairs safely and quietly
14. Fighting over things

One of the important procedures we use to discuss specific school-related issues is called Talking the Problem, which includes seven steps that are posted on a chart (see Photo 1–6). Usually I initiate the first Talking the Problem in September to familiarize the children with the procedure. For example, at the beginning of the year I noticed that during group children were sitting up on their legs so that those behind them couldn't always see. I was hearing frequent whispered comments such as, "Sit down," "Sit on your butt," "I can't see," often in a negative tone. Children were also talking to the person next to them or poking them. During class meeting we talked about the problem by referring to the seven steps, and I wrote our responses on a special form, which we consulted throughout the year as the need arose (see Appendix A1–3).

Other important issues we discussed by Talking the Problem were whether to allow cutting in line, how to include everyone who wants to play tag on the playground, keeping the coat area orderly, cleaning up after snack, and ways to clean up the room at the end of the day.

Sometimes the most productive solution to a classroom issue is to establish a list of rules together. In fact, children usually can recite most of the rules that are part of school (such as no running in the hall and no hitting), but sometimes lack the control or become too enthusiastic to follow them. Framing rules as either negotiable or nonnegotiable (Seigle & Macklem 1993), gives the children, as members of our classroom community, areas in which they have a say in what happens and gives us a common language for discussion. I encouraged the class to

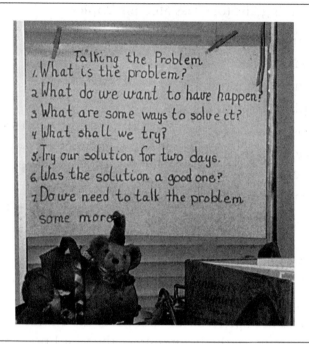

Talking the Problem
1. What is the problem?
2. What do we want to have happen?
3. What are some ways to solve it?
4. What shall we try?
5. Try our solution for two days.
6. Was the solution a good one?
7. Do we need to talk the problem some more

PHOTO 1-6 *Seven steps of Talking the Problem*

keep our list of nonnegotiable rules in positive wording—for example, keep your hands to yourself, walk in the halls, be a good listener, and be a good learner.

Rules for Blocks

1. Do not knock down blocks.
2. Build only to your shoulder.
3. No throwing blocks.
4. Share the blocks.

Many of our nonnegotiable rules address behavior that is either dangerous or destructive, referred to as Double Ds in the Social Competency Program (Seigle & Macklem 1993). This concept helps the children solve many of their own problems instead of tattling and coming to me for help. For example, if someone reports to me that a friend won't share the colored pencils, I ask if that's a Double D. We agree that it isn't, and the child goes off to try to work things out without adult help.

This doesn't mean that I don't address social issues that are not dangerous or destructive. But we are more apt to discuss them during class meeting, when the emotion of the incident has dissipated and after the children have had the opportunity to try to work out the specific problem among themselves. For example, sharing the colored pencils began to take a lot of time away from writing, so we addressed the issue during class meeting. I also make it clear that if their continual efforts to solve a problem are unsuccessful, I will help them work it out. For example, one child in my class made continual efforts to ask a classmate not to stare at him during group. The three of us got together to discuss the concern, which opened up better dialogue between the two.

I believe that trusting children to be responsible for their own learning and behavior is at the heart of establishing community in my classroom. It is an ongoing process, which requires my commitment to allow the children time and opportunities to share in the responsibility for creating and maintaining a positive environment for thinking and learning.

FOR FURTHER READING

BERMAN, SHELDON, AND PHYLLIS LA FARGE. 1993. *PROMISING PRACTICES IN TEACHING SOCIAL RESPONSIBILITY.* ALBANY, NY: STATE UNIVERSITY OF NEW YORK PRESS.

CAMBOURNE, BRIAN. 1988. *THE WHOLE STORY: NATURAL LEARNING AND THE ACQUISITION OF LITERACY IN THE CLASSROOM.* NEW YORK: ASHTON SCHOLASTIC.

HOLDAWAY, DON. 1986. "THE STRUCTURE OF NATURAL LEARNING AS A BASIS FOR LITERACY INSTRUCTION." IN *THE PURSUIT OF LITERACY: EARLY READING AND WRITING,* EDITED BY MICHAEL SAMPSON. DUBUQUE, IA: KENDALL/HUNT.

KOHN, ALFIE. 1993. *PUNISHED BY REWARDS: THE TROUBLE WITH GOLD STARS, INCENTIVE PLANS, A'S, PRAISE, AND OTHER BRIBES.* NEW YORK: HOUGHTON MIFFLIN.

PETERSON, RALPH. 1992. *LIFE IN A CROWDED PLACE.* PORTSMOUTH, NH: HEINEMANN.

SMITH, FRANK. 1988. *JOINING THE LITERACY CLUB: FURTHER ESSAYS INTO EDUCATION.* PORTSMOUTH, NH: HEINEMANN.

2

Generating Curriculum

"It sure is nice to be able to study what you're interested in." Alex offered this comment one morning as the children moved about the room during workshop time. At the beginning of the year we had brainstormed a list of different topics that had interested us and I had gotten to know the children's interests and ways of learning by filling out an Inquiry Interview with each child (See Appendix A2–1). Now the children were involved in pursuing those topics, as well as generating new ones. They worked independently and in small groups. Some went to the library and some found books in the classroom. Some drew pictures and painted, and some made constructions out of recycled materials. They talked. A generative curriculum began.

Brainstorming List—Topics of Interest

1. Flying
2. Out-of-doors
3. Top gun
4. Singapore, Asia
5. Germany
6. Deserts
7. Japan—writing
8. Swamps
9. Human bodies
10. Volcanoes
11. Mammals
12. Languages—names
13. Prehistoric animals
14. Trees
15. Long ago places
16. Blood
17. Plants
18. How to make a playground
19. Bugs
20. Reptiles

21. Dinosaurs
22. Nature
23. Earthquakes
24. Jungle
25. Fish
26. Elephants
27. Seals
28. Claws
29. Spirits and Gods
30. United Kingdom
31. Bunnies
32. Angels
33. Pirates and treasure
34. Guinea pigs
35. Soccer
36. Rides
37. Sports

WHAT IS A GENERATIVE CURRICULUM?

I first heard the term from Don Holdaway while Pat Cordeiro and I were having breakfast with him one morning in Colorado. He used it to describe what he perceived as the next step in curriculum development (Cordeiro 1992a). During the past three years in my first grade, I have developed and used a generative curriculum to support children in becoming lifelong learners in a democratic society.

In a generative curriculum one focus of inquiry generates another. As interests are initiated and pursued throughout the year, connections and relationships are made. The cumulative effect is an environment in which study topics and projects spring from one another and learning is ongoing and dynamic. Life and learning are seen as a whole in which a book, topic, area of study, art project, or science experiment reflects and suggests the entire curriculum of life, just as tiny holograms each contain the much larger whole object within themselves (Fisher 1995).

A generative curriculum helps learners apply the processes of reading, writing, speaking, listening, art, music, drama, and mathematics to gain meaning and understanding from the content areas of social studies and science, with children's literature playing a central part in integrating both processes and content areas. There is always an interplay between content learning and process learning, as we learn content through process, and process through content (Fisher & Cordeiro 1994).

Holdaway's (1986) Natural Learning Classroom Model, with opportunities for *demonstration, participation, practice/role-play,* and *performance* is applicable to a generative curriculum. The traditional application of this model calls for demonstrations by the teacher and participation by the student during group time and shared reading, practice/role-play by the student during independent work or choice time, and performance by the student as a culmination.

In a generative curriculum Holdaway's model becomes more dynamic. For example, new demonstrations arise from practice/role-play, and performance becomes ongoing and incidental, as well as formal. Children sometimes become demonstrators (teachers), and teachers often become participants, role-players, and performers (students).

SOURCES OF CURRICULUM

In practical terms the generative curriculum in my class derives from three sources: the interests of the children; my personal interests and experiences as a teacher; and the prescribed school curriculum (Fisher & Cordeiro 1994). This curriculum cannot be planned in detail. Although in September I start with some general areas of inquiry that I want us to pursue and then continually watch, listen to, and talk with the children about their interests. I keep in mind the school system's prescribed curriculum, which we integrate with our personal interests. The classroom soon develops a dynamic quality, as one area of interest generates another and connections are made between them (see Photo 2–1).

Children's interests

The interests of the children are the driving force in a generative curriculum. When learners pursue their own interests, engagement is at its highest. Cambourne (1988) suggests that if the learner is not engaged, all the other conditions of natural learning are not sufficient for meaningful learning. Goodman (1986) states that "Language [learning] should be whole, meaningful, and relevant to the learners." Short and

PHOTO 2-1 *Busy room*

Burke (1991) talk of "Learning as an active and intentional search for meaning (1991, p. 13)," and Harste discusses inquiry as "an alternative way to organize curriculum (1993, p. 3)." Edelsky, Altwerger, and Flores (1990) discuss theme cycles as a way of engaging children in creating ongoing curriculum. In *Engaging Children's Minds,* Katz and Chard (1989) describe how four major learning goals–knowledge, skills, dispositions, and feelings–become integrated as children do project work. A generative curriculum provides opportunities for children to pursue ongoing and new interests by building on past experiences. For example, as we learned about different habitats, Alex related what he was learning to his experience of owning a pet lizard.

Teacher's Interests

A generative curriculum also takes into account the personal and pedagogical interests of the teacher. Pedagogical interests include an entire array of skills and strategies that the teacher knows support learning and which she uses in the classroom. These include knowledge of reading, writing, and math processes, the field of literature, and the content areas of social studies and science.

Personal interests include topics and subjects that the teacher is presently pursuing. Last year I became interested in mythology and a recent trip to Scotland generated an interest in islands, island life, and seals. I read myths to the class and pursued my study of seals during workshop time. In sharing my personal interests, I modeled *how* I learn *as* I learn. The teacher becomes "a learner who teaches (Cordeiro 1992b) and establishes that give and take in teacher/learner roles.

Prescribed Curriculum

Most school systems have a core, prescribed, or mandated curriculum for each grade. In my system our social studies topics for first grade are Hopi Indians, Africa, and Japan. Science topics include: physical science (senses and properties); life science (organisms); and earth science (seasons, sun, and shadows). We have a large amount of flexibility in the depth and extent of involvement with each topic and in the teaching methods we use.

I tell the children that we are required to study the three social studies topics, and from these we generate the focus, projects, and culminating activities. Most of the science topics generate easily and naturally from the children's interests. I capitalize upon these by introducing information and demonstrations to extend the children's understanding. A developing process of science observations focusing on the senses and properties continues throughout the year.

STRANDS OF LEARNING

Within a generative curriculum three strands of learning usually weave their way throughout the flow of the day: incidental learning; mini topics; and whole class topics that the entire class studies together for an extended length of time (Fisher & Cordeiro 1994). Each arises from one or more of the sources of curriculum, the children, teacher, or school focus.

Topics, such as heroes, seals, or Scotland, are concrete areas of study. As topics are pursued, themes, such as how animals live together or what makes a hero, emerge. For example, an information book that Jacob wrote was entitled, *Differences, Differences, Differences.* The topic of the book was crickets and grasshoppers, and the theme was ways that the two insects are similar and different.

Incidental Learning

Incidental learning is spontaneous learning in the daily classroom life that has not yet developed into a topic but may do so. Examples of this type of learning include responses to questions, inquiries, and suggestions that come up during group time through *demonstration* and *participation,* such as when a child asks why the queen ant in the photograph in the big book *Ants, Ants, Ants* (Cutting 1992) is bigger than the other ants; when I ask the children what they think will happen next in the home/adventure/home story of *The Tunnel* (Browne 1989) that we are reading; or when someone suggests that we read the book *Emily* (Bedard 1992) again. Other incidental learning occurs during *practice/role-play* as part of the daily routine of reading and writing process, science observations, block building, and art experiences.

Mini Topics

When a child begins to explore incidental learning in more depth, it generates into a mini topic for that child, for a group of children, or sometimes for the entire class. The topic of sharks that Carl picked for a topic during workshop generated into a mini topic for several children. Jake, Paul, Danielle, and I got together and shared our interests in sharks, whales, and seals and made a chart comparing the three animals (see Photo 2–2).

Mini topics are small areas of study that individuals or small groups of children decide to pursue, especially during workshop time, or that the entire class focuses on for part of a day or two. Examples of these are author studies, making a maze book, doing a set of experiments about color, or conducting a survey and making a graph about it. They

PHOTO 2–2 *Comparative chart—seals, sharks, whales*

are expressed through all four conditions of the natural learning classroom model in varying degrees: we get demonstrations, participate and practice through books, conversations, writing and drawing, and creating artifacts, and then we share what we have learned with each other.

Whole Class Topics

Whole class topics are focuses of study that the entire class investigates in depth for at least a month and which conclude with a group project (*performance*), such as a museum. Class topics sometimes initiate from incidental learning or mini topics generated from the children's and teacher's interests, and often they are topics from the prescribed school curriculum. Regardless, there is a point when the class decides that it will study a topic in depth together. Some examples of whole class topics described later in this book are Westward Ho!, Immigration Study, Africa (see Chapter 12), and The Waterworks (see Chapter 11).

WORKSHOP

Generative curriculum really takes off during workshop. Throughout this interactive time, which is scheduled about three times a week, the children explore books and create projects as they pursue their own topics of inquiry or contribute to class projects that have generated from mini topics. Workshop provides time for multiple expression through the arts: painting, three-dimensional constructions, murals, drama, puppetry, block building, and science experiments. During a typical workshop time children might be building with unit blocks, painting together at a side-by-side easel, drawing pictures or creating a three-dimensional object for a topic project, writing, reading alone or with a friend, listening to a story on a tape, making a science observation or experiment, going to the library, or working with puppets.

During workshop my roles are facilitator, teacher, and learner. I provide children with materials, help them focus on a topic, and confer with them about their work (see Photo 2–3). When I work side by side with them on my own project, they see me as an authentic learner. We ask each other questions, share resources, and talk about ideas for projects.

Project Demonstrations

The natural learning model in action in a generative curriculum includes the different ways that learners gather information (*demonstration* and *participation*), create projects and artifacts (*practice/role-play*), and share (*performance*) what they have learned as they actively pursue curriculum interests. The natural learning model encompasses how children represent, portray, depict, illustrate, express, practice, explain, create, invent, communicate, describe, display, exhibit, experiment, produce, and express learning. The different ways to gather information include making big books, creating posters with diagrams and information, taking surveys and then making a graph, and creating models out of recycled materials.

Children become especially involved in these projects during workshop as they work alone or in groups, reading, building, drawing, painting, inventing, constructing, experimenting, making books, taking surveys, and creating murals and posters. At the beginning of the year I

PHOTO 2-3 *Working and talking together*

give many demonstrations of possibilities for projects and often require that the children give them a try. I continue giving demonstrations throughout the year, building on the children's interests and literacy development. Very soon they come up with their own projects as one project generates possibilities for other projects. The children become demonstrators, too. For example, Laura and Kate decided to take a mini trip around the school to find words to add to their spelling dictionaries, and very soon other children wanted to do the same thing.

Extensions and Innovations

Extensions and innovations encourage children to make connections between a familiar book, poem, or song and their areas of interest and inquiry. They keep the same syntax and general format of the original book, poem, or song. One child or a group of children can contribute a

30

page to a new class text, or an individual or small group can make up their own.

Extensions retain the original text and children either add more information or tell what might happen next in the story. For example, everyone in the class wrote an extension to the series of books, *On Sunday the Giant . . .* (Grater 1988), which told about the adventures of a giant who spent Sunday through Friday at a small village. The children wrote their own story about what happened to the giant on Saturday.

Innovations substitute new text for the original text. *Somewhere in the Universe* (Drew 1988) became the model for a book we made during a mini topic about the universe. After becoming familiar with the big book through repeated readings, the children made their own book with themselves as the main characters. They started at the back of the book and drew themselves in their houses. They marked where their houses were located on a street map of the town and drew themselves on maps of Massachusetts, the United States, the earth, and on a diagram of the planets.

Laura wrote her own version of *Along Comes Jake* (Cowley 1988), substituting names and creating her own family incidents. Everyone contributed their own rhyme to a class book of Down By the Bay. During a mini topic on animals, the children made their own innovations on the books *I Spy* (Drew 1990) and *Creature Features* (Drew 1988).

Visual Arts

One major way that children learn and express what they are learning in a generative curriculum is through visual arts. Throughout the year they gain experience with a variety of art materials such as crayons, paint, clay, paper, wood, and recycled materials as they draw pictures, create murals, and make three-dimensional artifacts. Marina painted a map of Greece and several children drew portraits of gods and goddesses with crayons and collage material.

Three-Dimensional Building

Many of the topics of inquiry in a generative curriculum are best explored and expressed through three-dimensional building (see Photo 2–4). Materials include a variety of blocks (unit blocks, geoblocks,

31

PHOTO 2–4 *Block building*

and pattern blocks), other math manipulatives (rods, unifix cubes), recycled materials for construction, and paper (origami, pop-up books). Cara made a bird in its nest out of paper and recycled materials.

Note Taking

I introduce note taking early in the year and continue giving different demonstrations of note taking possibilities as the year goes on. I encourage the children to take notes while I read and offer opportunities for note taking from visual observations (a nature walk around the school yard) as well as from texts. Notes can be in the form of pictures (see Figure 2–1) or words (see Figure 2–2), depending on the literacy development and learning style of the child as well as the nature of the subject matter. The children took notes as I read books about Japan and then used the notes to make a book (Fisher 1995).

FIGURE 2-1 *Note taking with pictures*

Interviews

There are many interviewing possibilities in a generative curriculum. Early in the year the children see interviewing as a normal way to gather information as I interview them about their reading, writing, math, and learning interests. They interview each other, school personnel, and people outside of school for our classroom newspaper or to obtain information on a topic of interest that they are pursuing.

I demonstrate how to plan for and conduct an interview, and during group time I choose someone to interview. The children help me draft appropriate interview questions and I conduct the interview. The children then interview each other, and as the year goes on they gain experience as they interview school personnel, family members, and experts in a field of inquiry.

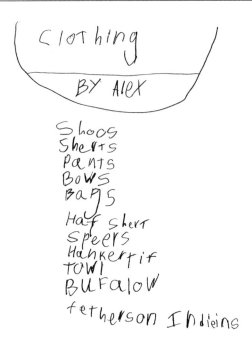

Clothing
BY Alex

Shoos
Sherts
Pants
Bows
Bags
Half shert
Speers
Hankertif
towl
BuFalow
fetherson Indieins

FIGURE 2-2 *Note taking with words*

Surveys

Surveys are a simple form of interviewing. On the first day of school I introduce the children to a class list in box form and show them how to check off their name when they have completed a task. I start a survey, asking them to write their favorite number in the box with their name and then we make a graph of the results. This single beginning generates different surveys and graphs, invented by the children, that continue to be produced throughout the year. Andrew took a survey of everyone's favorite color and soon many other children were taking surveys of favorite foods, sports, and numbers.

Mini Field Trips

Mini field trips are excursions taken anywhere on school property, in the building and outside. Sometimes we go as an entire class. Other times teams of two or three set out to obtain some information (these

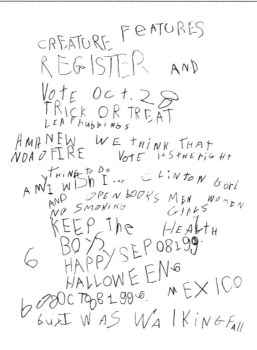

FIGURE 2-3 *Notes from an environmental print walk*

trips are always inside). Almost always the children use clipboards to take notes. During some mini field trips we search for environmental print (signs such as exit, gym, nurse's office—see Figure 2-3); properties (colors, shapes); or things that magnetize. Other times we make texture rubbings or take a five-senses walk, using our different senses and recording what we notice.

Sharing

Sharing (*performance*) completes the cycle of the natural learning model and often starts a new cycle. As the children share what they have learned, they become the demonstrators or teachers. This performance often generates new curriculum or further inquiry because it engages the learner and gives purpose and focus for new demonstrations, participation, and practice.

PHOTO 2–5 *Informal sharing*

In my classroom sharing happens incidentally and informally throughout the day as we work and talk with each other (see Photo 2–5). Other daily sharing is more structured and formal. During the Author's Chair a child or group of children present work in front of the class and take responses from the audience. Circle share is when we all bring our work to the rug and briefly explain what we are doing and how it is going. For quick share time I hold up the children's work and make a few positive comments. Around the room share involves everyone moving from one area to another to see and hear what individuals or groups have been doing. More elaborate forms of sharing include museums, plays, festivals, fairs, video presentations, and visitor days.

QUESTIONS TEACHERS ASK

1. We have system wide required curriculum. Where do I find the time to cover it and still give kids opportunities to pursue their own topics?

I think that you can give children a lot of choice even within a prescribed curriculum. For example, at the beginning of the year, find out their special interests and areas of inquiry and then look over the curriculum to find matches. Be flexible and involve the children in planning study topics within the curriculum so that they can include their own interests. Finally, allow them to go off on their own as they become engaged in a pursuit of learning.

As we go up the grades, there seems to be more required curriculum that teachers feel they must cover. *Theme Immersions* (Manning, Manning & Long 1994) offers many useful ways to involve the children in curriculum planning.

FOR FURTHER READING

CORDEIRO, PAT. 1995. *Social Studies, Whole Language, and Literacy: Classroom Profiles Grades K-5.* Portsmouth, NH: Heinemann.

FISHER, BOBBI, AND PAT CORDEIRO, EDS. 1994. "Generating Curriculum: Building a Shared Curriculum." *Primary Voices K-6* 2(3).

HARSTE, JEROME. 1993. "Inquiry-Based Instruction." *Primary Voices K-6,* Premier Issue.

KATZ, LILLIAN, AND SYLVIA CHARD. 1989. *Engaging Children's Minds: The Project Approach.* Norwood, NJ: Ablex Publishing Corporation.

MANNING, GARY, MARYANN MANNING, AND ROBERTA LONG. 1994. *Theme Immersion: Inquiry-Based Curriculum in Elementary and Middle Schools.* Portsmouth, NH: Heinemann.

SHORT, KATHY, AND CAROLYN BURKE. 1991. *Creating Curriculum: Teachers and Students as a Community of Learners.* Portsmouth, NH: Heinemann.

WIGGINTON, ELLIOT. 1985. *Sometimes a Shining Moment: The Foxfire Experience.* Garden City, NY: Anchor Books.

3

Organizing for Learning

Primary teachers often arrive at school early in the morning and leave long after the kids have gone. We are usually the ones who start setting up our classrooms in the summer as soon as the custodians have cleaned the floors. We know that the daily schedule will flow more smoothly if the physical set up of the classroom and appropriate teaching materials are well organized. There are a lot of equipment and materials involved in teaching primary grades, and what's more, we have to plan the environment for the same group of children for the entire day. (See floor plan in Figure 3–1).

SCHEDULE

Organizing time is one of the most challenging aspects of teaching, especially in a generative curriculum. There needs to be a natural flow of the day, with a balance of group times and individual practice times, active times and calm times, talkative times and contemplative times. Throughout the day we as teachers try to be attentive and responsive to the children's interests. The ideas and interests that they bring up during settling-in time and group meeting expand during writing, workshop, math, and reading. My daily schedule seems to satisfy this pacing and promotes and supports a generative curriculum.

First Grade Schedule

8:40	Settling-in time
9:10	Group meeting
9:40	Writing and/or workshop
11:10	Recess
11:30	Workshop or Specialist
12:15	Math
12:50	Recess and lunch
1:35	Reading
3:10	Home

Settling-in Time

The children arrive in the classroom within a fifteen-minute time span. On a clipboard I write a list of things that they have to do to get ready for the day, such as sign in, perform committee work, put their writing folders at their places, and add the daily spelling word to their dictionaries (see Figure 3–2). These are all starred. The list also suggests activities they can choose to do, such as estimating the number of color cubes in a jar, making an observation comment about the elephant plant leaf on the science table, adding some news to the new board easel, and recording their response to a survey about their favorite animal. They also have time to chat with each other and with me informally, show something they have brought from home and display it on the sharing table, exchange a book at the school library, read a book, or start their writing.

Settling-in Clipboard Possibilities (in alphabetical order)

- Add a word to the word family envelopes.
- Answer the graph question.
- Answer the math question.

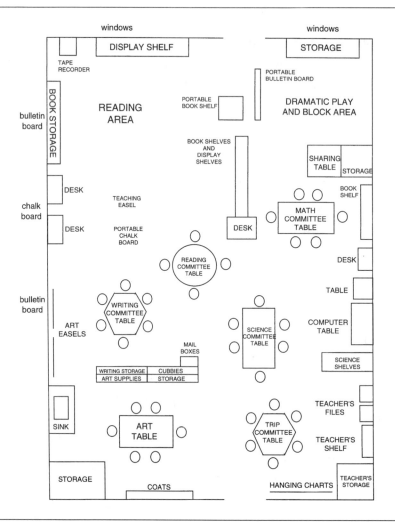

FIGURE 3-1 *Room floor plan*

- Before you ask me a question, try to get the answer from at least three classmates.
- Bring five different Cuisinaire Rods to the rug.
- Clear out your writing folder.
- Committee work.
- Do one box math.
- Do the math paper.

Tuesday, June 9

#1. Check in
2. Finish box math
#3. Numberline math
#4. Write 5 have-a-go words in your dictionary
5. See me — Tell me what you learned this year
6. Equation for 60

FIGURE 3-2 *Morning clipboard*

- Fill in the weather on your calendar.
- Get your writing ready.
- Give someone a compliment.
- Greet four friends.
- Paste the poem in your poem book.
- Paste Amanda's poem in your poem book.
- Put a notice in your bag.
- Put a unifix cube in each of your pockets.
- Put the papers in your front file in the envelope at your seat. Put the weekly news in, too. Give me the folder.
- Read a book with a friend.
- Read the big letter from our pen pal class.
- Read your pen pal letter.
- See me with a word beginning with *c* or *k*.

- Sign in.
- Sign in on the computer.
- Start the observation of the amaryllis.
- Start your writing.
- Survey question: How many books will be read this year?
- Take a big white envelope.
  Put your name on it.
  Put some of your April writing in it.
  Put it in the basket and take it home tonight.
- Take a notice.
- Tell me a kindness that you are going to do for someone today.
- Tell me a word that begins with *w* or *wh*.
- Tell someone a kindness.
- Write the word *can* in your have-a-go dictionary.

The generative curriculum is already underway. For example, Scott has brought in a snake skin that will become the object for our weekly science observation. Gary has decided to survey his classmates about their favorite snack. I notice several children making mazes (I will ask the librarian to come in and tell the story of Theseus and the Minotaur). Some children will continue their interest in mazes during workshop by creating mazes with blocks or on paper.

Morning Group Time

The children have been active and talkative since they first came through the door. But as we gather together as a community group at the rug area, activity and talk becomes more focused. This first group meeting of the day offers many opportunities to capitalize on curriculum generated on previous days, as well as introduce new possibilities. It is the first of several times during the day for shared literacy (see Chapters 4 and 5), when we read and discuss stories, focus on skills and strategies, and explore social studies and science topics (Photo 3–1).

I signal the children to come to the group area by singing a familiar song and we continue singing, reciting poems, and talking about them

Photo 3-1 *First group meeting of the day*

before I read a story. The songs, poems, and books either relate to a topic we are studying, an interest of a particular child, or a topic or strategy that I want to pursue. Sometimes a child has suggested a song or written a poem. I write it on a chart, she illustrates it, and we add it to our collection. The child leads the class, pointing to the words and directing the action. Our roles are reversed, as the child becomes the teacher and I become the learner.

On a large piece of easel paper I have written the schedule for the day and a question or statement that relates to either a process or content topic that we are examining. Examples are: "What questions do you have to ask our visitor, Ms. Lewis, who will be showing us slides of the Hopi Indians?", "What words describe Mathius in *Island Boy* (Cooney 1988)?"; "What do you do when you come to a word you don't know?"; "Brandon's mom is visiting today. Sign up with Brandon if you want to read to her."

Group time ends with community circle time, which has come to be called Passing the Rock in my class. We sit in a circle and each person can share something important with the group. We have a special rock, which is held by the person talking and then passed to the next speaker. In order to give everyone a chance to share daily, we try to limit comments to one or two sentences. These comments might include:

"My grandmother is coming to visit."

"Hornets are building a nest next to my window, and my dad says we have to take it down."

"I'm going to Florida on vacation to visit my grandparents and I'm excited."

"I can't wait to work on our mural during workshop today."

"Paul is coming over to my house today."

These comments offer excellent opportunities for further learning in a generative curriculum. They give indications of the interests of the children, which can become powerful topics during writing or workshop. I'm always listening so I can encourage the children to pursue these interests, help them make connections with common interests of their classmates, and provide books, artifacts, and projects for future pursuit. They also form the foundation for building a community of learners who are willing to work together and help each other.

Writing Time

After this interactive group time, the children are ready and willing to concentrate more independently and quietly (see Photo 3–2). Consequently we move into writing time, with children pursuing individual interests as they choose their own topic, genre, and format (see Chapters 7 through 9). Some write (and draw) a new piece each day, some make books, some work alone, and others collaborate. At the end of writing the children share their work.

Workshop Time

Workshop, which either follows or substitutes for writing, takes place about three days a week. It is the foundation of a generative curriculum because it gives the children time and opportunities to become engaged in learning through reading, writing, art, science, social studies,

PHOTO 3-2 *Writing time*

dramatic play, and three-dimensional building with blocks. It includes a combination of student and teacher choice, and as the year progresses, the children take on more responsibility for their own planning and projects (see Chapter 11).

We usually first meet at the rug area to plan. I might give demonstrations of possibilities for projects. If I am meeting with small groups, we go over the schedule. The children discuss their individual plans for the day and we begin. At the end of workshop we clean up and share.

One day I looked up during workshop and wrote down all the things that were happening at the moment. Two children were creating a scene from *Arrow to the Sun* (McDermott) in the block area and two were painting at the easel. Several children were reading big books together and two were reading by themselves. A group was making charts about sharks and several children were writing and drawing. A few children were at the library looking for books on a new topic. A small group was experimenting with magnets.

45

Math Time

During the scheduled math time we continually focus on patterns, counting, numbers, the four basic processes (addition, subtraction, multiplication, and division), place value, fractions, estimating, geometry, and measurement (see Chapter 10). These same processes are also addressed throughout the day as part of a generative curriculum. For example, later on we estimated the cost of buying hamsters and equipment for them. Carl measured the length of paper needed to cover a big box for the waterworks project by using Unifix Cubes. A group studying the solar system arranged their papier mâché planets according to size and proximity to the sun (see Photo 3–3).

Reading Time

Reading time gives many opportunities for the children to continue to generate their own interests as they make choices about reading material (see Chapter 6). It starts with silent reading, which lasts for five minutes in September, is up to fifteen minutes in October, and is at least a half hour by spring. Since the children are not allowed to move about the room or to talk to anyone during this time, they learn to select enough books to interest them for the session (see Photo 3–4). I encourage them to use the school library and bring books from home to share. I also make available books about topics we are studying. As I get to know their interests and independent reading levels, I provide appropriate books to individuals. During this time I read with the children, individually.

After silent reading, the children have more opportunities to pursue their interests as they read together and write in their response journals (see Chapter 4).

Shared Literacy Throughout the Day

There are three or four opportunities for shared literacy during the day, with the first session usually part of morning group, the other two before and after recess, and the last at the end of the day. During shared literacy I do a lot of explicit teaching as we read and discuss

Photo 3-3 *Math time*

stories, focus on skills and strategies, and explore social studies and science topics (see Chapter 5).

SPACE AND MATERIALS

The physical organization of the classroom is critical for a generative curriculum because both the teacher and the children need appropriate work spaces and easily accessible materials for their work. My classroom has tables for large projects and cooperative learning, individual desks for small projects and individual pursuits, and specific areas for reading, writing, science, sharing, art, and blocks. Materials are easily accessible so the children can be as independent as possible and so I can spend my time talking with them about what they are learning. I set up the classroom in September, but as the year goes on the children and I

47

PHOTO 3-4 *Reading time*

make changes to fit our curriculum. For example, when the science committee started planting seeds, they moved a table to the window for better light.

Display Areas

A sharing table displays things of interest that the children have brought from home or made at school. On a typical day the table might contain a fall leaf, a postcard from a grandparent in Florida, a beetle in a bug cage, some shells from the beach, a bow and arrow made at the art table, and a kimono from Japan. These items could become part of a mini topic or act as a catalyst for a theme immersion. This is another way to get to know the children's interests so I can plan and incorporate them into my planning for group time, shared literacy, and workshop. The table also gives me the opportunity to share some of my own interests.

In addition to this table, items are shared in related areas around the room and pictures, drawings, and paintings are hung on bulletin boards.

Reading

Books and other reading materials are central to a generative curriculum because they are one of the primary ways through which we gain new understandings and information. I help the children make connections between books and what they are learning and encourage them to refer to printed material while working on a project.

The reading area (called the rug) is where the whole class gathers for group times. Books and magazines are sorted in cardboard boxes and plastic bins according to categories and are placed on the floor around the edge. Big books are organized and stored according to fiction and nonfiction. A calendar, chalkboard, and a United States and world map are hung on the surrounding walls of the area. A teaching easel, which displays charts, plain chart paper, and big books stands in one corner. Poems and songs on wire hangers hang from hooks and nails and are easily accessible to the children and me. A shelf with reading games, puppets, pointers, beginning reading books, sentence strips, a tape recorder, ear phones, and tapes with books on it is along one wall. Science books are located in the science area and selective books are placed around the room. For example, books about hamsters are near our pets' cages and books about buildings are in the block area.

Writing

There are several desks and five large tables in my classroom where the children do most of their writing and work on projects. During workshop, children working on a common topic usually work at the same table so they can share ideas and materials. Often they take a box of books on their topic to the table.

General supplies (paper, pencils, markers, crayons, date stamp and pad, alphabet strips, scissors, hole punchers, and staplers) are on a shelf accessible to the children. Writing folders are kept in hanging plastic file boxes. A computer sits on a desk along the wall.

Math and Science

Math and science materials constitute an important part of a generative curriculum because they provide opportunities for hands-on experiences. The math and science area is defined by three shelves and a large table. The shelves store math manipulatives (Cuisenaire Rods, pattern blocks, attribute blocks, Unifix Cubes, number bars, chip trading materials, geoboards, color cubes, calculators), science supplies (empty containers, magnifying glasses, eye droppers), science boxes with artifacts and specimens (topics might include magnets, birds, wasps and hornets, the ocean, and weather), hamster cages and book boxes categorized according to science topics. At the table the children record observations, perform experiments and talk about the ever changing displays of objects that we all bring in.

Dramatic Play Environment

Dramatic play within a generative curriculum gives children the opportunity to role-play what they are learning and to share with others what they have learned. In my class, the use of the dramatic play area changes throughout the year. It is usually the focus for social studies topics and has been made into many different environments, such as a Japanese home, a television studio, a homestead, and public waterworks. When there is no dramatic play environment set up, the children build with unit blocks in the area.

Art Area

A generative curriculum acknowledges the importance of the visual arts. The art area is one of the more permanent givens of the room since it has a six-by-twelve-foot linoleum floor (the rest of the room is carpeted) and a sink. The area consists of a table, two side-by-side paint easels, a bulletin board and storage shelves that store paper, recycled materials, stamps and ink pads, glue, scissors, chalk, crayons, Cray-pas, and watercolors.

LESSONS PLANS

Throughout the year I use different forms to help me plan and I keep changing them to fit my current needs. Sometimes I write detailed plans to guide instruction and other times I only write down a few key points to remind myself of the direction I plan to take (Appendix A3–1, A3–2, A3–3, and A3–4).

FOR FURTHER READING

DEPREE, HELEN, AND SANDRA IVERSEN. 1994. *EARLY LITERACY IN THE CLASSROOM: A NEW STANDARD FOR YOUNG READERS.* BOTHELL, WA: THE WRIGHT GROUP.

FISHER, BOBBI. 1994. *CLASSROOM CLOSE-UP. BOBBI FISHER: ORGANIZATION AND MANAGEMENT.* BOTHELL, WA: THE WRIGHT GROUP. VIDEOTAPE.

GOODMAN, YETTA, WENDY J. HOOD, AND KENNETH GOODMAN, EDS. 1991. *ORGANIZING FOR WHOLE LANGUAGE.* PORTSMOUTH, NH: HEINEMANN.

GRAVES, DONALD. 1991. *BUILD A LITERATE CLASSROOM.* PORTSMOUTH, NH: HEINEMANN.

HARP, BILL, ED. 1993. *BRINGING CHILDREN TO LITERACY: CLASSROOMS AT WORK.* NORWOOD, MA: CHRISTOPHER-GORDON.

MILLS, HEIDI, TIMOTHY O'KEEFE, AND DIANE STEPHENS. 1992. *LOOKING CLOSELY: EXPLORING THE ROLE OF PHONICS IN ONE WHOLE LANGUAGE CLASSROOM.* URBANA, IL: NATIONAL COUNCIL OF TEACHERS OF ENGLISH.

ROUTMAN, REGIE. 1991. *INVITATIONS.* PORTSMOUTH, NH: HEINEMANN.

4

Literature

Authentic and meaningful literature experiences form the core of literacy learning in my classroom. Literature offers my students and me a common experience that we use to expand our real and imaginary worlds as individuals and as a classroom community.

It is common knowledge that the cumulative process of literacy learning begins long before formal schooling, as children hear stories and are involved in experiences with literature as emergent readers. It continues as they unfold as beginning readers, focusing on reading aloud the printed word, and as they mature to fluency, reading for a variety of purposes. I believe that the extensive reading aloud that takes place in my classroom community leads to the children developing a love of reading. This love of reading encourages and supports a love of writing. Both are sustained and strengthened when children continue to be engaged in oral reading opportunities, not just in the early primary years, but throughout the elementary grades and beyond. Bill Martin Jr. (1972) correlates all of the linguistic skills with reading in the following way and it all starts with "the sounds of language:"

> as one learns to listen, he is learning to speak;
> as one learns to speak, he is learning to read;
> as one learns to read, he is learning to write;
> as one learns to write, he is learning to listen. (17)

Although literacy develops through continuous experiences with all forms of writing, such as notes, lists, charts, newspapers, and graphs, in this chapter I describe literacy learning through the conventional forms of literature, namely storybooks, information books, information storybooks, and biographies. First, I describe the different ways that we categorize books in my classroom, and then I discuss some of the ways that we look at literacy.

FAVORITE BOOK FROM HOME

The newsletter I send to the children in the middle of August (see Appendix B2–1) asks them to bring a favorite book from home on the first day of school. This project suggests to the children and their families that books are important in this class, that their interests are valued, and that I want to know what they like to read. It offers parents and children opportunities for discussion. Chuckie's mom said that there was lots of talk at home about which book he would choose.

During those first days, this exercise gives me a starting point for discussions with the children and enables those who don't know each other to find common interests. For example, David and Dawn both brought in dinosaur books and shared their books together. A favorite book might suggest a writing topic. Chuckie brought his book about snakes and made a copy of his favorite kinds as a starting place for topic inquiry.

On the first day the children bring their books to the rug area and we place them on the display shelf. I write each title and child's name on a chart. During the next few days they each get a turn to show their book to the class and tell why they picked it. As the children take their turn being moderator for the day, they share the book more fully. They select pictures to show, read the book, or ask me to read it to the class. We briefly discuss if their book is a storybook, information book, or information storybook (Leal 1993). At reading time they look at their books informally with each other.

One year we made a class quilt about our favorite books. To introduce the project, I brought a quilt from home and read *The Quilt* (Jonas). We talked about quilts as reflecting memories and discussed what was important about their favorite book that they would like to remember on a quilt square. I asked them to write the title and their name and a picture on a five-by-five-inch piece of paper. The squares were mounted on a larger piece of paper and we had our first quilt hanging on a bulletin board.

ORGANIZING BOOKS

There are many reasons for spending time organizing the books in a classroom and many different ways of doing it. When books are organized, it is easier to keep the room neat and to find a particular book. However, I believe that a very important result of the process of categorizing literature is the understanding and learning that derives from the many discussions the children and I have as we go about the process.

Categorizing Books

Many of our classroom books are organized in boxes according to categories or text sets. A text set is a collection of books (two or more) that is assembled on the basis of some common criteria. Harste, Short, and Burke (1988) list story variants, story versions, story structures, themes, text types, topics, different illustrators of the same text, characters, authors, illustrators, and cultures as possible text set categories.

I keep an ongoing list of the children's books I use on a File Maker Pro database and group the books according to the different ways that we organize them in the classroom and according to the topics we're apt to study during the year. Presently, along with standard bibliography information (author, copyright date, title, city, and publisher), the books are organized according to category, text pattern, writing/reading process, story structure, social studies, science, and animals (see Figure 4–1). Over the years I've changed the categories to reflect current areas of study.

At the beginning of the year I create four text sets and label each box with a word and picture label: ABC Books, Singing Books, Repetitive/Rhyming Books, and Counting Books (see Chapter 10). On the first or second day of school I group the children in pairs and give each pair three books to look at from the different boxes. Then I line up the boxes and ask any team with an ABC book to return it to the ABC box. We do

Last Name

First Name

Title

Publisher

City

Date

Category
☐ Storybook ☐ Info/stbook
☐ Information ☐ Biography

Pattern
☐ Alphabet ☐ Interlocking ☐ Music ☐ Poetry ☐ Rhythmic
☐ Cumulative ☐ Math ☐ Nursery ☐ Repetitive ☐ Wordless

Process
☐ Art ☐ First person ☐ Learning ☐ Quilts ☐ Vocab
☐ Borders ☐ Inquiry ☐ Libraries ☐ Story telling ☐ Writing

Structure
☐ Character ☐ Folk tale ☐ Myth ☐ Big book
☐ Circle ☐ H/A/H ☐ Prob. solv ☐ Big print
☐ Fairy tale ☐ I Can Read@ ☐ R/F/R

Social studies
☐ Africa ☐ Community ☐ Family ☐ South America ☐ West
☐ Asia ☐ Democracy ☐ Immigration ☐ Slavery
☐ City/country ☐ Europe ☐ Maps ☐ Trips

Science
☐ Animals ☐ Experiments ☐ Ocean ☐ Seasons/weather
☐ Day/night ☐ Food ☐ Plants ☐ Space
☐ Dinosaurs ☐ Human body ☐ Properties ☐ Water
☐ Ecology ☐ Machines ☐ Rain forest

Animals
☐ Ants ☐ Cats ☐ Fish ☐ Plains ☐ Spiders
☐ Bees/wasps ☐ Desert ☐ Forest ☐ Reptiles ☐ Tundra
☐ Birds ☐ Dogs ☐ Mammals ☐ Seals ☐ Whales
☐ Bugs/insects ☐ Farm ☐ Mountain ☐ Sharks ☐ Woodland

FIGURE 4-1 *Bibliography on database*

this for each box, discussing that many books could go in different boxes, depending on the category we choose. For example, Liam noted that *Roll Over! A Counting Song,* illustrated by Merle Peek, could go in either the singing or counting box. I do this activity early in the year to coincide with the start of silent reading so that the children will begin to be aware of the different kinds of books available, and know where to return them.

Other fiction books are stored on shelves and throughout the year we add boxes and change the categories of some of the text sets to fit our needs and interests. For example, one year we had boxes labeled "Silly Stories," "Mother Goose," and "Myths and Fairy Tales." Although poetry has its own text set, some poetry books are located throughout

PHOTO 4-1 *Display books relating to whole class topic*

the classroom with predictable books, singing books, and even with the science books. If we are working on a whole class topic, we put small, colored, circle stickers on each book relating to that topic and keep them on the display shelf for the duration of the study. We did this with books about westward expansion (see Photo 4-1) during our immigration study (see Chapter 12).

Science books are categorized according to topics and shelved in standup folder boxes in the science area. The children read these books during silent reading and often take one of the boxes to their work area during workshop. We start with the following: "Dinosaurs," "Fish and the Sea," "Insects," "Mammals," "Reptiles," "Outer Space," "Plants," "Space and Weather," and as the year goes on, categories are changed and new text sets are added.

One year there was a lot of interest in snakes, so we created a box just for books about snakes. Often the box for mammals becomes too full, so we divide the books into subcategories for farm, woodland, plains, and jungle animals.

Organizing by Type

I organize the different kinds of literature we read into four categories or type: storybooks (fiction), information books (nonfiction), informational storybooks (the gray area between fiction and nonfiction), and biographies. Leal (1993) defines a storybook as "a fictional narrative picture book," an information book as "expository text-like literature with illustrations intended to transmit or explicate information," and an informational storybook as "a piece of literature containing characteristics drawn from both the storybook and the information book" (62–63).

The children and I discuss some of the characteristics of these different types of books. They come to understand that storybooks are about characters who have an adventure or solve a problem. They notice that all stories have a beginning, middle, and end and that many have a home-adventure-home pattern, such as *Two Bad Ants*, by Chris Van Allsburg. In this book the ants start out safe at home, leave home and have an adventure in which they almost die as they look for sugar, and finally make it back home safely.

The children concluded that information books tell "true" facts about science or history and that there is no story in the writing, such as in *Sea Animals,* by Angela Royston in the Eye Opener Series. We discussed that *The Magic Schoolbus at the Waterworks,* by Joanna Cole, an informational storybook, tells a lot of scientific information as part of the story. They also learned that biographies, such as *A Picture Book of Harriet Tubman,* by David Adler, tell about real people's lives.

Organizing Key Books

As we study different topics during the year, one book often becomes a key book for a particular study. I define a key book as a book that we read again and again throughout the year because it generates continued interest and in-depth study. Sometimes a key book becomes the focal point for a text set. For example, *A Letter Goes to Sea*, by Lore Leher, became a key book for a trips-around-the-world project that I introduced in September. We read it many times throughout the year as we took imaginary trips to different places. From this key book, we began to create a text set on maps and geography.

Key Books

- *A Letter Goes to Sea* (Lore Leher). I write a note to the children on the first day of school, telling them that we will be taking many imaginary trips around the world during the year. We keep a year long "passport" of countries we visit.
- *Will I Have a Friend?* (Miriam Cohen). We talk about making new friends during the year.
- *Fly Away Home* (Eve Bunting). We donate food to a food pantry.
- Tana Hoban's books. We observe properties of objects in science.
- *Mickey's Magnet* (Franklyn Branley & Eleanor Vaughn). We get involved in a study about magnets.
- *Chrysanthemum* (Kevin Henkes). We work toward developing a caring classroom community.
- *Arrow to the Sun* (Gerald McDermott). We study about the Hopi Indians.
- *Johnny Appleseed* (and other books illustrated by Stephen Kellogg). We connect details in illustrations with details in writing.

PHOTO 4-2 *Adding stickers to the read aloud books list*

- *Ten Apples Up On Top.* (Theo LeSieg). We take a trip to the apple orchard.
- *The Quilt* (Ann Jonas). We make a series of quilts about our year.
- *On the Day You Were Born* (Debra Frasier). I read this on each child's birthday.
- *My Great Aunt Arizona* (Gloria Houston). We connect this with other texts about the westward expansion.
- *The Boy Who Lived with the Seals* (Rafe Martin). This is an all encompassing book that I read again and again and each time we focus on a different reading perspective.
- *The Boy of the Three Year Nap* (Alan Say). We study about Japan.
- *The Magic School Bus at the Waterworks* (Joanna Cole). We use this book to learn about waterworks as part of a school-wide theme on water.

Read Aloud List

We keep a list of every book (big book and trade book) we read aloud in class, and each year we read about 250 different books. On chart paper I write the month and then, after we read a book, I write the title, author, publisher, and copyright date. The children usually spell the title aloud as I write and put a circle sticker above the number of the book (see Photo 4–2) to indicate if it is a storybook (red sticker), information book (green sticker), informational storybook (yellow sticker), or biography (blue sticker). At the end of the month I send a list of the books home with the children.

INTRODUCING LITERACY PERSPECTIVES

At the beginning of the year, through extensive oral reading and discussions, I give the children an overview of the main focuses of our engagement with literature for the year. I introduce them to the value of personal response (reader response perspective), to the structure of story (critical perspective), to the richness of learning social studies and science through information books (curriculum perspective), to the reading and writing connection (writer's perspective), and to reading process (reading process perspective). These perspectives are derived from the work of Tompkins and McGee in *Teaching Reading with Literature.*

Reader Response Perspective

"The reader response perspective focuses on reading as a lived-through experience that involves the feelings, images, thoughts, and associations called to mind at the moment of reading. Readers respond to those feelings during and after reading" (Tompkins & McGee 1993, 165).

"What do you think?" I ask as I finish *The Boy Who Lived with the Seals*, by Rafe Martin. After reading a story aloud, I usually start with this question and the responses are rich and varied based on the children's own experiences. These personal responses are activated prior to hearing the story, as the children predict what the story will be about and expanded and deepened during and after the reading. In this case, the children shared what they knew about seals. They told of occasions when they wandered off or got lost from their parents and they talked of times they like to be alone, like the boy in the story.

"Literacy begins in hearts, not heads" (Sloan 1984, 13). The children's personal response to any piece of literature becomes the natural starting place for literature discussion in my class. The children demand it by their insistence to tell their personal stories, to express their feelings and emotions, to use their imaginations, and to ask their unique questions. For example, *The Boy Who Lived with the Seals* elicits responses about the times the children got lost from their families.

Holdaway (1979) writes of the deep meaning in literature that draws young children into a book and of the emotional power of the favorite storybook, which provokes young children to demand repeated readings as part of the bedtime story and evokes discussion and reaction during read alouds in school. Those same favorite stories offer children opportunities to understand language and develop a literary set. Deep familiarity with one text, supports understanding of other texts as children make connections.

This same emotional power encourages response as children become independent readers and continues to stimulate us as adults. It focuses on the deep developmental issues that direct our lives and make us uniquely human: issues of love and hate or fear, issues of power and control, issues of gender identity, issues of separation and autonomy, and issues of fantasy and reality.

Louise Rosenblatt (1978) describes reading as an experience between the reader, the poem (the reader's response or transaction), and the text. She uses the terms "aesthetic" and "efferent" reading to describe the different stances or transactions that are activated by past experiences and our present situation while reading. At one end of the continuum is aesthetic reading, a personal, emotional response. At the other end is efferent reading, more concrete, sequential, tangible, and measurable. In my class we usually start discussions about a book with our aesthetic response and move back and forth along the continuum.

Weaver (1994) calls our attention to the importance of our schematic context as part of the reading process. "This refers to knowledge in our heads: a mental schema is simply an organized chunk of knowledge and experience" (17). As we read, we start with our personal schemas, which include our background knowledge, experiences, feelings, and emotions, and we continually add new knowledge and insights to our schema.

Reader response starts in our minds, within our private thoughts. Some of these responses never get put into words, while others, written in diaries, are never shared with anyone else. In school our responses become public as we respond orally, in writing, and through artistic expression.

Oral Response

The predominant expression of reader response in my class is through talk and discussion. Before I read a book to the class, we refer to the title and pictures to predict what the book might be about. After reading, we discuss our responses and feelings. The invitations to respond are general and varied. For example, if I read a story about someone losing a tooth, I don't need to initiate the conversation—the children just start talking. Before I read *Galimoto*, by Karen Lynn Williams, I guide the conversation because I know that most of the children won't know that a galimoto is a toy made of wire.

In order to become more conscious of our own reader response, we generate a list of ways to initiate response in the form of questions and ways to begin an answer. We display the list in the reading area, adding to it throughout the year and periodically reviewing and discussing the differences between these inquiry words.

Inquiry List

- What do you notice?   I noticed . . .
- What do you wonder?   I wonder . . .
- What did you think?   I thought . . .
- What did you like?   I liked . . .
- What did you learn?   I learned . . .
- What did you discover?   I discovered . . .
- How did you feel?   I felt . . .
- What did you consider?   I considered . . .

After reading a story, I usually start the group discussion by asking one of the open-ended questions from the list. Almost immediately the children include the other inquiry terms. They seem to know the subtle differences in meaning between notice, wonder, think, like, learn, discover, feel, and consider and intuitively choose the specific word they need to make their point. The discussion quickly moves away from a question and answer format to an interactive exchange of ideas, with one person talking at a time so we can all hear each response.

When I notice that many children are having trouble listening because they all want to respond, I ask them to share their ideas with the person next to them. A buzz of conversation immediately fills the room. Sometimes I ask a specific question, which calls for a short, individual response, to help draw everyone into the discussion. For a yes or no question, I ask for a show of hands. "Do you think the boy was happy at the end?" For a short answer question, the children respond at the same time. "What was the one thing you noticed most?"

Written Response

The children's repeated experiences with oral response act as demonstrations for written response in response journals (see Photo 4-3). For these, we use stenography notebooks, which are inexpensive, sturdy, convenient to store, and easy to use because the spiral on the top doesn't get in the way of the child's hand when writing.

I introduce the journals toward the end of October. After silent reading the children come to the rug with a pencil and a book they have been reading, and I give them a journal with their name and "Reading Journal" written on the front. (One year I wrote "Math Journal" on the back and we used these same notebooks as math response journals). I have a journal, too. We turn to the first page and write the date and title of our book at the top, underline the title so it will be easy to find on the page, and circle the letters *S, I, IS,* or *B* to indicate if the book is a storybook, information book, information storybook, or biography. Then we respond. I ask everyone to write and/or draw a picture telling something about their book. I keep my instructions brief and general so the children can take ownership and have a go. The less directive I am, the more confident they become in their ability to respond in their own way. (Figure 4-2).

The room is quiet, except for the rustling of pages and the sputter of ear spelling in which children say a word and write the letters that they hear. Occasionally a child asks someone how to spell a word, or shows a drawing or illustration to a friend, but for the most part we're all engaged in our own work. As children finish, they look up, indicating they are ready for sharing. Those who choose to share, give the title of their book, tell what kind of a book it is, and read what they have written or tell about their picture. We put the journal in their storage box and put the books away.

After school I respond in their journals, writing in pen so the children can easily locate what I have written. I try to reply as I would to a friend who had written me about a book she or he had read. I write briefly, such as:

> "I liked this book, too, especially the part where the third little pig doesn't do what the wolf wants."
>
> "I never noticed that every other page is drawn in black and white. I'm glad you pointed that out to me."

PHOTO 4–3 *Response journals*

"Do you know the book, *Lions Book?* It's another book-inside-a-book."

"Jan Brett has a new book coming out. I'll try to get it."

"Your picture of the Berenstain bears has a lot of action in it, just like the book."

When we first start journals, many of the children are comfortable just responding through drawing. Although I encourage illustrations, my goal as the year goes on is for written response to dominate and for illustrations to support. These journals become a record of the children's growth as writers and readers and offer ongoing evaluation for them and for me (see Figure 4–3).

After we have written in the journals three or four times and the routine is established, I start the Inquiry List described on page 62, writing the first two phrases "I liked" and "I noticed" on a chart and asking the children to pick one, write it in their journal, and finish the sentence.

Throughout the year, as we focus on other literature perspectives, I periodically suggest something specific that the children *might* want to

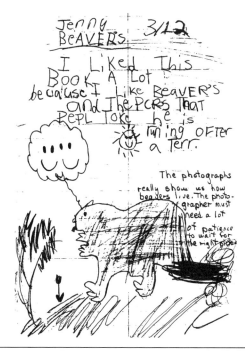

FIGURE 4-2 *Response journal entry*

address in their journal that day. A sample of prompts that I've found successful are:

- Tell how your feelings and the book character's feelings are alike or different.
- What was important about the setting?
- If you have an information book, tell what in it has helped you to get information.
- What words did the author use that you might use in your own writing?

I use these prompts as suggestions and choices, rather than as assignments, because I don't want to take away the children's control of what and how they respond. Some may have been thinking about what they want to write during silent reading. An assignment from me could

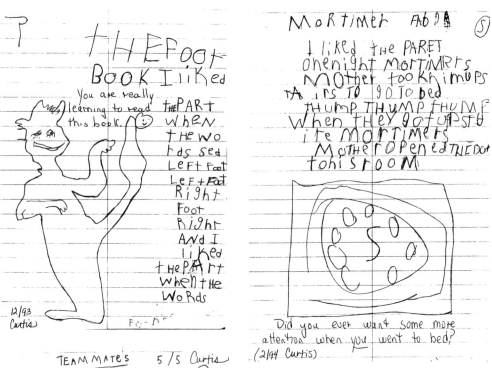

THE Foot
BOOK I liKed

You are really
learning to read
this book. THE PART
wheN
the wo
rds sed
LeFt Foot
LeFt Foot
Right
Foot
Right
ANd I
liKed
the PArt
wheN the
WoRds

12/93
Curtis

MoRTiMer AbD 5

I liKed the PARET
onenight MortiMRts
MOther took him ups
TAirs to go To bed
THUMP THUMP THUMP
when tHEy got UPSTU
ite MoRTiMers
MOther opened THE DOr
to his room

Did you ever want some more
attention when you went to bed?
(2/94 Curtis)

TEAMMATES 5/5 Curtis
115

I LiKed THE PART
In THE BACK OF tHe
BOOK WHeN THey
MAde FriehdS
Oh THE cover OF THe
THe Book You CAn
See THem ANd THere
AutograpH is
uNder THem THEY Bied
if THEy wher ALive tHey
Wood Bee very good
Jackie Robbth DieD FroM
A hardaTack THEy wher
very good THey BoTh wher
oh THE Dodgers THis
WASAvery serXes Book
THis WAS A AutograPHeD
Book IM READing THis
To THE CLASS I LoveD THis Bok

I loved this book, too. I'm glad that
blacks and whites are on the same
teams now.

FIGURE 4–3 *Journals record children's growth as writers and readers*

detract from their ownership, motivation, and self-regulation. I also notice that children sometimes respond to a suggestion on another day, when it becomes meaningful to them.

My authentic participation as a learner in this process is extremely valuable to me and the children. As Donald Graves (1991b) states, "Why should kids have all the fun?" I like to have some time to read during the school day. As I write, I sort out my thoughts and gain new insights into what I have been reading. I also like to share what I have written with the children.

The children are intrigued with what I am reading and how I respond. Daily, as they come in from lunch and get their books for silent reading, they might see me reading a novel, a nonfiction book, a book about teaching, a magazine, or a children's book. As they become aware of my particular interests and notice that I value reading and writing, they begin to view me not just as teacher, but as a learner who is also a teacher. For example, Julie often asked me what I was reading and if I'd finished the book I had the other day. She encouraged me to read the responses in my journal along with the rest of the class.

Also, because I am involved in my own reading and writing at these times, the children become more independent about their selection of books and about what they write in their response journals. They stop relying on me for the right answers and start depending on themselves for appropriate solutions.

Artistic Response

Don Holdaway (1979) reminds us of the importance of multiple forms of expression or response. "It is not only listening to stories that is important in this sense: probably of greater importance is the way children enter into the story world expressively as they repeat, re-enact, read again, or live out in many expressive modes the story language which fulfills multiple functions in their experience" (149). Glenna Davis Sloan (1984) states that, "There are many ways to understand a story and they are *not all translatable* into descriptive prose. A more appropriate test of the child's comprehension of the stories he reads and hears is an artistic or creative response" (107).

Responding through drawing   As I read picture books to the class, we mention the illustrations and their relationship to the text. We notice the details that different artists choose to include to support the story. We talk about information that is expressed in both words and pictures, descriptive phrases that stand alone as an integral part of the text, and visual details that extend and enhance it. This focus becomes an automatic part of our general conversation about books and begins to support the children in their own writing as they gradually use more words to describe what was previously depicted primarily through their illustrations.

During writing time, the children have daily opportunities to express themselves through drawing, and I also plan specific demonstrations and activities to encourage response to literature through art work. As a way of making explicit the value of both text and illustrations, and of helping the children make the connection between the two forms of expression, I sometimes ask them to illustrate a story while I read it orally, without showing them the pictures. The instructions are simple: "Write your name, date, and the title on the top of your large drawing paper; listen to the story and illustrate it any way you want, using just a regular pencil; you can add color later." During this activity, the children work on their own without talking, since they are listening to the story. When I read the story first and then ask them to illustrate it, they often work together and talk as they draw.

I have different reasons for picking various texts. For example, most of the fairy tales in *Tales from the Enchanted World* by Annabel William-Ellis are not familiar to the children, so the author's words, rather than the children's previous experience with the story, guide their drawings. Chapter books, which rely almost solely on the text to tell the story, demonstrate the power of the author's words to create meaning. When the children illustrate an unfamiliar picture book, the rereading, accompanied with the pictures, enables them to compare their drawings with the illustrations of the artist and to discuss how the pictures supported and/or extended the text. After studying several versions of *Little Red Riding Hood,* illustrating another version gave the children the opportunity to construct personal meaning as they worked with a familiar text.

Responding through drama   When children step into the role of a story character and take on the point of view of that character, their response assures a new dimension. They have the opportunity to develop empathy and a deeper understanding of what it is like to be someone or something else—to be another living thing, whether it be a human, another kind of animal or creature, or even a plant. Second-grade teacher, Sheryl McGruder (1993) states that, "Pretending, being other than who we are, helps us become more adaptable, more able to accept people and other beings as they are. Being other than who we are enables us to comprehend what might be" (145).

There are many kinds of dramatic response in primary classrooms, from a simple pantomime by the entire class during shared reading to a full production on stage before an audience. Some of the simple ways we incorporate dramatic response into our shared literacy time are through singing, acting out a book, and using puppets (see Photo 4–4).

The songs we sing to start each group time invite us to respond to text as a classroom community. Each song encourages a distinctive emotional response and helps set the mood for the group. *Hush Little Baby* (Aliki) quiets us down. *The Lady with the Alligator Purse* (Wescott) encourages laughter. *Teaching Peace* (Grammer) builds community and produces a united class spirit.

Big books lend themselves to dramatic interpretation that can be performed often and quickly. The simplest performance is for the children to pick a character in the story and act it out at their places as we read the book together. Sometimes we make a stage in front of the group, and selected children act out a part while the rest of the class takes the role of narrator and reads the familiar story. To keep the characters straight, I write their names on index cards, which are attached by clothespins to pieces of yarn and hung around each child's neck. Variations of this dramatic response can also be performed with puppets.

These demonstrations often generate other dramatic responses that the children initiate. For example, two or three children may decide to act out a book on their own, and soon other groups will start planning presentations with big books, sometimes including props and costumes.

Critical Perspective

When we discuss literature from a critical perspective in my classroom, we concentrate on literary elements, structures, and text types. Although we refer to these informally, from time to time we specifically

PHOTO 4-4 *Acting out a big book with puppets*

focus on one element. The thinking and reasoning behind the discussion is what is important, not any *one* correct answer, although we do return to the text to support, clarify, and confirm what we say. Three aspects of a critical perspective that we focus on include:

- Story elements: character, setting, time, mood, theme, and plot
- Story structures: circle stories, home/adventure/home stories, and reality/fantasy/reality stories
- Text categories: storybook, information book, information storybook, and biography

Story Elements

When discussing the elements of a story in my classroom, we use the terms character, setting, time, mood, theme, and plot (story structure) because they are easy for the children to understand and talk about. At

FIGURE 4-4 *Character web*

the beginning of the year I mention the various elements informally as I read and as we discuss a story. Over time, I focus on each one, usually starting with character.

For example, during the second reading of *Letting Swift River Go*, Jane Yolen's account of the flooding of the land and towns near her present home in central Massachusetts to make the Quabbin Reservoir, we made a web describing some of the feelings a young girl growing up at that time might have had (see Figure 4-4).

The elements of story are written on a Storybook Plan form (Appendix A4-1) and displayed on a chart in the reading area. Specific questions we might ask are also listed for everyone to see. We often

Name _The Class_ Date _3/14_
STORYBOOK PLAN
TITLE _The Tub People_
by Pam Conrad

CHARACTERS Tub People

PLACE Bathtub

TIME Day and night

MOOD Happy, sad, happy

FIGURE 4-5 *Storybook plan form*

refer to these charts during discussions and sometimes fill in a Story-book Plan form (see Figure 4-5) during group, or an individual or group of children fills it in for us during writing. Children also use the form to plan a story they want to write (See Chapter 7).

Story Questions

Character

    Is there a main character?

    Who is it?

    How is main character important to this story?

    Are there several main characters?

    Are there other important characters?

    How are they important to the story?

Setting

    Where does the story take place?

What is important about the setting?

How important is the setting to the story?

Are there several important settings?

Time

What is time frame in the story? part of a day, day, week, year, season, lifetime, etc.

How important is the time setting to the story?

What is important about it?

Mood

What is the mood(s) of the story? happy, sad, scary, etc.

How is the mood of the character important?

How is the mood of the plot important?

Plot

What is the story structure of this story?

Cycle story

Home/adventure/home

Reality/fantasy/reality

Is this a realistic story? Could it really have happened?

Story Structures

While focusing on the first four elements of story described above, the elements of plot and story structure are automatically included in the discussion. In my class our dialogue about plot focuses mainly on circle (cycle) stories and problem-solving stories, which have a conflict to be solved. In a circle story, such as *There's a Hole in the Bucket* (Wescott), the end of the story is almost the same as the beginning, and the same story could start over again. Problem-solving stories have a beginning, middle, and end, such as in the home/adventure/home story, *The Story About Ping* (Flack) and the reality/fantasy/reality story, *No Jumping on the Bed!* (Arnold).

We've also made group charts describing some of our favorite books that fit different structures or text sets. Usually I create the initial categories and we fill some of them in during group. Then individual children complete the chart over time, often working during settling-in

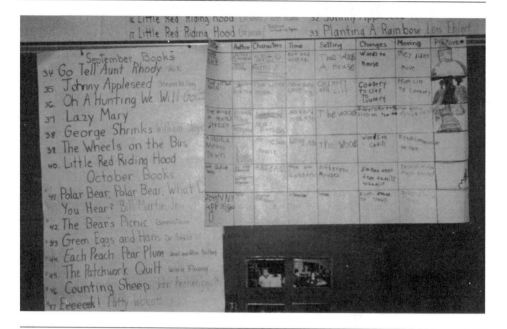

PHOTO 4-5 *Chart of different storybooks about westward expansion*

time or workshop. We've made charts describing circle stories, different home/adventure/home stories, and various versions of *The Mitten* and *Little Red Riding Hood.*

During our study of westward expansion we made a chart describing some of the common features of different storybooks about settling this country (see Photo 4–5). We divided a large piece of tag board into sections. Down the left hand side we listed five different books: *Home Place* (Dragonwagon); *The Little House* (Burton); *The House on Maple Street* (Pryor); *Aurora Means Dawn* (Sanders); *The Quilt Story* (Johnston); and *Johnny Appleseed* (Kellogg). Along the top we labeled some important features: title, author, characters, time, setting, changes, moving, and a place for a picture.

Curriculum Perspective

When we examine literature from a curriculum perspective with the children, we focus on the content areas of science and social studies. We do this primarily through information books and information storybooks, which are used extensively in my classroom as Read Alouds, independent reading resources, and references for inquiry during workshop.

I read many information books to the class, modeling different ways that readers use nonfiction and demonstrating study skills, or different ways to obtain, organize, and use information. For example, I explain that instead of reading the entire book, I might go to the table of contents or index to find what I am looking for and just read the pertinent chunks of texts or focus on pictures, graphs, or maps. I might also explain how I skim the pages for the key words about a topic (see Chapters 11 and 12).

Writer's Perspective

Read like a writer, write like a reader (Smith 1988). The two go hand in hand. When we view literature from a writing perspective we take a writer's point of view, stepping into the writer's shoes and linking what we know with what he/she has written. The rich discussions that accompany Read Alouds and the stimulating interactions when the children share their own writing are two powerful times when we think about literature in the class from a writer's perspective.

"Where do you think this author got the idea for this story?", "What did she have to know to write it?", "What kinds of things interested him?" These questions, which we discuss during story time, and think about as we write, become the questions we ask each other when the children share their writing. "Where did you get the idea for your story?", "Where do you get all the information in your story?", "I notice that you're interested in dinosaurs."

When I read *Letting Swift River Go* (Yolen), I told the children that the author, Jane Yolen, lived in the area that had been flooded for the Quabin Reservoir. We discussed that in writing the book, she imagined how a young girl growing up in the area might have felt as the land became flooded. We talked about important things that have happened to us that we have written about. We discussed why we wanted to write about certain important topics in our lives and how we felt after we had written about them.

We also discussed style and voice in writing as part of author studies. Jane Yolen wrote *Letting Swift River Go* in the first person, using "I" because she identified with the children of the time and wanted to keep it personal. Jan Brett's story orientation is different. In *Berlioz the Bear*, she wrote in the third person as she told about Berlioz and the musicians' adventures in getting to town. The illustrations enhance the story and even tell a story within a story through the use of borders surrounding the text on each page.

I sometimes talk about myself as an author, showing the children the drafts, copyedited manuscript, and galleys of *Joyful Learning*. I tell them that I wrote the book because I wanted to remember, and more clearly understand, what I did as a kindergarten teacher, and because I thought that other kindergarten teachers would be interested in what I did. I show them an example of a part I had to rewrite because the copyeditor didn't think it would be clear enough to the readers. I also explain that as the author, I had the choice of whether to make that change or not.

Vocabulary discussion is also prominent when we look at literature from a writer's perspective. We talk about a word an author has used and what different words would make sense and sound right in its place. I often start the discussion by saying, "If you were the author, what word might you use instead of _____ in this sentence?" For example, the following discussion ensued from this text by Jane Yolen:

> When it got dark
> the stars came out, reflecting in the water,
> winking on and off and on like fireflies.

"Jane Yolen uses the word "winking" to describe the reflection of the stars on the water in *Letting Swift River Go* (unpaged). If you were the author, what word might you use instead of winking, or would you use the same word?"

"Blinking," "turning," "flashing," and "sparkling" are some of the responses. I might write the sentence on the easel and list the words. We could focus on the semantic cueing system and be assured that all our choices made sense. We might refer to the syntactic cueing system and note that all the words we picked needed to end in *ing* in order to

76

sound right. We might draw our attention to the graphophonemic cueing system and talk about the beginning sounds to predict and confirm our reading of the word.

Reading Process Perspective

During the early elementary years a great deal of attention is given to ways to support children's growth as independent readers of the printed word. Chapter 5, "Shared Literacy," describes ways that teachers can help children grow toward independence in reading while they learn as a classroom community. Chapter 6, "Helping Individual Readers," suggests ways that teachers can work with individual readers.

QUESTIONS TEACHERS ASK

1. What do you do about children who have not been read to before coming to school?

Read to them—a lot. We have to start with what the children know and with what they have experienced. If they haven't heard lots of stories during their first five or six years of life, we must read to them so that those patterns of language and rich story structures become a deep part of their experience. School can be a second chance for some children and give them that "foundation of literacy," as Don Holdaway would say, that we know is essential for reading and writing. We have to give them lots of "bedtime stories."

FOR FURTHER READING

AVERY, CAROL. 1993. *. . . AND WITH A LIGHT TOUCH: LEARNING ABOUT READING, WRITING, AND TEACHING WITH FIRST GRADERS.* PORTSMOUTH, NH: HEINEMANN.

HARRIS, VIOLET, ED. 1992. *TEACHING MULTICULTURAL LITERATURE IN GRADES K-8.* NORWOOD, MA: CHRISTOPHER-GORDON.

HARSTE, JEROME, AND KATHY SHORT, WITH CAROLYN BURKE. 1988. *CREATING CLASSROOMS FOR AUTHORS.* PORTSMOUTH, NH: HEINEMANN.

HART-HEWINS, LINDA, AND JAN WELLS. 1990. *REAL BOOKS FOR READING: LEARNING TO READ WITH CHILDREN'S LITERATURE.* PORTSMOUTH, NH: HEINEMANN.

HARWAYNE, SHELLEY. 1992. *LASTING IMPRESSIONS: WEAVING LITERATURE INTO THE WRITING WORKSHOP.* PORTSMOUTH, NH: HEINEMANN.

HICKMAN, JANET, AND BERNICE E. CULLINAN, EDS. 1989. *CHILDREN'S LITERATURE IN THE CLASSROOM: WEAVING* CHARLOTTE'S WEB. NORWOOD, MA: CHRISTOPHER-GORDON.

MOSS, JOY F. 1990. *FOCUS ON LITERATURE: A CONTEXT FOR LITERACY LEARNING.* KATONAH, NY: RICHARD C. OWEN.

PETERSON, RALPH, AND MARYANN EEDS. 1990. *GRAND CONVERSATIONS.* NEW YORK: SCHOLASTIC.

TOMPKINS, GAIL E., AND LEA M. McGEE. 1993. *TEACHING READING WITH LITERATURE: CASE STUDIES TO ACTION PLANS.* NEW YORK: MACMILLAN.

YOLEN, JANE. 1992. "ON WRITING AND ILLUSTRATING *LETTING SWIFT RIVER GO.*" *BOOK LINKS: CONNECTING BOOKS, LIBRARIES, AND CLASSROOMS* 2(1), SEPTEMBER.

TEXT SET: ALPHABET BOOKS

AGARD, JOHN. 1989. *THE CALYPSO ALPHABET.* LITTLETON, MA: SUNDANCE.

ARGENT, KERRY. 1989. *ANIMAL CAPERS.* NEW YORK: DIAL.

AYLESWORTH, JIM. 1992A. *OLD BLACK FLY.* NEW YORK: HENRY HOLT.

———. 1992B. *THE FOLKS IN THE VALLEY.* NEW YORK: HARPER.

AZARIAN, MARY. 1981. *A FARMER'S ALPHABET.* BOSTON, MA: DAVID R. GODINE.

BAYER, JANE. 1984. *A MY NAME IS ALICE.* NEW YORK: DIAL.

CAMERON, POLLY. 1961. *"I CAN'T," SAID THE ANT.* NEW YORK: SCHOLASTIC.

CHRISTENSEN, BONNIE. *1994. AN EDIBLE ALPHABET.* NEW YORK: DIAL.

ELTING, MARY, AND MICHAEL FOLSOM. 1980. *Q IS FOR DUCK.* NEW YORK: CLARION.

FEELINGS, MURIEL. 1974. *JAMBO MEANS HELLO.* NEW YORK: DIAL.

HOBAN, TANA. 1987. *26 LETTERS AND 99 CENTS.* NEW YORK: GREENWILLOW.

KITAMURA, SATOSHI. 1985. *WHAT'S INSIDE?* NEW YORK: FARRAR, STRAUS & GIROUX.

KNOWLTON, JACK. 1988. *GEOGRAPHY FROM A TO Z.* NEW YORK: HARPERCOLLINS.

MAYERS, FLORENCE C. 1986. *ABC: MUSEUM OF FINE ARTS, BOSTON.* NEW YORK: HARRY N. ABRAMS.

McDONALD, MARY. 1988. *DEBRA'S DOG.* CRYSTAL LAKE, IL: RIGBY.

MODESITT, JEANNE. 1990. *THE STORY OF Z.* SAXONVILLE, MA: PICTURE BOOK STUDIO.

OWENS, MARY BETH. 1988. *A CARIBOU ALPHABET.* NEW YORK: FARRAR, STRAUS & GIROUX.

PALLOTTA, JERRY. 1991. *THE UNDERWATER ALPHABET BOOK.* WATERTOWN, MA. CHARLESBRIDGE.

SHELBY, ANNE. 1991. *POTLUCK.* NEW YORK: ORCHARD.

SLOAT, TERI. 1989. *FROM LETTER TO LETTER.* NEW YORK: E. P. DUTTON.

TEXT SET: FAVORITE SINGING BOOKS

ALIKI. 1968. *HUSH LITTLE BABY.* NEW YORK: SIMON & SCHUSTER.

———. 1974. *GO TELL AUNT RHODY.* NEW YORK: MACMILLAN.

BANGS, EDWARD. 1976. *STEPHEN KELLOGG'S YANKEE DOODLE.* NEW YORK: PARENTS' MAGAZINE PRESS.

BRAND, OSCAR. 1974. *WHEN I FIRST CAME TO THIS LAND.* NEW YORK: G. P. PUTNAM.

EOVALSI, MARYANN. 1987. *THE WHEELS ON THE BUS.* BOSTON, MA: LITTLE, BROWN.

GERSTEIN, MORDICAI. 1984. *ROLL OVER.* NEW YORK: CROWN.

GILMAN, ALEX. 1990. *TAKE ME OUT TO THE BALL GAME.* NEW YORK: FOUR WINDS.

HAGUE, MICHAEL. 1992. *TWINKLE, TWINKLE, LITTLE STAR.* NEW YORK: MORROW.

JONES, CAROL. 1990. *THIS OLD MAN.* BOSTON, MA: HOUGHTON MIFFLIN.

KOVALSKI, MARYANN. 1987. *THE WHEELS ON THE BUS.* BOSTON, MA: LITTLE, BROWN.

LENSKI, LOIS. 1987. *SING A SONG OF PEOPLE.* BOSTON, MA: LITTLE, BROWN.

PEEK, MERLE. 1969. *ROLL OVER! A COUNTING BOOK.* NEW YORK: CLARION.

———. 1985. *MARY WORE HER RED DRESS.* NEW YORK: CLARION.

———. 1987. *THE BALANCING ACT.* NEW YORK: CLARION.

QUACKENBUSH, ROBERT. 1973. *GO TELL AUNT RHODY.* NEW YORK: LIPPINCOTT.

ROUNDS, GLEN. 1990. *I KNOW AN OLD LADY WHO SWALLOWED A FLY.* NEW YORK: HOLIDAY HOUSE.

WESCOTT, NADINE B. 1988. *THE LADY WITH THE ALLIGATOR PURSE.* BOSTON, MA: LITTLE, BROWN.

———. 1990. *THERE'S A HOLE IN THE BUCKET.* NEW YORK: HARPER.

WICKSTROM, SYLVIE. 1988. *THE WHEELS ON THE BUS.* NEW YORK: CROWN.

ZEMACH, MARGOT. 1976. *HUSH LITTLE BABY.* NEW YORK: E. P. DUTTON.

TEXT SET: RHYTHMIC AND REPETITIVE BOOKS

BAER, GENE. 1989. *THUMP, THUMP, RAT-A-TAT-TAT.* NEW YORK: HARPER & ROW.

BARCUS, SARAH. 1975. *I WAS WALKING DOWN THE ROAD.* NEW YORK: SCHOLASTIC.

BENNETT, JILL. 1986. *TEENY TINY WOMAN.* NEW YORK: G. P. PUTNAM.

CARLE, ERIC. 1993. *TODAY IS MONDAY.* NEW YORK: PHILOMEL.

COWLEY, JOY. 1984. *I'M THE KING OF THE MOUNTAIN.* KATONAH, NY: RICHARD C. OWEN.

FOX, MEM. 1995. *TOUGH BORIS.* NEW YORK: HARCOURT BRACE.

PEEK, MERLE. 1985. *MARY WORE HER RED DRESS.* NEW YORK: CLARION.

ROSEN, MICHAEL. 1989. *WE'RE GOING ON A BEAR HUNT.* NEW YORK: MARGARET K. MCELDERRY BOOKS.

SMITH, JUDITH. 1986. *THE THREE BILLY GOATS GRUFF.* CRYSTAL LAKE, IL: RIGBY.

VAGIN, VAGIN, AND FRANK ASCH. 1989. *HERE COMES THE CAT.* NEW YORK: SCHOLASTIC.

VAUGHN, MARCIA. 1989. *THE SANDWICH THAT MAX MADE.* CRYSTAL LAKE, IL: RIGBY.

WEISS, NICKI. 1989. *WHERE DOES THE BROWN BEAR GO?* NEW YORK: GREENWILLOW.

WESCOTT, NADINE B. 1980. *I KNOW AN OLD LADY WHO SWALLOWED A FLY.* BOSTON, MA: LITTLE, BROWN.

WILLIAMS, SUE. 1989. *I WENT WALKING.* NEW YORK: HARCOURT BRACE.

WOLCOTT, PATTY. 1991. *WHERE DID THAT NAUGHTY LITTLE HAMSTER GO?* NEW YORK: RANDOM HOUSE.

WOOD, AUDREY. 1984. *THE NAPPING HOUSE.* NEW YORK: HARCOURT BRACE.

TEXT SET: HOME/ADVENTURE/HOME BOOKS

ARNOLD, TEDD. 1987. *NO MORE JUMPING ON THE BED!* NEW YORK: DIAL.

BROWNE, ANTHONY. 1989. *THE TUNNEL.* NEW YORK: KNOPF.

BUCKNALL, CAROLINE. 1988. *ONE BEAR IN THE PICTURE.* NEW YORK: DIAL.

COLE, JOANNA. 1986. *THE MAGIC SCHOOL BUS AT THE WATERWORKS.* NEW YORK: SCHOLASTIC.

CONRAD, PAM. 1993. *THE TUB GRANDFATHER.* NEW YORK: HARPERCOLLINS.

DUVOISIN, ROGER. 1953. *PETUNIA TAKES A TRIP.* NEW YORK: KNOPF.

———. 1961. *VERONICA.* NEW YORK: KNOPF.

EASTMAN, P. D. 1960. *ARE YOU MY MOTHER?* NEW YORK: RANDOM HOUSE.

FLACK, MARJORIE, AND KURT WIESE. 1933. *THE STORY ABOUT PING.* NEW YORK: VIKING.

HALL, DONALD. 1979. *OX-CART MAN.* NEW YORK: VIKING.

KLINTING, LARS. 1987. *PEARL'S ADVENTURE.* NEW YORK: RAND S. BOOKS.

KRAUS, ROBERT. 1986. *WHERE ARE YOU GOING LITTLE MOUSE?* NEW YORK: GREENWILLOW.

LEAF, MUNRO. 1988. *WEE GILLIS.* NEW YORK: VIKING.

LOCKER, THOMAS. 1984. *WHERE THE RIVER BEGINS.* NEW YORK: DIAL.

MARTIN, RAFE. 1993. *THE BOY WHO LIVED WITH THE SEALS.* NEW YORK: G. P. PUTNAM.

MURROW, LIZA KETCHUM. 1989. *GOOD-BYE, SAMMY.* NEW YORK: HOLIDAY HOUSE.

POTTER, BEATRIX. 1988. *PETER RABBIT.* NEW YORK: VIKING PENGUIN.

SAY, ALAN. 1993. *GRANDFATHER'S JOURNEY.* BOSTON, MA. HOUGHTON MIFFLIN.

VAN ALLSBURG, CHRIS. 1988. *TWO BAD ANTS.* NEW YORK: HOUGHTON MIFFLIN.

5

Shared Literacy

Whole Class group time is one of the essential components of a process-oriented classroom. This time, traditionally known as shared book (Holdaway 1979) or shared reading (the term used by many North American teachers) has often been considered as a teaching technique that teachers use only with emergent readers in kindergarten, using big books, charts, and a pointer. But I believe that it has value throughout the grades and encompasses a wider range of literacy learning than just reading skills.

I have come to call this group time "shared literacy." It includes all the times in the day when the entire class gathers together to learn in community. A noncompetitive, risk-taking environment is created as the class engages in literature, social studies, science, and math discussions, and as I demonstrate reading and writing skills and strategies (see Photo 5-1).

Shared literacy includes the demonstration and participation components of Holdaway's (1986) Natural Learning Classroom Model in which the teacher demonstrates and the children participate in literacy learning. It is the prime instructional time for the reading (and writing) process.

This chapter specifically focuses on the role of shared literacy from a reading process perspective. First I examine the components of explicit instruction and then describe specific skills and strategies that I use during group to help children develop fluency in reading.

PHOTO 5–1 *Shared literacy*

EXPLICIT INSTRUCTION*

In my classroom shared literacy is one of the main instructional times during the day. As it's interactive and fast paced, I videotaped several sessions in my classroom and analyzed the transcripts and tapes of those sessions, and then developed an "Explicit Instruction Planning and Evaluation Form," which I now use as a guide to plan and evaluate my teaching (see Figure 5–1 and Appendix A5–1).

I use the term explicit instruction, rather than direct instruction, to describe my teaching because it reflects the dynamic relationship and interaction between me and the children. Direct instruction is a phrase

*This research was part of the work done through a Teacher-Researcher Grant that I received for the 1992–93 school year from the Massachusetts Field Center for Teaching and Learning.

82

EXPLICIT INSTRUCTION
PLANNING AND EVALUATION FORM

Date	3/7		
TEXT	Three Billy Goats Gruff		
CLASSROOM CONTEXT	Have heard many times. Popular		
CATEGORIES OF LEANRING			
Strategies	To ke parts of narreter goats,		
Skills	" "		
Content	Other words for "said"		
SOURCES			
Teacher knowledge	✓		
Teacher observations	✓		
Children's questions	✓		
TYPES OF EXPLICIT INSTRUCTION			
Physical demonstration	Cover words w. th post. its		
Questioning	What other words makes ase?		
Making statements			
Eliciting practice	Read rest with different words		
Validating			

FIGURE 5-1 *Explicit instruction planning & evaluation form*

with a history. It recalls past teaching days when how and what I taught came from what adults—teachers, curriculum coordinators, school committees, writers of basals and college texts—thought the children needed to know. I would stand at the front of the room, tell the children what I was going to teach and then lead them through rote drill. Sometimes they would write or do a follow-up worksheet and I would correct it. Eventually I would give them a test to see what they had learned.

Explicit instruction requires a classroom organization that includes demonstration, participation, practice role-play, and performance (Holdaway 1986). It presumes a classroom atmosphere that allows for the open expression of the conditions of natural learning (Cambourne 1988), and it assumes that the personal and collective experiences (schema) of students and teacher are not separate from the teaching and learning that takes place. It is based on understanding that when children read together and talk about text, each one is predicting, approximating, self-correcting, and confirming to make sense of the text; each is working toward developing a self-extending system for literacy learning (Clay 1991). As Holdaway (1979) observed, "The unison situation, properly controlled in a lively and meaningful spirit, allows for massive individual practice by every pupil in the teaching context" (129).

Classroom Context

The classroom context, as well as the background knowledge and personal history of the children, always affects explicit instruction. This includes family background, daily personal life, health, the weather, the season, classroom interests, and what else is going on during the day, as well as the children's particular interests and association with a particular text. For example, one class often requested *The Three Billy Goats Gruff* (Smith), which they loved to dramatize. This familiar, popular text allowed us to delve deeper and deeper into meanings, text structure, and skills strategies and content.

Text

If as teachers we believe that learning is meaning driven, then the purpose of learning skills and developing strategies is to apply them as we read and write to construct meaning. Therefore, the skills, strategies, and content we explicitly teach should always relate to a text (poem, song, chant, big book, trade book) rather than be taught in isolation. We usually work with familiar texts, although an unfamiliar one offers distinctive opportunities for predicting experiences, which are not available after a first reading.

Categories of Learning

There are three major categories of learning that I explicitly teach: skills, strategies, and content. I refer to skills as small, concrete units of knowledge, and strategies as patterns of learning that help the learner construct meaning from the text. Skills and strategies go hand in hand, so I continually make explicit to the children how they relate to each other. For example, knowing letter names and sounds is a skill. Applying them while reading to predict, sample, and confirm or self-correct to construct meaning is a strategy. I show the children that skills and strategies work together in order for us to learn content, which includes concepts, facts, vocabulary, and knowledge.

As we worked with *The Three Billy Goats Gruff*, we discussed the different words that we could substitute for *said* before or after a direct quotation. As we examined the text, we tried out different possibilities that would be appropriate for the different billy goats and for the troll, continually checking to see if our text sounded right and made sense. I wrote the words on Post-it Notes as we discussed their letters and sounds.

Sources of Explicit Instruction

Explicit instruction in my classroom generates from three sources: my knowledge as a teacher; skills and strategies that I notice the children practicing as they gain control of reading and writing; and direct questions. My knowledge as a teacher includes all that I know from my experience teaching and observing children, from professional readings, courses and workshops, and from conversations with colleagues and parents. What I observe, as the children read and write, is also an important source for group instruction. For example, when I notice that many children are putting a lot of apostrophes in their writing, I consider discussing contractions and possessives. Finally, direct questions from children provide an obvious source of explicit instruction because the children are asking me to respond to what they want to control in a meaningful context. When Dawn asked, "What are those marks?" as she pointed to quotation marks, I gave her a brief explanation.

Although one source usually initiates instruction, all three are critical to the dynamic teaching and learning inherent in shared literacy. During a single session we address many skills, strategies, and areas of content and daily sessions allow for numerous and repeated opportunities for explicit instruction from all three sources. For example, explicit teaching relating to the word *said* in *The Three Billy Goats Gruff* came from all three sources. I knew that beginning readers come across synonyms for *said* as they read and that attention to this helps their reading. During writing conferences I noticed several different spellings for *said.* One child asked, "Does *said* begin with a *c* or an *s*?"

Experience has shown me that what I notice as a teaching moment for one child can often benefit others. Many times I focus on a similar explicit teaching lesson with the entire class after exploring it with an individual. One time, when reading to me, Bobby seemed stuck with words beginning with *a,* such as *around, about,* and *ahead.* Since I knew that he was ready to deal strategically with words with this pattern, I made explicit some of their graphophonemic complexities. The next day during shared literacy the class and I focused explicitly on words with the prefix *a,* generating a list of words beginning with *a* and discussing their similarities and differences. Our list included words with different sounds of *a,* such as *acorn, ahead, alley,* and *also.*

Types of Explicit Instruction

Explicit instruction includes physical demonstrations, questioning, making statements, eliciting practice, and validating. In a typical session all are usually employed rapidly and repeatedly.

Physical demonstrations are actions by me and the children. They include pointing, masking words, writing, dramatizing a word, phrase or story, and asking children to physically respond (for example, by writing a letter in the air).

Questioning calls attention to a skill, strategy, or content and is followed by an answer by the students or me. I either call on a volunteer to answer, ask for a group response, or answer the question myself. Children come to the easel and point or frame their response in the text. Sometimes my tone of voice encourages a child to continue a chain of responses that are leading to an answer.

Making statements is one of the primary ways that I explicitly teach. As we work with a text I might state:

- We put quotation marks before and after the exact words that someone says.

- When you add *ing* to a word, don't keep the silent *e*.
- This is important: People's names begin with a capital.

Eliciting practice is another form of explicit instruction, and is also directed at the entire group, rather than an individual child.

- Let's all spell *said* out loud five times: "s-a-i-d, s-a-i-d, s-a-i-d, s-a-i-d, s-a-i-d."
- Close your eyes and picture the periods and the end of the sentences on this page. Then open your eyes and check.
- Trace a question mark on the rug in front of you.

Validating the children's responses is a more subtle form of explicit instruction. It is usually done by nodding my head or by saying, "Right" or "Yes." Since shared literacy is a time when we learn in community, the children are not particularly singled out for a correct answer. Therefore, the purpose of this validation is primarily to encourage them to stay involved or let them know that they are on the right track, not to motivate them to perform for their peers or to win praise from me.

Planning and Evaluating

I use the Explicit Instruction Planning and Evaluation Form when I want to analyze my teaching more formally. In using the form as a planning tool, I write down what I *think* we will do during shared literacy. Then, after the session, I record what actually happened. I don't try to stick to my plan rigidly, however, because it is important to maintain spontaneity and ensure that the children are controlling their own learning. Shared literacy sessions need a balance of leadership between the teacher and children to be effective.

Explicit teaching is based on a transactional model of learning, rather than a transmission model of teaching (Weaver 1994). Instruction is initiated from several sources: the knowledge of the teacher, observations of children at work, and questions children ask. It is always related to a text and not taught in isolation. Therefore skills, strategies, and content are practiced and learned in context, not as an isolated drill. They are learned through the process of reading and writing for authentic purposes and are revisited often, rather than taught sequentially and for mastery in and of themselves. Finally, the learning from explicit instruction is evaluated by the teacher, not by a test or worksheet, and applied for future instruction as the learner uses the skills, strategies, and content.

SHARED LITERACY SESSIONS

Throughout shared literacy I am demonstrating and the children are participating in a variety of strategies as we read and write for meaningful purposes. Often this is done very naturally. For example, as we wrote a group letter to our pen pals in Olga McLaren's first grade in Houston, we kept rereading to keep our train of thought, to check what we had said, and to decide what to write next. When I was reading *The Keeping Quilt* (Polacco) to the class, I had to slow down and sound out some of the unfamiliar names.

I also explicitly teach reading strategies, often with big books. When I introduced the big book, *The Little Yellow Chicken* (Cowley) I covered some of the words with Post-it Notes. First, we predicted words that would make sense and sound right in the text and I wrote them on the note. Next, we looked at the first letter of the word and confirmed any words that had the same beginning letter as possibilities. Then we made a new list of possible words beginning with that letter before looking at the word that the author had chosen.

Benefits of Shared Literacy

All of the strategies I described from my experiences in kindergarten in *Joyful Learning* are applicable for teaching in the primary grades. The benefits of shared reading to support kindergartners listed here apply to primary age children as well. In fact they are universal and apply to all readers. I believe that shared literacy:

- develops a sense of community in the classroom, building upon the value of the group experience of culturally significant language, which is transmitted through group participation;

- promotes a community of learners where everyone has something to contribute and learn from one another;
- acknowledges that language is social;
- gives opportunities for all children to attend to what is personally meaningful, interesting, and functional and to share it with others;
- engages all children in reading-like behavior;
- enables children to share more of themselves by allowing for repeated opportunities to take risks, approximate, self-correct and comprehend within the safety of the group in a noncompetitive atmosphere;
- brings children in contact with the literary experience of books and the language of the outside world;
- validates reading for meaning;
- provides demonstrations of appropriate selection and use of the three language cueing systems;
- enables individuals to develop and internalize their own learning style;
- gives opportunities for children at all levels on the reading continuum to be successful learners;
- offers optimum quality and quantity time each day for the teacher to demonstrate.

THE THREE LANGUAGE CUEING SYSTEMS

Successful readers have control of the three language cueing systems: the semantic, or meaning system; the syntactic, or language system; and the graphophonemic, or system of relationship between letters and sounds. Successful readers apply these three systems strategically to construct meaning. My goal is to help the children in my class gain and keep control of the cueing systems as they grow as independent readers.

Goodman, Watson, and Burke (1987) explain language cueing systems as "the sources of information readers use in their transactions with the text as they seek to comprehend. Three language cueing systems operate during reading—graphophonemic, syntactic, and semantic systems. The interrelationships of these three linguistic systems, with the social-cultural context in which they occur is the pragmatic system, which must also be considered" (25).

"The semantic system refers to the system of meanings in language" (27). Meaning is at the center of our reading. It is the reason we read, so when we focus on semantic reading strategies during shared literacy or individual reading, I ask, "Does it make sense?"

"The syntactic system refers to the interrelationships of words, sentences, and paragraphs within a coherent text" (26). When we focus on syntactic reading strategies, I ask, "Does it sound right?"

"The graphophonemic system is the set of relationships between the sounds and the written forms of the language" (25). When we focus on this cueing system, I ask if the letters and sounds of a particular word match what they think the word could be.

The goal is to use these systems strategically to construct meaning. "When people read, they are actively involved. As they transact with a written text in their long-distance conversation with the author, they are engaged in a wide variety of plans, or *reading strategies,* building or creating their own meaning or comprehension . . . . It is in this transaction that readers at all ages and of all materials use the same overall reading strategies" (29).

The skills and strategies I demonstrate during shared literacy to integrate the three cueing systems include: predicting, vocabulary development, conventions of print, spelling conventions, masking, and ways to figure out unknown words.

Predicting

Frank Smith (1983) writes that ". . . prediction is essential for reading, that everyone who can comprehend spoken language is capable of prediction, and that prediction is routinely practiced in reading by beginners as well as by fluent readers" (26). Although humans automatically predict, which Smith defines as "the prior elimination of unlikely alternatives," during shared literacy we often spend some time as a group activating prior knowledge and predicting what a book will be about before we read it. We share personal experiences that the book brings to mind. We discuss what the book might be about from the title, cover, and pictures. As we read the story we predict what might happen next.

Sometimes I make the role of predicting more explicit. I tell the children that readers often spend time before reading predicting what the book will be about so they can understand and enjoy it more. Then I guide them through some predicting strategies. Before reading a storybook we sometimes use the Storybook Plan (Appendix A4–1) to predict the characters, place and mood, and what the problem or adventure might be. After reading we confirm our predictions. If it doesn't make sense or sound right, we self-correct and then confirm what we have read. Before reading an information book we discuss what we know about the topic and what we would like to learn. Then we look at the table of contents or index and select a part to read.

Vocabulary Development

Discussing vocabulary is one of the best ways to demonstrate the integration of the three cueing systems because we are reading strategically to create meaning. I am continually helping the children to do this by asking, "Does this make sense?" (semantic); "Does it sound right?" (syntactic); and "Do the letters and sound confirm our predictions?" (graphophonemic).

One way to extend and enrich vocabulary is to talk about other words that would make sense and sound right in a specific text. I often ask the children, "If you were the author, what word might you use instead?" For example, in *The Little Yellow Chicken* (Cowley) we discussed alternative words and phrases for "laughed at" in the sentence, "His friends laughed at him" (2). Suggestions included "teased," "ignored," "made fun of," and "went with." We had to reread and read ahead in the story as we discussed which phrases would sound right *and* make sense within the whole story.

Conventions of Print

Throughout the primary years, children continue to internalize the conventions of print and apply them more and more automatically (Holdaway 1979). I consider conventions of print as the skills and strategies needed to make sense of print. We learn them so that we can apply them strategically as we read and write for meaning. Therefore, during shared literacy I demonstrate these conventions in the context of meaningful texts, not as isolated skills.

Conventions of Print

Book knowledge

- Front of the book
- Back of the book
- Reading the left-hand page before the right-hand page
- Holding a book and turning the pages
- Distinction between pictures and print
- Title
- Author

Directionality

- Where to start reading on the page
- Reading left to right
- Return sweep
- Page sequence

Visual Conventions

- Difference between a letter, word, and sentence
- Spaces between words
- Punctuation (period, question mark, exclamation mark, comma, quotation marks)
- Letter recognition (upper and lower case)

Auditory Conventions

- Sound-symbol relationship
- Hearing use of punctuation
- One-to-one correspondence (Fisher 1991, 50–51)

Spelling Conventions

Spelling conventions come up frequently as we look at texts. Two things that help spelling develop is the predictability of letter patterns and the frequency of letters. We find words with *e* at the end and discuss how it affects the spelling of a word. We notice that *oa* is a frequent spelling pattern, but that there aren't many words with an *ao* pattern. We also focus on homographs and discuss that the meaning of a word guides its spelling. We talk about vowels and practice spelling high-frequency words (see Chapter 10 for more details of spelling during shared literacy).

Masking

A list of masking questions from *Joyful Learning* that I ask children during shared reading as a strategy to help them focus on print is reprinted here. (outlines of the masks are in Appendix A5–2):

Masking Questions

Who would like to mask . . . ?

- a letter they know
- a word they know
- the letter that their first (last) name begins with
- a letter in their name
- their favorite letter
- the letter that their friend's name begins with
- the letter ____
- the letter with the sound ____
- the letter before ____
- the letter after ____
- the letter between ____ and ____
- a lower case letter ____
- an upper case letter ____
- a small word
- a medium-sized word
- a large word
- a word with one (two, three, etc.) letters

- a word that begins with ____
- a word that ends with ____
- a word with the blend ____
- the word ____
- a word that means about the same as ____
- a word that is the opposite of ____
- a compound word
- a color word
- an action word
- the name of a person, place, or thing
- a word with the ending *ing* (*ly*, *ed*, etc.)
- a period (question mark, quotation marks, etc.)
- the contraction for *I am*
- the first word on the page we are going to read
- the last word on the page we are going to read

I use these questions and masks extensively in my first grade, and many teachers in the primary grades have told me that the questions are appropriate for the children they teach. The questions allow us to focus on many of the skills, concepts about print, and writing conventions that come up naturally as we discuss texts, as I write in front of the class, and as the children read and write throughout the day. Masking is always done strategically as part of the meaning-making process because we always talk about the functions of the words we mask in the text.

When I want to focus on a particular convention, I ask specific questions. For example, as part of one shared literacy session, using the text *Bear Facts* (Gentner), I asked, "Who can mask a lower case *b*?" "A lower case *d*?" and "Who can find a question mark?" We talked about the differences and similarities between the two letters and then got into a discussion about upper case *B* and *D*. After we located some question marks, we compared other marks of punctuation in the text, such as commas, periods, and ellipses.

Children gain control of the session when I ask the open-ended question, "What do you notice?" Some responses from *I'm the King of the Mountain* (Cowley) were: "I notice the word *top* in the word *stop*.", "I notice that *Rooster* begins with the same letter as my name.", and "I notice a lot of quotation marks."

Children also gain control when they ask the masking questions and call on their classmates to respond. For example, they came up with the following questions from the big book, *Where the Forest Meets the Sea* (Baker). "Who can find a word with two-*l*s?", "Who can find a word with a *y* sound?", "Who can find the word *an* in a bigger word?" Both of these approaches give the children control over our discussions, and gives me the opportunity subsequently to build upon items in which they have shown interest.

Although I have described the children's responses to print, it is important to note that often they notice the illustrations, especially at the beginning of the year and when we first focus on a book in detail. Illustrations relate to the meaning of the text, and many readers use pictures to make sense of print. This semantic strategy especially supports beginning readers as they work to integrate the semantic, syntactic, and graphophonemic cueing systems.

Ways to Figure Out Unknown Words

In the middle of the year we began to generate a list of strategies that we use when we come to a word we don't know. One year our list included the following:

1. I look at the sounds.
2. I read on and try to figure out what makes sense.
3. I do my "ear spelling."
4. I try to read it—sound it out.
5. I think about how to write the first letter.
6. I look at the pictures.
7. I skip the word.
8. I skip the word and figure it out later.
9. I read it again.
10. I look for little words in a big word.

We reviewed and added to it, and it became a resource as children read together or independently, and as I worked with individual children. The list, along with my observations, were authentic evaluation tools. The children were reading strategically.

QUESTIONS TEACHERS ASK

1. You talk about explicit teaching during group sessions of shared literacy. Do you teach explicitly when you work an individual child?

When I work with individuals, I do the same type of explicit teaching as when I do shared literacy with a group. However, since I am just working with one child, I am able to match this teaching more closely to the child's specific, individual needs.

FOR FURTHER READING

CLAY, MARIE. 1991. *BECOMING LITERATE: THE CONSTRUCTION OF INNER CONTROL.* PORTSMOUTH, NH: HEINEMANN.

FISHER, BOBBI. 1991. *JOYFUL LEARNING: A WHOLE LANGUAGE KINDERGARTEN.* PORTSMOUTH, NH: HEINEMANN.

GOODMAN, KENNETH. 1993. *PHONICS PHACTS.* PORTSMOUTH, NH: HEINEMANN.

GOODMAN, YETTA, DOROTHY WATSON, AND CAROLYN BURKE. 1987. *READING MISCUE INVENTORY: ALTERNATIVE PROCEDURES.* KATONAH, NY: RICHARD C. OWEN.

HOLDAWAY, DON. 1979. *THE FOUNDATIONS OF LITERACY.* PORTSMOUTH, NH: HEINEMANN.

WEAVER, CONSTANCE. 1994. *READING PROCESS AND PRACTICE: FROM SOCIO-PSYCHOLINGUISTICS TO WHOLE LANGUAGE.* 2D ED. PORTSMOUTH, NH: HEINEMANN.

TEXT SET: FAVORITE BIG BOOKS

BAKER, JEANNIE. 1987. *WHERE THE FOREST MEETS THE SEA.* NEW YORK: SCHOLASTIC.

BARCUS, SARAH. 1975. *I WAS WALKING DOWN THE ROAD.* NEW YORK: SCHOLASTIC.

COWLEY, JOY. 1984. *I'M THE KING OF THE MOUNTAIN.* KATONAH, NY: RICHARD C. OWEN.

——. 1988A. *GREEDY CAT.* BOTHELL, WA: THE WRIGHT GROUP.

———. 1988b. *The Little Yellow Chicken.* Bothell, WA: The Wright Group.

Rendall, Jenny. 1986. *When Goldilocks Went to the House of the Bears.* New York: Scholastic.

Rose, Gerald. 1975. *Trouble in the Ark.* New York: Scholastic.

Smith, Judith. 1986. *The Three Billy Goats Gruff.* Crystal Lake, IL: Rigby.

Vaughn, Marcia. 1989. *The Sandwich that Max Made.* Crystal Lake, IL: Rigby.

Williamson, Fraser. 1993. *Why Frog and Snake Can't Be Friends.* Crystal Lake, IL: Rigby.

TEXT SET: FAVORITE SONG BIG BOOKS

Belanger, Claude. 1988. *I Like the Rain.* Bothell, WA: The Wright Group.

Daniel, Alan, and Lea Daniel. 1992. *The Ants Go Marching.* Bothell, WA: The Wright Group.

———. 1994. *Once an Austrian Went Yodeling.* Bothell, WA: The Wright Group.

Gentner, Norma. 1993a. *Bear Facts.* Bothell, WA: The Wright Group.

———. 1993b. *Dig a Dinosaur.* Bothell, WA: The Wright Group.

———. 1993c. *Gravity.* Bothell, WA: The Wright Group.

Lawrence, Lucy. 1990. *Fly Fly Witchy.* Crystal Lake, IL: Rigby.

Peek, Merle. 1985. *Mary Wore Her Red Dress.* New York: Clarion.

Valley, Jim. 1993. *Rain Forest.* Bothell, WA: The Wright Group.

Van Bramer, Joan. 1992. *Whale Rap.* Crystal Lake, IL: Rigby.

6

Helping Individual Readers

First grade has traditionally been considered the year when children learn to read, and, indeed, most five- to seven-year-olds do become independent readers as they focus on the print and read the words of simple texts that they have never seen or heard before. When I taught first grade seventeen years ago I believed that learning to read meant being able to "read the words." I considered that my main responsibility as a teacher was to help the children do just that, and I primarily taught through phonics. The meaning-centered reading that went on during read alouds, silent reading, and science and social studies projects seemed to be something separate. I didn't see the connections, but the children must have been making them on their own, using all the language cueing systems and applying a variety of reading strategies that I know about today. As I look back, I realize I could have made it a lot easier for them.

My understanding of reading has changed since then. I believe that meaning is at the heart of reading, and that my role is to help my students become independent language users for a variety of purposes. This chapter looks at reading from a reading process perspective, with specific emphasis on ways that I help individual children gain control of the three cueing systems and apply appropriate reading strategies as they develop into independent readers.

READING ROUTINES

My goal every September is to establish the main reading routines for the year. The class participates in shared literacy during group time in the morning and at other times during the day. After lunch we spend more than an hour reading, beginning with independent silent reading, moving to quiet reading with friends, then gathering together for some kind of sharing, which includes literature projects or writing in response journals, and concluding with an end-of-the-day bedtime story.

Silent Reading

On the first day I ask the children to take a few books and find a place in the room to read by themselves. Some sit at the tables or individual desks, and others stretch out in the reading area (see Photo 6–1). The block and the science areas are off limits because these hold too many potential distractions while the children are learning the routine. We start with five minutes and by the end of a month we have extended the time to fifteen. In January the children can read silently for twenty minutes and by the end of the year the sessions usually last more than half an hour. During this time I read for about five minutes and then confer with individual children.

Silent reading means that the children read by themselves. Everyone can participate because I define reading broadly to include looking at pictures, making up the story, and/or reading the words at various ranges of competency. Since reading out loud helps many children, I encourage them to do so in a whisper. If it is too difficult for some to read quietly enough not to distract others, I ask them to sit by themselves (see Photo 6–2).

Quiet Reading

I announce the end of silent reading, and the beginning of quiet reading. Although many children continue to read by themselves, they are

99

Photo 6-1 *Silent reading*

Photo 6-2 *Silent reading rules*

now free to move about the room and read quietly with each other (see Photo 6-3). Some share the books that they had been reading, while others join together at the rug area to read big books and charts or to sing songs.

Sharing Reading

As quiet reading ends and the children put away their books, sometimes different children share a book with the class. At the beginning of the year, I start a list of sharers in order to give everyone a chance. Each child sits in my chair by the easel, reads the title and author of their book, tells why he or she chose the book, shows or reads a favorite page, and calls for comments and questions. Some share the favorite book they brought from home on the first day.

As the year progresses, the reading committee (see Chapter 2) keeps track of the class readers for the day. Usually two children take turns reading a book that they have practiced together. In order to keep the session engaging, they often use two copies of the book, so that while one is reading, the other is showing the pictures.

SELECTING BOOKS

Learning to select books is an important part of the process and the children have almost complete freedom in choosing their reading materials. Since during silent reading they are not allowed to talk or move about the room, they learn to pick the number and kinds of books they will need ahead of time. They are free to choose from the storybooks, information books, trade books, beginning readers, and magazines, as well as read their school library books and books from home. Organizing the books in categories and text sets helps them locate the books they want and think about the different kinds of books and subjects that interest them. For example, Tyler knew where to go to find singing books, Alex went to the science area to find books about reptiles, and Elizabeth often took books from the I Can Read shelf.

PHOTO 6-3 *Reading together during quiet reading*

Sometimes I suggest or introduce specific books. For example, when I want to add new books to the classroom library, I select a special one for each child and put them at the children's places to be found when they return from lunch. I choose the books by matching interests and/or instructional reading ranges. Once I asked everyone to take a book from the science area. This encouraged a burst of interest in information books and helped many of the children realize that they *could* read from this type of book.

Periodically, I take out books for everyone from the town library. I give a brief book talk about each, the children select one for silent reading or quiet reading and during sharing time, they tell about their book. We keep them in a special library box and for the next month the books are available for everyone. Other times, the children read a book from the box and then give a book talk about it. Children usually go to the school library when they *need* a book rather than at a specific library time. However, once in a while we go as a class and each child picks a book for silent reading.

A month or so into the school year, after the general routines are established and I know the children's reading competencies, I suggest that everyone take some books to practice their reading. Most children are already practicing, and as the year goes by they spend more and more time attending to the print. I make this comment for the few children who are satisfied just to be looking at pictures and who I believe need to attend to the print more on their own. I keep this request very general because the reading materials for specific practice vary widely with each child and I don't want to foster comparisons and competition. However, I am aware of those who might need individual help choosing books within their current instructional range. One way to encourage this is to create a text set of big print books (see page 117), which includes trade books with a limited number of words in big print on each page.

READING GROWTH CONTINUUM

As a kindergarten teacher I developed categories to describe young readers as they developed toward independence (Fisher 1991). I watched and listened to children read, and I wrote down what they did. I referred to descriptions by Don Holdaway, Cochrane et al, and Marie Clay, and then watched some more. I added to my list and incorporated descriptive phrases that were significant to what I was observing.

As a first-grade teacher, I have continued to refine my understanding of what children do when they read. I have reread *The Foundations of Literacy* and *Independence in Reading* by Holdaway and *Reading, Writing, and Caring* by Cochrane, Cochrane, Scalena, and Buchanan. I have become familiar with running records through ELIC (Early Literacy In-Service Course) and with miscue analysis through *Reading Miscue Inventory: Alternative Procedures* by Goodman, Watson, and Burke. I have furthered my understanding of what young readers and writers do by reading *Becoming Literate: The Construction of Inner Control* and *An Observation Survey of Early Literacy Achievement* by Clay.

The Reading Growth Continuum, which lists general ranges and specific descriptors of reading behaviors, is an update of the "Stages of Reading Development" described in *Joyful Learning*. There I stated that, "I consider this descriptive list a draft. It will continue to change and never be complete because I am always learning as I observe children read and write and as I grow professionally through reading, attending conferences, talking with other teachers, presenting workshops, and reflecting. I encourage teachers to make their own list as they work with children in their classrooms" (79). The same can be said of the Reading Growth Continuum which is discussed in the next section and followed by a discussion of instruction books for each level. The main characteristics of each range on the continuum are summarized below and listed in detail in Appendix B6–1.

Reading Growth Continuum

Introduction to Books

- Emphasis on meaning of the story and the sound of language
- Emphasis on semantic and syntactic cueing systems

1. Book Awareness
2. I Am a Reader!

Print Range

- Attention to print when reading
- Attention to graphophonemic cueing system

3. Print Range One
4. Print Range Two

Independent Range

- Integration of semantic, syntactic, and graphophonemic cueing systems
- Reading for a variety of purposes

5. Becoming an Independent Reader
6. Independent Reader
7. Mature Reader

CONTINUUM RANGES

Introduction to Books and I Am a Reader Range

I have never had a child enter first grade at the Introduction to Books range, but I have many displaying I Am a Reader behavior. These children need extensive shared literacy experiences and daily opportunities to read and write. When I work with them individually, I have to be careful not to try to force them along the continuum. They need time. So we work very slowly, reading lots of books and interacting as we would if I were reading a bedtime story. We talk about different strategies for enjoying books. We recall prior knowledge, predict what the book will be about, match the words with the pictures, focus on beginning sounds, and point word for word as we read the text. We work with alphabet books and books with a small amount of print, which the children read over and over again.

Print Range

Readers within the print ranges concentrate heavily on the print, reading slowly, word for word (sometimes called voice pointing) and need to read out loud. Often they concentrate so intensely on the graphophonics that they lose track of the meaning and syntax of the story. Therefore, one of my jobs is to help them use all three cueing systems. We discuss the story as we read and I ask them if what they're reading makes sense and sounds right. They look at the pictures to predict the text and at the beginning letter(s) of the words to confirm their predictions. Readers in this range need lots of practice and benefit from reading the same books over and over again.

Print Range One:

Readers in Print Range One are beginning to attend to the print when reading and consequently benefit from pointing word for word, which they often do automatically. At the beginning they may be able to point to two words, but with six they get lost. Therefore, the number of words on a line and size of the print makes a big difference to their success.

When these children read with me, I ask them to point to the words so they will stay focused on the print and so I can monitor what they are doing. By the time they are successful reading a line of print, I reduce my requests for pointing, because I notice that they're usually able to monitor their reading strategies and automatically point when needed. If they lose their place or become confused, I refocus them and encourage them to point.

Print Range Two:

Print Range Two readers display many of the same characteristics of print one readers, but are able to read two or three lines of continuous text on a page. Although they still voice point and focus intensely on the print, they demonstrate some fluency, especially with familiar material. I use the same strategies described under print range one to support their reading.

Independent Range

By January, the majority of the children in my class are reading somewhere in the Independent Range on the continuum, which includes a wide range of competencies—from reading simple, short, unfamiliar texts, to more complicated and lengthy ones; from an uneven application of the cueing systems, to their strategic use; from one genre, usually the story, to a variety of genre, including informational texts and biographies; from reading out loud to silent reading; and from requesting to read to an adult to preferring to read to themselves.

The children and I spend a lot of our individual conference time talking about meaning starting with a general discussion, which often includes a retelling or a detailed discussion of a favorite or interesting part. This gives me an idea of what to listen for when the children give an oral reading of a self-selected part. If they seem to have understood the story, the oral reading acts as a catalyst for a discussion of vocabulary, metaphors, analogies, plot development, and so on. If comprehension seems confused, I listen for miscues that will give me a window into ways to help. For example, if the child doesn't self-correct, we focus on semantic strategies, such as predicting what will happen next and looking at the pictures for cues. I ask, "Does that make sense?" and "What would make sense?"

Becoming an Independent Reader:

Readers in this range are learning to read strategically as they integrate the three cueing systems. For example, they will go back and reread if the passage doesn't make sense or sound right and will look at the beginning letters to predict what to read. They often display uneven reading behaviors, which are greatly affected by the difficulty of the text and by what they bring to the reading—their personal schema or individual background, interests, knowledge, and experience. For example, when they have adequate background knowledge of the subject, their reading is more fluent and they use the semantic and syntactic cueing systems along with the graphophonics. With unfamiliar subjects their fluency is uneven and they sometimes return to print range strategies.

Independent Reader:

Fluency increases with independent readers as they more easily adjust their reading to the degree of difficulty of the text. They automatically employ a variety of reading strategies to fit the particular situation. As needed, they predict, confirm, reread, read ahead, and self-correct to make sense of what they are reading. My goal is to help these children gain a self-regulating, self-monitoring, and self-sustaining system with increasingly complex texts and different genre. Our conferences include sharing personal or aesthetic responses (Rosenblatt, 1978) discussing complex story structures, expanding vocabulary, and exploring different book formats, such as the table of contents, index and charts, and diagrams in information books. For example, Carolyn and I examined a chart about the different body parts of various insects in the information book *Creepy Crawlies* (Davidson), and Jake and I discussed the home/adventure/home format in *Pearl's Adventure* (Lars).

Mature Reader Range

It is very rare for a first grader to read in the Mature Range. These readers display many of the characteristics of adult readers. They read widely and have enough background knowledge to understand new material. They think conceptually and critically and understand nuances, metaphor, and symbolism. They read for information and enjoyment and can adjust the pace and focus of their reading to different genre, vocabulary, and content. My conferences with these readers mostly take the form of discussions, which help support them in expanding their knowledge, understandings, and interests.

Sometimes we develop an ongoing focus that generates from the interest of the child. For example, Jake and I started discussing the themes in the books he read after he wrote about them in his response journal.

INSTRUCTIONAL BOOKS

The emergent and early reading books from the Story Box, Sunshine Books and Twig Books (Wright Group), and Literacy 2000 (Rigby) form the core of instructional materials in my classroom (see Literature Resources, p. 383). These supportive texts help children move toward independence in reading. They change in complexity in the number of words and lines of text on a page, size of the letters, and the spaces between the words. They also change in the relationship of the text to the pictures. The texts develop from oral language patterns—talk written down—to various forms of written language and begin with predictable events and repetitive texts, from which the children can easily draw upon their prior knowledge, and continue to include different genre, such as myths, legends, biographies, plays, and science books. The books also change in the sophistication of story structure: characters, setting, time frame, plot, mood, and theme and develop in richness of vocabulary, metaphor, and symbolism (see Appendix B6–2).

In order to facilitate the selection of appropriate books, I've categorized them into eight levels. These are based on decisions I've made about their degree of difficulty as I observe children reading them. I have also taken into account suggestions from the publishers and the work by Marie Clay (1991) and Reading Recovery teachers (DeFord, Lyons and Pinnell 1991).

PHOTO 6-4 *Books categorized and stored in boxes on shelf with correspond-ing labels*

I mark each book at the top right hand corner (1-1, 1-2, 1-3, 1-4, 1-5, 1-6, 1-7, 2, 3, 4, 5, 6, 7, 8) and store them in boxes with correspond-ing labels on a special shelf (see Photo 6-4). Level 1 is divided into seven parts; each part corresponds to the number of words on a page. (There are usually eight pages.) For example, a 1-2 book such as *A Toy Box* (Literacy 2000) has two words on most of the pages. A 1-7 book, such as *My Friend* (Sunshine Books) has seven words on a page. The books in level 2 have between eight and fifteen words on a page and are eight or sixteen pages long. Levels 3 and 4 have more text on sixteen or twenty-four pages. Levels 5-8 continue to increase in complexity in story structure, genre, vocabulary, and the amount and size of the print.

In general, level 1 corresponds to Print Range One, levels 2-4, to Print Range Two, levels 5-6 to Becoming an Independent Reader, and levels 7-8 to Independent Reader. I also include trade books and I Can Read Books with big print and few words between levels 4 and 5 for those children who need more practice with controlled text features. As the children move along the continuum, the specificity of reading levels for instructional purposes becomes less important for their reading progress. Books at this level often are I Can Read Books, chapter books of various length, science books, and trade books.

ENVELOPE BOOKS

One part of my reading program that encourages *practicing reading* is called envelope books because the children take books home in a large manila envelope to read to their parents and then bring them back to read with me. The purpose of envelope books is to help each child practice reading at her instructional range.

The General Procedure

I usually start the envelope book procedure during the third week of school, explaining to the class that one part of their work in first grade is to practice reading so that they will be able to read more and more by themselves. I work with them individually with books that will help them do this.

To start, I mix the books from levels 1–1 to 6 (I save levels 7 and 8 for later in the year) and spread them out on the tables, requesting the children to look them over and bring me one or two that they would like to read to me. I record the title and level and put them aside to read with the child in the next few days. After school I sort the remaining books according to levels and put them in the labeled boxes on the shelf in the reading area.

The next day I briefly explain how envelope books work and what I will be doing with everyone to get started. I show the children what they will be taking home: a brown manila envelope with their name on it, Books I Can Read, a recording form to document their reading growth over time, and a letter to their parents describing the procedure and their role in it (see Appendix B6–3). I also send along a publication about reading "Getting Parents Involved" (see Appendix B6–4). Then I meet with the children individually. I listen to them read the book they selected the day before and help them choose a few books at their instructional range to take home in their envelope.

The children are encouraged to bring the books back about every three days and place the envelope in a basket in the reading area. During silent and quiet reading, and at other times during the day when I have a few minutes, I take an envelope from the basket, meet with the child, and listen to her read. Most children are consistent about bringing the books back, and I make certain that I also read regularly with the few children who don't return them often.

Working at the Appropriate Instructional Range

It takes a few weeks to settle on the appropriate instructional range for each child, since the ease, pace, and procedure varies with the individual and with his place on the reading continuum. For example, some children appear to go through the ranges very sequentially while others move along, but occasionally return to easier books. Some seem to just take off and all at once are reading books with a much higher degree of difficulty. A few children thrive on reading books that seem too difficult because they have the patience to stick with them. Some children seem to prefer other kinds of books, such as I Can Read Books, as the primary material for practicing their reading.

As I work individually with children I keep in mind that each child's reading is unique, and that it is my job to support each in developing a self-motivating, self-monitoring, and self-sustaining system (Clay 1993). Regardless of where the children are on the reading continuum, I always start with a discussion focused on meaning. For example, I talk about what they like, don't like, or wonder about. Daniel usually would open his book and with great enthusiasm show me a humorous part. Marina often would give a retelling of the entire book before reading a favorite part.

When I listen to children read orally, I keep in mind Clay's (1993) comment that "Oral reading remains important as the only situation that the teacher can use to observe, check, and reinforce appropriate reading behavior in the first few years" (251). It helps our teaching start with what the children can do and then work within the "zone of proximal development" (Vygotsky 1978), where with help they can learn new skills and strategies.

111

RECORDING READING PROGRESS

I keep records of each child's reading progress in a file folder with pockets, which I store in a plastic file box. I stand the file folders vertically in the file box, and after I read with a child I replace that child's folder horizontally. When I have read with everyone in the class, I turn the folders vertically and begin again. This way I keep track of the children with whom I have read and those I need to call up to read. In order to locate the folders easily, I write the children's names on both the vertical and horizontal right-hand corners. In these folders I keep the "Letter Identification Score Sheet" (Clay 1993), Reading Conference Recording Forms, Miscue Recording Forms, and parent recording forms for spelling assessment (see Chapter 8).

Letter Identification Score Sheet

At the beginning of the year I evaluate the children's knowledge of letters and sounds, using the "Letter Identification Score Sheet" in Clay's *Observational Survey of Early Literacy Achievement* (45–46). I sit with the children individually and record the letters they can name (and the substitutions they make) and the consonant and vowel sounds they can say. This baseline information guides some of my planning for shared literacy and directs my work with specific children during reading and writing conferences.

In January, using the same sheet but a different color pen, I reevaluate and share the children's progress with them. We talk about what they think they need to work on to continue their learning and what I'll do to help them. I make specific plans for those who would benefit from more explicit teaching of the graphophonemic cueing system.

Reading Conference Recording Form

Over the years I have developed various ways of recording children's progress as I have observed them reading. The Reading Conference

READING CONFERENCE RECORDING FORM   Name _____

DATE	TITLE	STRATEGIES	MISCUES	TEACHING OPPORTUNITIES	COMMENTS
10/12	Ouch _1-5_	Points when necessary			Deliberate
10/18	Shark in the sack 1-7		Skipped words	needed help getting started	
10/21	Guess What? 1-7				fluent
10/28	Where Are You Going		Ian for I'm Self-correcting	Read again when you're stuck	
11/2	My Home (2)	Sounds out reread	mother for dad (sc) mother for sister (sc)	Keep conscious of meaning!!!	Very pleased with her progress

FIGURE 6-1 *Reading conference recording form*

Recording Form (see Appendix A6–1) gives me an ongoing record of the children's progress, indicates ways that I have supported their reading in the past, and helps me consider future instructional practices. It is simple to use. Each time I have a conference I write down the date, title, and instructional level of the book they read. I also record the reading strategies I observe, their miscues and self-corrections, specific teaching opportunities, and other information that helps describe the reader (see Figure 6–1).

Miscue Recording Form

I created this form from the work of Goodman, Watson and Burke (1987) to use when I need specific information about a child's reading (see Appendix A6–2). For example, the children may have had difficulty telling me about a story they have read or they may be making many miscues when reading orally. Recording their various miscues helps me know more specifically how to help them self-monitor and apply the cueing systems. If their miscues change the meaning, we focus on what makes sense. If they change the syntax, we talk about how the text sounds. If the miscues are related to the graphophonics, we focus on auditory and visual matching. Sometimes a child just needs help selecting appropriate texts.

Parent Recording Forms

The children and their parents fill in this form, which lists the envelope books they read during the year (see Appendix A6-3). Parents record the book title, date, practice level (E = Easy; R = Just Right; Ch = Challenge; H = Too Hard), and comments. The column for teacher and parent comments is a convenient vehicle for ongoing communication. For example, if a parent notes that the books seem too easy, I pay special attention to what the child is reading. I may change the book level or explain why I want the child to continue on the same level. If a parent comments that the child is looking at the pictures for clues, I explain the value in this behavior.

ASSESSMENT PROFILES

I do everything I can to keep my evaluation record keeping simple and have continued to use the same procedure I followed in kindergarten with the Class Assessment Profile Form and the Individual Assessment Profile (Fisher 1991, 128). This evaluation procedure is for my use only, although I refer to it extensively before writing report cards, conferring with parents and school personnel, or planning individual or group instruction.

I have separate profiles for reading (see Appendix A6-4), writing, spelling, and math (see Chapters 7, 8, 9, and 10), which list the main descriptors or characteristics of the discipline. Each class profile chart lists the children's names in a column on the left, followed by columns to the right and the descriptors along the bottom. In the corresponding boxes I record my observations about each child (see Figure 6-2).

I find that a flexible coding system allows me to describe most accurately what I have observed. I use the following number and/or symbol system. Often I write a few words to clarify.

Number System	Symbol System
1. Most of the time	* Has full command
2. Some of the time	+ In control
3. Not noticed yet	0 Needs time

Reading September	Interest in books	Retells a story	Watches text/shared reading	Practices during silent reading	Recognizes upper case	Recognizes lower case	Letter/sound correspondence	Word/sound identification	Word/space/word match	Semantic cueing system	Syntatic cueing system	Graphophonemic cueing system	Self-corrects	Reading range
Pam	✗	3	2	3	18	13	+	+	0	need time				P1
Peter	✗	✓	+/+	+	24	18	+	+	5^one	need time				P2
Sam	✗	✓	✗	✗	24	26	✗	✗	✗	+	+	+	✗	I

FIGURE 6-2 *Class reading evaluation profile*

I keep the profiles for each discipline on separate clipboards so I can easily record my observations. Sometimes I record while the children are working and other times I record after school as I go over their work and reflect on their learning. Periodically, I transfer the information from the class profile to each child's Individual Assessment Profile (see Appendix A6–5), which has reading, writing, and spelling on one page and math on another. This profile has space to record four times a year, but I usually fill it out three times, in September, January, and May.

The reading assessment part of the profile lists the main indicators that I consider indicative of progress toward becoming an independent reader. They include engagement in reading, concepts about print, skills, and strategies pertinent to many readers in the primary years, and the three cueing systems.

QUESTIONS TEACHERS ASK

1. Are you involved with Reading Recovery in any way?

My school system has not adopted Reading Recovery, but I have many friends who are Reading Recovery teachers and I highly respect their work. I think that Reading Recovery in this country has been a successful response to children who need individual, specific support in reading. Each year I have one or two children who would have benefited from such a program.

2. Do you do running records or miscue analysis?

There are many ways for teachers to record the ongoing reading behavior of individual students. Running records and miscue analysis are two of them. I think that it is important for teachers to work out the best procedure for themselves. I have found that the Reading Conference Recording Form that I fill out when I listen to children read works well for me.

Miscue analysis is very helpful when I need very specific information in order to understand and help a child with reading difficulties. That's when I use the miscue recording form. Also, miscue analysis is an excellent way for teachers to learn about the reading process.

3. Our system is replacing our old scope and sequence charts with learning rubrics. What is your opinion of them?

There's a lot of talk about rubrics in education today. For my purposes, I think of a rubric as a list of markers within a range of learning. My Individual Assessment Profile could be considered a rubric. This profile is valuable to me because I created it and I have complete control of how I use it. I believe that rubrics must remain under the classroom teacher's control, however, and not become another method of standardized assessment.

FOR FURTHER READING

CLAY, MARIE. 1991. *BECOMING LITERATE: THE CONSTRUCTION OF INNER CONTROL.* PORTSMOUTH, NH: HEINEMANN.

———. 1993. *AN OBSERVATION SURVEY OF EARLY LITERACY ACHIEVEMENT.* PORTSMOUTH, NH: HEINEMANN.

DeFord, Diane E., Carol A. Lyons, and Gay Su Pinnell. 1991. *Bridges to Literacy: Learning from Reading Recovery.* Portsmouth, NH: Heinemann.

Department of Education, Wellington (New Zealand). 1985. *Reading in Junior Classes.* Katonah, NY: Richard C. Owen.

Goodman, Yetta, Dorothy Watson, and Carolyn Burke. 1987. *Reading Miscue Inventory: Alternative Procedures.* Katonah, NY: Richard C. Owen.

Holdaway, Don. 1980. *Independence in Reading.* Portsmouth, NH: Heinemann.

TEXT SET: BIG PRINT BOOKS

Aliki. 1974. *Go Tell Aunt Rhody.* New York: Macmillan.

Baer, Gene. 1989. *Thump, Thump, Rat-a-Tat-Tat.* New York: Harper & Row.

Barton, Byron. 1987. *Machines at Work.* New York: Thomas Y. Crowell.

Berenstain, Stan and Jan. 1969. *Bears on Wheels.* New York: Random House.

Dunrea, Oliver. 1985. *Mogwogs on the March!* New York: Holiday House.

Eastman, P. D. 1961. *Go Dog Go.* New York: Random House.

Ehlert, Lois. 1991. *Red Leaf, Yellow Leaf.* New York: Harcourt Brace.

Fox, Mem. 1994. *Time for Bed.* New York: Harcourt Brace.

Gilman, Alex. 1990. *Take Me Out to the Ball Game.* New York: Four Winds.

Hill, Eric. 1981. *Spot's First Walk.* New York: G. P. Putnam.

Hutchins, Pat. 1983. *You'll Grow into Them, Titch.* New York: Greenwillow.

Kraus, Robert. 1970. *Whose Mouse Are You?* New York: Macmillan.

Krauss, Ruth. 1948. *Bears.* New York: Harper.

LeSieg, Theo. 1961. *Ten Apples Up On Top.* New York: Random House.

Martin, Bill Jr., and John Archambault. 1985. *Here Are My Hands.* New York: Holt.

Sis, Peter. 1989. *Going Up.* New York: Greenwillow.

Tafuri, Nancy. 1989. *The Ball Bounced.* New York: Greenwillow.

Ward, Cindy. 1988. *Cookie's Week.* New York: G. P. Putnam.

Williams, Sue. 1989. *I Went Walking.* New York: Harcourt Brace.

Wolcott, Patty. 1991. *Where Did that Naughty Little Hamster Go?* New York: Random House.

7

Writing

"This book about my trip to California is going to be over one hundred pages long." Brian is in the middle of writing his second book of the year, but stops to write a home/adventure/home story entitled *Ants Go Marching,* which ends up being twelve pages and takes him a couple of weeks to finish.

"I don't usually write books. I have so many different ideas to write about." Beth likes to finish a new piece each day. She often writes about friends.

"I'm going to write a poem." At the beginning of the year Cara asked for reassurance that it was okay to write poetry. Her work is lyrical whether it's poetry or prose.

"This is going to be an information book about cars," Martin reports as he asks to go to the library for a book.

These comments, made in March, are typical as the children become engaged in their own daily writing. Commitment to writing deepens as they learn the classroom writing routines, become familiar with the process, and have many experiences with literature.

In my class, writing is the different ways that the children express themselves on paper and includes drawings and pictures, as well as letters and words. The writing discussed in this chapter refers primarily to the personal writing the children do during writing time, often referred to as writing workshop (Graves 1983; Calkins 1994). I describe how we get started in September, ways I encourage children as writers, and different opportunities for sharing in my class. Chapter eight discusses writing evaluation, including management techniques to keep work organized and portfolio assessment and strategies that support my teaching and that keep parents informed.

THE FIRST DAYS OF WRITING

Writing begins after the first group time in the morning, about an hour after the children have arrived in the room. We have settled in, sung some songs, heard a story, shared in community circle, and talked about the plans for the day. After a writing mini lesson, the children move to tables and desks around the room to write independently or collaboratively. They choose their own topic, genre, paper, and writing utensils.

My writing goals in September are for the children to love writing; to believe that they are writers; to understand that writing is meaning centered; and to feel confident to have-a-go and write the best they can. I want to get writing routines started—the habit of writing every day; the procedures for managing materials; the ways to share the work; and the portfolio evaluation.

Day One: Introducing Routines

When children write every day, they become deeply committed to their work, so we start writing on the first day and rarely miss a day throughout the year. My mini lesson is brief. I explain to the children that they are going to write and draw about something they know and that interests them and that they are to bring their work to the rug area when they are finished. I ask them to follow four steps: draw a picture, do some writing, and put their name and the date on the paper. They have the choice of either a plain piece of white paper or one with lines on the bottom with a space for a picture at the top. I call on a few children to select their paper, tell the group about what they are going to write, and start writing. Afterwards, the rest choose their paper and join them at the tables (see Photo 7–1).

I write along with the children for a few minutes and then move about the room, observing and talking to individuals about their work. As they finish, we sit in a circle on the rug and informally share our pieces. We check to see that our name, the date, a picture, and writing are included. Individual children are asked to go back and add any part that they left out. They put their work in the sharing basket in the writing area and at the end of the day I look them over and begin to record

119

PHOTO 7–1 *Children joining at tables to write*

what I notice about each child as a writer on the Class Writing Evaluation Profile (see Appendix A7–1).

Day Two: Four Steps for Writing

During the mini lesson on the second day we review the four procedures or "steps" for writing (draw something, write something, and put your name and the date on the paper). We call this a proofreading list, and as I write, I talk through what I am doing. For example, I mention that I am putting a space between each word as I write, I demonstrate ways to use ear spelling by saying a word slowly many times, and mention that we also need to use our eye spelling and look at the word. Kathryn thinks of a fifth rule, "Do the best you can." This then becomes a standard part of the list.

1. Write your **name** on your paper.
2. Write or stamp the **date** on your paper.
3. Read your writing. **Add** or **change** something if you need to.

4. Look at your drawing. Add more **detail** if you need to.

5. Do the **best** that you can.

The children then write and share their work informally with each other at the rug.

Day Three: Modeled Writing

On the third day I do some modeled writing, telling the children something that has happened to me and talking through how I select what I want to write. My primary purpose is to encourage them to begin to make the link between their own experiences and what they write about. We've already listened to stories during these first few days and have begun to talk about where the authors may have found their ideas. Now I want the children to begin to make the connection with their own writing.

As I write, I also demonstrate some of the important conventions the children will be working on throughout the year—lower case letters, spaces between words, ear and eye spelling, capital letters and periods, details in pictures. Paper with lines encourages writing, and this time I notice that more children select it than plain paper.

I spend writing time going to the different tables, listening to what the children want to tell me about their work, and continuing to fill in parts of the Writing Evaluation Profile. This day the children have a choice of where to put their writing. If they want to share, they put it in the sharing basket. If they don't want to share, they place it in a green nine-and-a-half by eleven-and-a-half-inch pocket folder that I have put in the file box at their tables that morning. The six-by-twelve-inch plastic file will hold the folders of the children assigned to that table, and when we change seating, the children will take their folders with them to their new places.

Day Four: Refining the Routines.

At the beginning of writing we review where to put finished work: file it or put it in the basket if you want to share it with the class. I also point out the sharing board, a bulletin board on which the children can hang their work. While they write, I continue to kid watch. At the end of the session two of the children who put their work in the sharing basket sit in the author's chair and share their work.

Day Five: Demonstrating Spelling Development

The next day's mini lesson concentrates on different ways children write. I use myself as an example, noting that when I was a child learning to write and spell, I probably wrote in different ways. I put a piece of half-plain, half-lined paper (*experience paper*) on the easel, pick a topic, and draw a quick picture. Then I begin to show the different ways I might have written as a little girl, demonstrating the general developmental stages of spelling (see Figure 7–1).

I say, "When I was a little girl I might have done scribble writing." I demonstrate and comment as I write. I repeat the procedure with the following writing possibilities, starting each with, "When I was a little girl I might have. . . ."

- written different letters that I knew.
- labeled the pictures.
- written the first sound that I heard as I said the words.
- written the first and last sounds that I heard.
- written the first and last sounds and some vowels.
- written some words and parts of words that I knew, leaving spaces between words.
- written the sentence in conventional spelling.

Since I can assume that there are children in the class writing in all of these ways, I purposely don't refer to specific ages or grade levels in this demonstration. The children need to know that however they write, it is just fine for them. This group demonstration gives me a reference point as I work with individual children and as I plan individual strategies for them.

For the prealphabetic writers, who know very few letters but who have wonderful stories to tell, it offers the freedom to scribble write as part of their development as a writer. I will focus on the story they tell me as they talk about their drawings and encourage them to try scribble writing and adding letters.

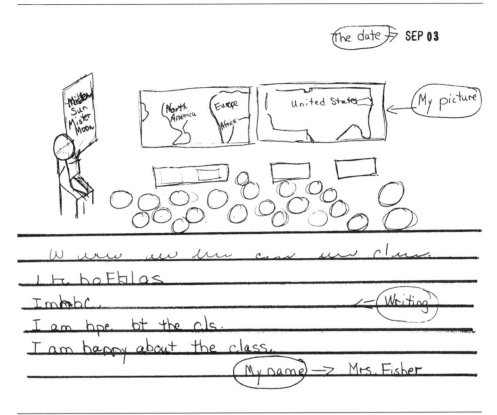

FIGURE 7-1 *Demonstration of spelling development*

Raymond had come from another school system and had not had experience with ear spelling. I sat with him and listened to his story. He was overwhelmed at the suggestion of writing all that he said, but was comfortable labeling his picture. He continued with the same subject, houses, well into October (he had just moved into a new house). Then he began to write phrases instead of labels and his drawings offered more details. He always put his work in the sharing basket, indicating that he felt confident enough to share his work in front of the class. After a successful time in the author's chair, I noticed that he began to write more.

Dawn wanted to spell everything correctly and kept asking for correct spellings. She wanted to please me and needed to know that she would get my approval by using her ear spelling. I also observed that she had a lot of conventional spellings in her work and was ready for other spelling strategies.

Karen was a very fluent writer and an active participant when we wrote and spelled during group. I asked her to read her writing before she shared it in front of the class and she was able to make several corrections to help her read more fluently. She was ready for some proofreading strategies.

During writing I begin to evaluate the children's letter and sound knowledge, administering the "Letter Identification" task (Clay 1993) individually to about five children a day (see Chapter 6).

Day Six and Beyond

Up to this point the focus of the writing mini lessons during shared literacy has been on procedural demonstrations to help the children establish the classroom routines for writing. Throughout the year I write in front of the children, demonstrating different genre, such as stories, science reports, invitations, thank-you notes, lists, and signs and specific writing conventions, such as left to right sweep, spaces between words, letter/sound correspondence, capital and lower case letters, and punctuation. Shared literacy becomes an amalgamation of reading and writing. It is difficult to tell where one begins and the other ends as we read like writers and write like readers.

ENCOURAGING CHILDREN AS WRITERS

Time to Write and Freedom of Topic Choice

In order to become engaged in writing, writers need to write every day. I believe a predictable routine helps, and in my class the children know that they will be writing after group time almost every morning.

At the beginning of the year most children write what I call a single piece, which consists of one idea, written on a single piece of paper, and finished in a day (see Figure 7–2). As the year goes on, many children begin to write books. One day in October Michael told me that he had to use several pieces of paper and that he was making a book. It all happened naturally because he had enough time and materials.

This is two flowers
with a rainbow.

The ocean is filled with
different animals.

Stacey
12/17

FIGURE 7–2 *Single pieces written at beginning of year*

Children also write books together. Tony and Ian spent four months writing a book entitled *The Attack of the Destroyer Peanut.* Every day they would get out their folder, pencils, and markers and write. The finished product shows their growth as writers. For example, in the early pages there were no spaces between words, but by the end, this convention had been mastered. The final sixty-nine page book is a demonstration of the social nature of writing as these two friends grew as writers.

When children have time to write and freedom to choose their own subject and format, they develop their own style and voice. Brian writes chronologies of family trips. Maybe he will be a news reporter. Billy and Daniel write books about soccer. Maybe they will be sports writers (Figure 7–3). Elizabeth writes about friends and family. Maybe she will write novels.

Mini Lessons

Mini lessons refer to the different demonstrations that teachers give to children about writing. Carol Avery, in *. . . And With a Light Touch,* using Mary Ellen Giacobbe's categories of mini lessons (procedures, strategies writers use, qualities of good writing, and skills) offers an extensive list of possibilities.

Sometimes mini lessons are formal. For example, I might write a list of the topics children have chosen to study. We might think of words that begin with *gr* and see if they would make sense and sound right in a big book we are reading. We might compose a group letter to our pen pals. As I write I'm also demonstrating letter formation, using a finger to leave spaces between words or writing from left to right.

Mini lessons are also informally embedded throughout the literacy discussions we have during the day as we read and write for a variety of meaningful purposes. Since their value lies in the authentic conversation surrounding them, it is often difficult to notice them as lessons.

Focus Times

As teachers, we find that the children's writing develops and remains dynamic when we orchestrate a rhythm of open times, when there is free-

He BLOKT IT

FIGURE 7-3 *A page from Billy and Daniel's book on soccer*

dom of choice, and focus times, when we put some parameters on their work. The open times are much longer than the focus times because we trust that when children have ownership and freedom as writers, they write what they need to write and learn what they need to learn.

Mini lessons offer the structure for focus times. It's when we ask the children to concentrate on a particular skill, strategy, or content as they write. An example of a skill focus is when I ask the children to think about including more lower case letters as they write. A strategy focus is when I suggest that they think about the lead in their piece as they start their writing. Content focus might emphasize vocabulary when I ask the children to include words that help us form a picture in our mind, which we call picture words. We often end focus time writing by sitting in a circle with our pieces in front of us at the rug area, sharing our work.

I consider focus times as times when I work within "the zone of proximal development" (Vygotsky 1978) both with the whole class and with each child individually. Although the particular focus is the same for everyone, each child is responding to his or her own developmental needs.

Special Writing

In my class the children often become so engaged in their own writing that they consider the special assignments I occasionally give them during writing as an intrusion. "What do you mean? I was planning to work on my book about my shells," Victor exclaims. "Ashley and I are in the middle of a book about flowers," Laura informs me. The children have taught me to warn them at least a day in advance that we will be having special writing, so they can adjust to the change in routine and think about the assignment in advance.

What we call special writing usually takes a day to complete. It is assigned about every three weeks when there is a particular strategy or topic about which I want the children to write. One year I noticed that several of the children were drawing during most of writing time and not putting much effort into writing. I helped them refocus by only offering choice of lined paper with no designated place for a picture and asking them to spend the entire writing time just writing. This strategy encouraged many to write more and to express their ideas in words, not just in pictures.

Writing to their pen pals in Olga McLaren's first grade in Houston, Texas or, as part of a social studies topic, writing about the one thing they would pack in the trunk if they were an immigrant child coming to this country long ago, were a few special topics. These assignments also provided me with similar set of writing samples from everyone in the class for evaluation purposes.

SHARING OPPORTUNITIES

Bob Wortman suggests that audience changes one's writing process (Wortman 1994). I consider sharing to include all the different exchanges about work that occur in the class, from informal conversations at the writing table to sitting in the author's chair, to publishing a book. Regardless of the manner of sharing, I believe that the children should make the choice of *if, when,* and *how* they want to share their work. Teachers should give them the opportunities.

Informal Sharing

Informal sharing goes on throughout the day as the children talk about their work (see Photo 7–2), show it to a teacher or peer, hang it on a bulletin board in the writing area, or collaborate on a piece of writing and continues when children take their work home to show family members.

I've noticed that this informal sharing often satisfies young children. They don't require elaborate vehicles for sharing because much of their motivation seems to come from within themselves. When a piece is finished, it is filed and forgotten. Work put on the sharing board is taken down after a few days and the children don't seem to care or notice if anyone has looked at it. Sometimes children want to take a piece of writing home and, other times, this doesn't seem important at all.

Large Group Sharing

Children who want to share their writing with the class place it in the sharing basket in the writing area, and at the end of writing we gather at the rug to share. When time is limited, I hold up each piece and acknowledge the author. Sometimes she reads the piece and briefly comments on it.

Other days we have what I call Circle Share because we all sit in a circle with a current piece in front of us. Everyone has the choice of sharing. The focus of this sharing varies. We read the piece, share a favorite part, word, or expression; or tell how our writing went that day.

> "I just couldn't get going today," Carl admits.
> "I really concentrated," Conrad reports.
> "I almost finished my book," Lea relates.

The Author's Chair

Several times a week two or three children share their writing from a special chair labeled Author's Chair (Hansen and Graves 1983). (See Photo 7–3.) I keep a list to assure that everyone who wants to share in this way gets a chance.

At the beginning of the year the children read their pieces and show their pictures. This activity might include giving an oral telling from their

PHOTO 7-2 *Informal sharing goes on throughout the day*

scribble writing or picture, reading the labels by saying, "I wrote 'h' for house," or slowly reading their ear spelling word for word. Next, the child in the author's chair calls on different classmates to comment on the piece and then responds before calling on someone else. I ask the audience to start with the phrase, "I notice" because this directs them to focus on what the author has done and keeps the remarks positive:

> "I notice you used different colors."
> "I notice you wrote a lot of letters."
> "I notice your dog looks like it's jumping."

As the year goes on and the children become greater risk takers as learners and develop trust in each other, they generate a wider variety of questions and comments:

PHOTO 7–3 *Sharing writing from the Author's Chair*

"Why did you draw the horse bigger than the elephant?"
"Why did you decide to write about buried treasure?"
"Are you going to change anything in the piece tomorrow?"
"I notice a lot of detail in the boat you drew."

The author's sharing and the audience's comments primarily focus on meaning through discussion of the author's words and pictures, not on writing conventions. Children are at different levels in their writing development and the power of the piece lies in their ideas and story. However, sometimes in the introductory sharing the author mentions a convention he or she has put in. One day, soon after we had discussed that every word has a vowel, Jeff commented that he had put a vowel in every word in his piece and therefore the words were spelled right. As author, he was in charge. Once in a while someone in the audience notices a convention. Lindsay told Stevie, "I notice that you left spaces between the words." He was validated for something he had done.

My role is to support the children in becoming more and more in charge of the Author's Chair by helping them develop a procedure for sharing and by modeling what writers (the author) and readers (the audience) do. At the beginning of the year, although I sit in the group as one of the audience, I am more directive about what goes on. I initiate the introductory reading by the author, the "I notice" questions, the procedure for calling on people to share, or by sharing a piece I have written. After two children have shared their work, we discuss what went on and begin to write some rules for the audience since everyone has participated in that capacity. The rules usually include:

> "Don't talk."
> "Wait to be called on."
> "Say what you notice."

After a few weeks, when most of the children have sat in the Author's Chair, we write some rules for the author, which we review, edit, and rewrite throughout the year:

> "Hold your paper so everyone can see it."
> "Don't be silly."
> "Don't call on the same people all the time."

I continually demonstrate different audience responses. At first I offer noticing comments. Then, when I feel that enough trust has developed in our classroom community, I model comments and questions that encourage the author to explain what he has done:

> "How did you learn to draw roofs on houses?"
> "Are you going to draw any more pictures about baseball?"

As the year goes on, children use the Author's Chair, small group sharing, or informal opportunities at their writing tables to get suggestions from their peers and to work on difficulties they are encountering with a piece in progress.

PUBLISHING

Publishing includes a variety of procedures in my class. Usually the children start publishing books on their own, and all at once we begin a text set of student made books. I follow the children's leads, watching to see when they are ready for suggestions, demonstrations of possibilities, and invitations of ways to publish their work.

The American Heritage dictionary's definition of publish is: (1) to prepare and issue (printed material) for public distribution or sale; (2) to bring to public attention, announce.

According to this definition, the children in my class publish all the time. Whenever they write something, they almost always end up discussing it in some way and thus bringing it to someone's attention.

At one end of the publishing continuum is informal sharing. Toward the other end are computer printed books illustrated by the children and edited for spelling and writing conventions. The most popular formal publishing format in my class falls in between the two. These are books that the children write and illustrate. They publish it with a cover and sometimes a dedication page and an about the author section, staple it together and put it in the box of student-authored books for others to read.

Children's Publishing Choices

As teachers, we notice some general characteristics or bench marks (Calkins 1994) in children's writing that help us respond to their publishing needs. I find that for those children whose writing relies heavily on pictures and who are not yet writing sentences with spaces between words or including many conventional spelling patterns, informal sharing usually satisfies them (see Figure 7–4). What is important to them is the process or the doing of writing and drawing. Sharing that has value occurs while they are writing or right after they finish. I watch these children write and notice how their physical involvement becomes an integral part of the process. They talk, move their mouths, wiggle, stand up, sit down, and when inhibited from moving, they have a hard time writing in a meaningful way. As I confer with them, they continue to

FIGURE 7-4 *Student piece that relies heavily on pictures with no writing*

mark on the page and talk about their piece. They add, change, delete, and elaborate, and continue making up the story as they go along. In a sense, the piece isn't finished until it's out of sight.

As children focus more on the mechanics of writing, evidenced by sentences, punctuation, and conventional spelling patterns in their work, some of these physical behaviors diminish and they become interested in more formal publishing. The focus shifts from the doing to what's on the page. When I confer with these writers, they concentrate on what they have written, and with pencil in hand, they edit the text. However, adding a cover and stapling the pages usually satisfies their publishing needs.

When children shift their focus to the meaning of the text they are writing, their piece takes on a life of its own. I notice that they are more interested in formally publishing their work. They become involved in proofreading and are more apt to want the text to be accurate. They take more time on each page of the text and make conscious decisions concerning all the parts of their book—the cover, title page, dedication, about the author page, and end papers.

Home/Adventure/Home Book: First Assignment

Last year I asked the children to write two books with a home/adventure/home structure—a familiar story structure in which the character

134

starts out at home, has an adventure and returns home at the end. Examples of this are *Peter Rabbit* (Potter), *Two Bad Ants* (Van Allsburg), and *Whose Mouse Are You?* (Kraus).

The children wrote the first one in December, after I noticed that many were already writing storybooks and would benefit from a specific focus assignment. We talked about the assignment for a few days before we began. This gave the children the opportunity to shift from their regular writing and to think about the topic before we started. It gave us time to read several home/adventure/home books and talk about the structure with the assignment in mind.

On the day we started, most children had their character and adventure in mind. I kept the parameters simple, using many of the organizational strategies introduced by Mary Ellen Giacobbe's work in classrooms and workshops.

- Take four pieces of paper with lines on the bottom and a space for a picture on the top.
- Page one: tell about your character at home.
- Page two and three: tell about the adventure.
- Page four: tell about your character back at home.

These simple instructions allowed all the children to write at their developmental level, to work at their own pace, and to express their own voice and interests. For example, Elizabeth used more than two pages for her adventure about her family, Tyler included conversation in his story about ants, Martin finished his in a day, and Peter took more than a week to complete his story.

On the fourth day, when most of the children had finished, we generated a list of some of the qualities of a good cover. The children designed a cover for each of their books and stapled the pages together. At the end of the day they read their books to each other, and either took them home or left them in the classroom library.

Good Book Covers
1. Title and picture are together
2. Picture is about the story
3. You can learn something

4. Action
5. Title reminds you of other things
6. Can see the title
7. Funny story—funny cover
8. Details
9. Borders tell about the story
10. Shows the characters
11. Decorations

Home/Adventure/Home Book: Second Assignment

The second home/adventure/home book that I asked the children to write included filling out a storybook plan (see Appendix A4–1), writing a draft, working with an adult editor, adding illustrations to a computer printed copy, and designing a cover. It took about two weeks for everyone to complete the procedure, which the children shared on Visitors' Day.

The process began about a week before the children started writing. This gave us time to discuss the upcoming assignment and allowed them to think about their story before starting to write. As the children decided on their characters and story plot, they told the class their plans, which gave the others ideas for their own story and created excitement and enthusiasm for the assignment.

Although the children would be writing independently, they would also be writing in community. There is something very powerful about a community of writers all working on the same kind of project. For example, Laura used this assignment to remember her grandfather, who died the day before we started the project, and to share her sadness with her classmates (see Figures 7–5 and 7–6).

Since this was the first adult edited, computer published book that the children had written, I wanted them to understand the procedure they would be following from start to finish. I showed them some of the stages that I went through to get *Joyful Learning* from an idea to a published book. I showed them my rough drafts, the editor's markings on the manuscript, the art work, and the galleys that all led to the final

Name Laura _____ Date 3/23 ____

STORYBOOK PLAN

TITLE 9RANdPA New Home _____

CHARACTERS 9RANdPA _____

PLACE Heaven and earth _____

TIME DAY Night _____

MOOD 2Ad hAppy _____

FIGURE 7-5 *Laura's storybook plan*

book. Then, in order for them to get an idea of what their final product would look like, I showed them a model of the computer printed book form we would be using.

Planning

Next, everyone filled out a storybook plan and home/adventure/home plan (Appendix A7-2). They did this at the rug area so I could easily respond to their questions and so they could discuss their plans with each other. Since they were already familiar with the forms, they got right to work within an atmosphere of collaboration and cooperation. Then I looked over the plans with every child and gave them a new manila folder and four pieces of half-lined paper to start. About half the class kept to four or five pages, although several wrote books of more than fifteen pages. I reminded them that since they would be drawing pictures on their final printed copy, they might want to consider doing their illustrations in draft form.

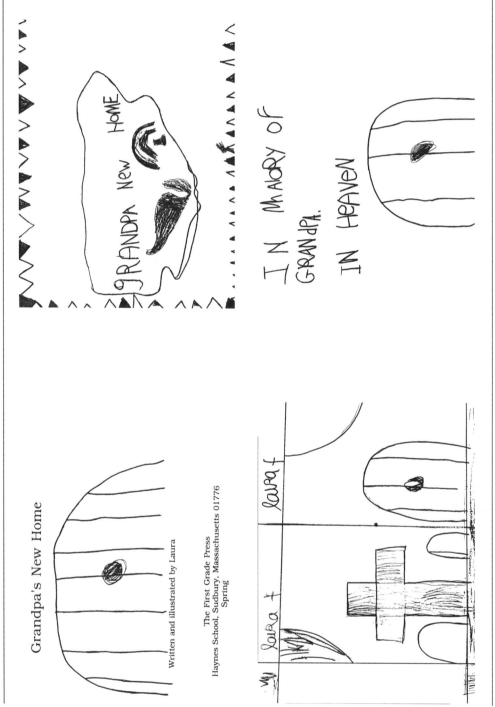

FIGURE 7–6 *Laura's writing to remember her grandfather*

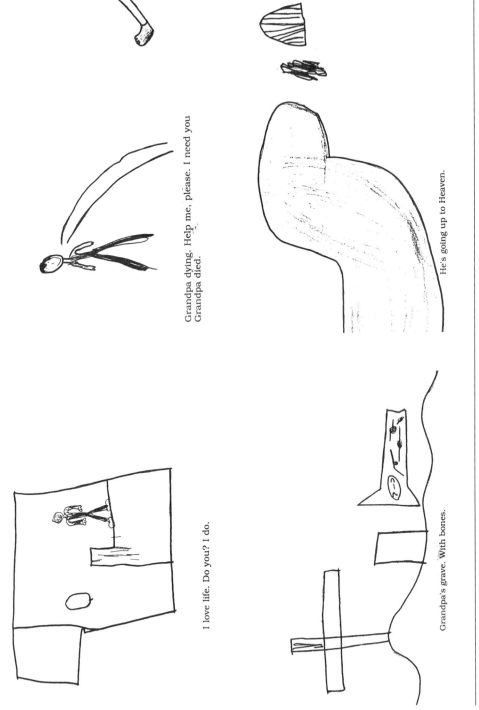

Grandpa dying. Help me, please. I need you
Grandpa died.

He's going up to Heaven.

I love life. Do you? I do.

Grandpa's grave. With bones.

FIGURE 7–6 *Laura's writing to remember her grandfather* (continued)

Writing

As the children got to work I realized that this was a good time for me to do some of my own writing. Everyone was engaged and no one needed me to interrupt with a teacher imposed conference. They were self-motivated and self-directed. As I wrote, children came up to ask me to spell a have-a-go word (see Chapter 9), and occasionally I would enter into the conversation at the table with those sitting around me.

Editing

In the next few days, as the children finished, I asked them to proofread their manuscript before giving me their folder. They returned to their regular writing and I called them over, one at a time, to edit their work.

First, we talked about their piece and went over the story and home/adventure/home plans again. We both had pencil in hand as they read their text out loud. Sometimes they would notice something to add, change, or delete, and, occasionally, I would ask them to make a change. Since I was the editor, I also wrote on their work, in order to make a teaching point or to clarify something I would need to know when I typed the story on the computer. This editing was very student specific and tailored to the development, interests, and personality of each child. For example, Carl and I worked on spelling, whereas Maria and I focused on indicating the beginnings and endings of sentences by adding capitals and periods.

Illustrating

When all the manuscripts had been typed, the children began their illustrations. During shared literacy we looked at drawings in favorite books and talked about the different artistic styles and what made them successful. I wanted the children to begin to consider their work from the point of view of the audience as well as creator. As they finished an illustration, they would show it to a friend for suggestions and received such comments as:

"You need to add more detail."
"The picture doesn't look finished. Put something in that space."
"Where is the character in your picture?"
"Why didn't you use any color?"

Creating the Cover

Designing, planning, and creating a cover took at least two days—one to design it and another to make the final copy. On the first morning, the clipboard list of things to do asked the children to, "Find a book cover you like. Bring the book to group."

During shared literacy they took turns showing the cover they had selected and telling what they liked about it. Liz Schreiner, my assistant, who works in the classroom twelve hours a week, added her comments about the artistic aspects. We discussed the size, spacing, and placement of letters, choice and contrast of colors, use of specific shapes, and selection of story details. We noticed that the title was easy to read, that the author's name was almost always on the cover, that use of color attracted our attention, that a circle was often used to highlight the title or main character, and that an important character and/or event in the story was often suggested in the illustrations.

The children then took newsprint and started designing their own covers. They were encouraged to use many pieces of paper and to try out different designs. There was a lot of conversation as they looked at each other's work, made comments and suggestions, and asked questions. The next day they transferred their drafts to a finer quality paper, added dedication and about the author pages if they wanted, and stapled their books together. That afternoon they read their books to each other in small groups. On Visitors' Day they proudly placed their books at their seats, ready to read to their own visitors, as well as the visitors of their friends.

QUESTIONS TEACHERS ASK

1. What do you do, especially at the beginning of the year, when children say that they can't write?

I tell them to draw a picture and write some letters. Remember, drawings are very important with young writers, and since we write every day, there is plenty of time for writing skills, strategies, *and* confidence to grow.

I learned a lot about risk taking, trust, and writing from Alan. For most of the school year he created meaning through drawings. Although he was willing to write, he was reluctant to try invented spelling. Rather, he developed strategies to obtain conventional spelling during writing: asking friends and me and copying his previous work and words around the room. The ideas expressed in his writing were limited by the fluency of his writing although his drawings were rich in story.

In looking closely at the way Alan approached learning, I began to realize that he desperately wanted to learn to read, and that he was methodically doing so through his daily writing. Spelling words correctly so he could read them was part of his learning process. He would read and reread the few words he wrote each day, and the meaning in his illustrations related to the words. Finally, in April, Alan started using invented spelling. He would write an entire page and often didn't include any illustrations. My assumption is that when he finally felt confident as a reader, he was ready to take on writing.

At first I felt that Alan wasn't writing enough, but I watched him carefully and trusted him as a learner. He was always conscientious and engaged, and taking risks in his own way. He was in control of his own learning as a reader *and* as a writer.

2. How have children used computers in your classroom?

The computer equipment in my classroom consists of one Macintosh SE, so our opportunities are somewhat limited. The children record their daily attendance using the program Excel, write stories, and play some games. Over one ten-week period, parents helped small groups of children publish their stories in the computer center, which had more and better equipment.

I believe that computers will play an increasingly important role in classrooms adopting a generative curriculum. For example, with the right equipment and classroom help, children today communicate online with pen pals around the world and access a wide variety of information as they research and pursue various topics and interests.

FOR FURTHER READING

AVERY, CAROL. 1993. *. . . AND WITH A LIGHT TOUCH: LEARNING ABOUT READING, WRITING, AND TEACHING WITH FIRST GRADERS.* PORTSMOUTH, NH: HEINEMANN.

CALKINS, LUCY M. 1994. *THE ART OF TEACHING WRITING.* NEW EDITION. PORTSMOUTH, NH: HEINEMANN.

DYSON, ANNE HAAS. 1989. *MULTIPLE WORLDS OF CHILD WRITERS: FRIENDS LEARNING TO WRITE.* NEW YORK: TEACHERS COLLEGE PRESS.

GRAVES, DONALD H. 1994. *A FRESH LOOK AT WRITING.* PORTSMOUTH, NH: HEINEMANN.

HUBBARD, RUTH S. 1989. *AUTHORS OF PICTURES, DRAUGHTSMEN OF WORDS.* PORTSMOUTH, NH: HEINEMANN.

OLSON, JANET L. 1992. *ENVISIONING WRITING: TOWARD AN INTEGRATION OF DRAWING AND WRITING.* PORTSMOUTH, NH: HEINEMANN.

8

Evaluating Writing

Peter Johnston states that all evaluation that does not directly benefit the child being evaluated is invalid (Johnston 1991). I want all the evaluation performed in my class to specifically support children as lifelong learners for a variety of meaningful purposes in their lives. This evaluation mainly consists of kidwatching (Goodman 1985), conferences with children, formal teacher evaluation, and portfolio assessment.

KIDWATCHING

I used to believe that teachers should almost always be interacting with the children. If I did just watch them, it usually was so I could tell them what to do and correct them right away before they developed bad habits. I certainly never believed that one of my teaching options was "to observe and do nothing at all" and to let the children continue to monitor their own learning

Now kidwatching is my starting point for evaluation. By kidwatching I mean watching *and* listening. My responses vary from child to child and take a different focus when I work with a group. For example, when Lynn wrote several lines, she didn't start each line at the same place, and so her writing moved to the right in a diagonal fashion. She and I talked about that together during a writing conference. Experience has shown me that what I notice as a teaching moment for one child can often benefit others. So during shared literacy I decided to focus explicitly on organizing lines of writing on a page.

CONFERRING WITH CHILDREN

The point of any writing conference is to help the children grow as writers, not to correct their work. I define a conference as any time when the children and I discuss their work. These opportunities arise periodically throughout the day and include both informal conversations and formal conferences.

Informal Conversations

I have many informal conversations with children during writing. Often I just walk around the room to check in and ask how things are going. Sometimes I get a status-of-the-class (Atwell 1987) and record on a class grid (see Appendix A8–1), information such as topic choice or level of engagement (see Figure 8–1), or fill in information on the Class Writing Profile (see Figure 8–2 and Appendix A7–1). Occasionally I sit at one of the writing tables and join in the conversation as one of the writers.

Formal Conferences

Formal conferences occur when I meet individually with my students to discuss their work (see Photo 8–1). I do this about once a week with each child, usually meeting for about five minutes. We sit together at a special desk and discuss a current piece of writing, work together on some guided writing, edit a piece to be published, or assess a piece for their writing portfolio. As we work, I often record my observations on an evaluation form.

CONFERRING ABOUT A PIECE OF WRITING

The student and I start by talking about the meaning of the piece, discussing where the idea came from, why they picked the subject, and what is important to them about their piece. They read it to me and tell me about their drawing. Next we focus on writing conventions, such as

Laura	Marina	Michael
Working with Ashley on book about flowers	Still working on story about the giant.	Writing series of books on plants as part of his committee work.
Paul	Sarah	Tyler
Hockey - in the middle of a book	Space - new piece	Sharks - almost finished. Will start new book

FIGURE 8-1 *Class grid*

leaving spaces between words or listening for sentences and putting capitals and periods. As we go along, the children make any additions or corrections that they feel are important, and I fill in the child's Writing Conference Recording Form (see Appendix 8-2). The form follows the same format as the Reading Conference Recording Form and is used in the same way. It helps me keep track of each child's growth and progress as a writer so I can support them individually and plan teaching strategies for shared literacy.

I fill out the form as I confer with the child. After writing the date, I record the type of the piece (story, informational, poem, letter, or newspaper article) and whether it is a single piece or part of a book. I note the meaning content, which includes what the piece is about, interesting phrases and vocabulary and any connections made with other subjects or pieces of literature. Next I write down any writing conventions that I believe are significant for the child. For instance, if I notice that a child is beginning to use spaces between words, I'll write "spaces." I then record any teaching opportunities that I take. For example, that we discussed the conventional uses of upper and lower case letters. Finally, we decide on a next step, which is usually one area on which the child will concentrate. It is often an area that I recorded during teaching opportunities or something that we have noticed or talked about during the conference (see Figure 8-3).

The form for each child is kept in a pocket folder in a plastic file box, along with other writing evaluation forms and samples. I place the

	Interest in writing	Drawing tells a story	Drawing predominates	Writing tells a story	Writing predominates	Reads back own writing	Spaces between words	Writes a sentence	Uses capitals and periods	Uses lower case letters	Pencil grip and direction	Hand writing and legibility
Pam	✓	yes	3	3	✓	✓	0	–	no	L?	0	
Peter	–	yes	3	3	✓	0	0	–	N	R/	✓	
Sam	✗	✗	2	2	✗	✓	✓	some	some	R/	✗	

Writing
September

FIGURE 8-2 *Class writing profile*

folder vertically in the box, and when I have worked with a child, I return the folder horizontally, which allows me to see which children still need conferences.

Collaborative Writing

Collaborative writing occurs when a child and I work together on a short piece, often just one sentence during a conference. My purpose is to explicitly teach specific skills and strategies, which I have noticed the child is working to control. For example we might focus on lower case letters, ear spelling, or spaces between words. We decide what we are going to write, and both of us, with pencil in hand, contribute what we know. Working within the zone of proximal development, I demonstrate, make statements, ask questions, and validate the child's responses.

PHOTO 8-1 *Formal writing conference*

FORMAL TEACHER EVALUATION

About three times a year I ask the children to do some special writing so I can formally evaluate their progress. My purpose is to determine the specific writing skills and strategies they are using, as well as writing content, so I can offer individual support, plan shared literacy lessons, and write report cards.

I tell the children that I will be asking them to do some special writing in a few days and that they should be thinking about what they want to write about. In October I offer them lined paper with space for a drawing at the top. In January they use paper with less space for drawing and more lines for writing. In May I give them paper with lines only. This way I get more lengthy writing samples as the children become more confident writers. I record my observations on the Writing Evaluation Profile and sometimes use the piece for one of the monthly portfolio assessments.

WRITING CONFERENCE RECORDING FORM   Name Daniel

DATE	GENRE	MEANING CONTENT	CONVENTIONS	TEACHING OPPORTUNITIES	NEXT STEPS
2|2	Book	Desert and Egypt	many lower case letters	periods	Put periods
2|9	Pen pal letter		lots of ? marks	Discussed I'm and I am	
2|16	Single	Theseus Pictures tell story	Periods at end of each line	Read to hear one sentence with and	Add more words to tell story

Theseus SLayed The Minitour.
and Got out of The Maze.
Feb. 16   For Mrs. S.

FIGURE 8-3 *Daniel's story and writing conference recording form*

Writing Assessment Form

This form covers writing content, drawings, writing conventions, handwriting, and spelling. It has a place for teacher, student, and parent comments. I send this home in February or March with a piece of writing and a cover letter explaining what we have been doing in writing and suggesting ways for parents to encourage their children's progress (see Appendix A8–3 and B8–1).

Spelling and Writing Skills Evaluation

This evaluation form focuses on the children's control of writing conventions, such as capital letters and periods to indicate the beginnings and endings of sentences, lower case letters and spaces between words, and spelling. I fill out the form and send it home along with the children's writing, and a letter to parents (see Appendix A8–4 and B8–2).

I want to demonstrate in measurable terms the children's competency in spelling. I divide the approximate number of words a child has written by the approximate number of correctly spelled words to get the percent of correct spellings and list all the different words the child has spelled correctly. (I use the word approximate here because sometimes it is difficult to get an exact count from young children's writing.) If the child has asked for have-a-go words I make note of them. In doing this several times a year, we notice that the list lengthens as the year goes on and becomes a very powerful display of spelling progress.

In the observations column I write comments that I believe are important about each child's writing. I always mention the meaning and content of the piece. Many of my other comments are in anticipation of questions parents might have. For example, I note the child's enthusiasm, specific conventions of which he or she is gaining control, or the fact that the child is beginning to write more. I also might point to some of the conventional spelling patterns that I notice in words that are not yet spelled correctly (see Figure 8–4).

Letter and Sound Identification Assessment

In September, I formally assess the children's letter and sound knowledge by administering the "Letter Identification" task (Clay 1993) individually to about four children a day during writing. I find that although kidwatching and ongoing evaluation of the children's writing gives me a lot of information about which upper and lower case letters each child is able to use and the extent of his or her letter/sound correspondence, this formal assessment gives me an organized and consistent record of everyone in the class. In March, I readminister the assessment to those children who didn't know most of the letters in September and share with them the progress they have made.

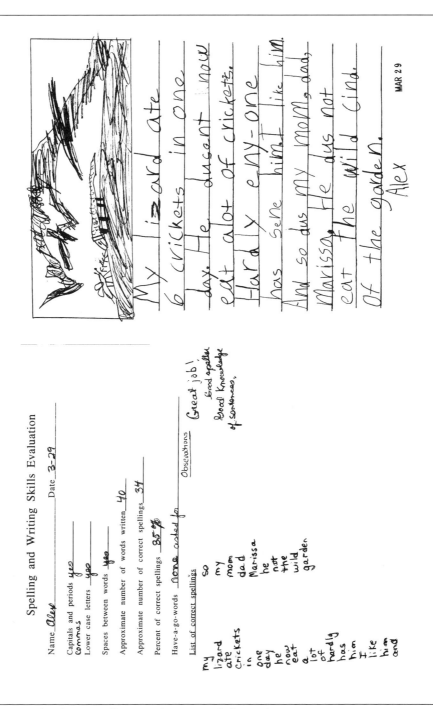

FIGURE 8-4 *Alex's spelling and writing skills evaluation*

Writing Evaluation Profile

The Writing Evaluation Profile (Appendix A7–1) addresses the major areas of writing that children focus upon during the early primary years. It includes the content and meaning of the writing and illustrations, writing conventions, and mechanics. The procedure I use with the evaluation profiles is described in Chapter 6.

PORTFOLIO ASSESSMENT

The purpose of writing portfolios in my classroom is to help the children grow as writers. Therefore, it is essential that they are involved in the process of selecting, organizing, and evaluating the pieces in their portfolio. They mainly use their portfolios to examine their own writing progress and make decisions about what do next as a writer. I use them to evaluate and plan instruction, to communicate with parents, and to inform interested school personnel and next year's teachers. A by-product for all of us is that portfolios contribute to beneficial classroom management. As the children learn to evaluate their work, their writing stays organized throughout the year.

Getting Files Started

When the children come in on the third day of school, they find a green pocket folder with their name on it at their table and a plastic file box with a labeled hanging file to keep the folder. At the end of writing I encourage them to put any unfinished work, referred to as work in process, in the folder. As the year goes on the folder will hold a personal dictionary and have-a-go papers (see Chapter 9), as well as a list of topics to write about.

During the second week of school I introduce the file in which the children put work that they finish during the month. This large plastic file holds a hanging file for each child and has a sign on the front indicating the current month, such as, "September Writing." Children file rough drafts, completed pieces, work that has hung on the sharing board for a few days, and work shared in the Author's Chair. They also file projects from workshop, math papers, drawings, and special projects. I add work that I have collected. At the end of September we start the portfolio file, which is set up the same way as the monthly file and will store special pieces from throughout the year (see Photo 8–2).

Monthly Procedure

I have developed a general organizational procedure for portfolios that we follow throughout the year. At the end of each month the children clear their daily writing folder of finished pieces and add them to the monthly file. From it they select at least three pieces to put into their portfolio file, although most children add many more. The remaining writing and an evaluation form are sent home. I usually either make copies of the form and evaluation pieces or ask the parents to return them to school.

The purpose of the evaluation form is to get the children thinking about themselves as developing writers and to help me evaluate their progress so I can be a more effective teacher. It also informs parents of positive ways to look at their children's writing and lets them know the kinds of things that we are working on as a group and individually in class. Each month, before I go over the form with individual children, we discuss it in group. This gets them thinking about their work and gives them the opportunity to hear the responses of their peers.

The focus of the monthly portfolio evaluation changes as we concentrate on different aspects of writing and as the children learn to manage their portfolios and become more engaged in their work. Their choices become more thoughtful and the analysis of their work over time becomes more specific.

September

At the end of September my main purpose is to introduce the children to the mechanical procedures of the files, to start them thinking about the value of saving their work so they can look at what they have learned over time, and to gather a baseline sample that we can use throughout the year to compare with current work and analyze progress.

PHOTO 8-2 *Portfolio file*

With both file boxes in front of me, I demonstrate the general procedure to the entire class. Then, while the others are writing, I work with one student at a time at the rug area. First they check their daily writing folder to see if there are any finished pieces. Then they take all their pieces out of the monthly file, add the date if it's missing, and spread their work out in front of them. I ask them to choose two pieces "that you like best." Sometimes I select another that I think represents them as a writer. As we look at these pieces, I fill out the My Writing in September form with them. I work with about six children a day in this manner (see Figure 8-5 and Appendix A8-5).

The September form focuses on the content of the children's work, both drawing and writing, emphasizing what we notice the children can do (what we see, not what is missing). It suggests that I am interested in writing conventions and mechanics and it draws attention to invented spelling, which we refer to as ear spelling and eye spelling, as well as conventional spelling. On the form I also record the number of upper and lower case letters that the children recognized when I administered the "Letter Identification" task (Clay 1993) earlier in the month. Finally, the children and I agree upon something specific that they will work on. This varies with each child and might include adding more details to pictures, writing more, putting spaces between words, or using lower case letters.

October

As we work with portfolios at the end of October, the children clear their files and select the October pieces on their own. They check their writing folders for finished pieces, take all of their work out of the October file, pick two or three pieces for the portfolio file, put the rest in a ten-by-thirteen-inch manila envelope, and put it all in a pile at my table. I call on them individually to discuss their work and fill out My Writing in October form, which goes in the envelope to be taken home. As they put the selected pieces in the portfolio file, I encourage them to look at their September pieces. Since the children have selected their pieces independently, I have time to work with about eight children a day.

The assessment form (see Appendix A8–6) is similar to the one we filled out in September. The changes draw attention to writing sentences and leaving spaces between words, two skills that we have been working on during shared literacy and individual conferences. Some children are writing sentences and developing a sense of capitals and periods. Others are mainly labeling, and I want to encourage them to write more.

November

The children follow the same general procedure as in October. However, now the monthly file also contains topic work, math papers, and other projects to be sorted. The assessment form, November Work (see Appendix A8–7) is in the form of a letter to parents and addresses what the children feel is important about writing, topics, reading, and math.

December

Portfolio assessment in December focuses on Visitors' Day, which is just before the holiday vacation. In preparation for the day, the children have cleared their writing folders and December writing file, filed their portfolio choices, and put the extra pieces at their writing places for their v

---

MY WRITING IN SEPTEMBER

Name Alex   Date 10/5

1. <u>What I have drawn and written about.</u>
Castles
Under the water
Basketball
Desert

2. <u>What Mrs. Fisher and I notice about my drawings.</u>
Color
Details

3. <u>What Mrs. Fisher and I notice about my writing.</u>
Spaces between words

4. <u>Some of the letters, sounds and "ear spellings" that I use in my writing.</u>
ear spelling

5. <u>In September I recognized:</u>
25 upper case letters and 25 lower case letters.

6. <u>Some of the words I spell in my writing.</u>
Went   at
to   the
a
barn

7. <u>What I plan to work on in October.</u>
Date
Do more writing

FIGURE 8-5 *My writing in September form*

to see and then take home. We haven't had time to fill out an evaluation form for this short school month, but as the children show their visitors around the room, writing from the portfolio is shared and celebrated.

January

The purpose of the January Writing Conference form (Appendix A8–8) is to encourage the children to think about themselves as writers and to inform me so I can better organize writing time and plan for individual children. The form focuses on the children's growth since September and their plans for the second half of the year. First we talk about the procedures of writing time. Then we discuss a current piece of writing and compare it with a September piece. Finally we decide on two goals for the rest of the year, one for writing conventions and one for content.

February

In February I conference individually with the children and we fill out the My Writing in February form together (see Appendix A8–9). I act as scribe for many of the children, but some write it themselves. As noted on the bottom of the form, the responses are the children's, not mine. This is a very powerful evaluation and planning tool, because it enables me to compare my perceptions of the children's progress with their own perceptions.

March

The March Portfolio Assessment (see Appendix A8–10) is the first one that the children fill out entirely by themselves. As they have done each month, they clear out their writing folder and monthly file and pick one or two pieces of March writing for their portfolio file. They look over all the pieces in the portfolio and select a September piece for comparison. I lead the class as they fill out the form, suggesting that they either use smiley faces or write "yes" or "no" to indicate how they did in September and how they are doing now (see Figure 8–6).

April

We are so busy writing books during April that we don't have time to write out a formal evaluation. The children are continually evaluating as they write their home/adventure/home and information books. Sometimes I make copies of selected pages. At the end of the month, as usual, the children clear the files and add first drafts, copies, final products and copies of their portfolios.

May

There is so much to do during the final two months of school that I have to be very organized and plan enough time to put closure on all the projects that we have been pursuing. Therefore, the children complete an end-of-the-year writing assessment with me in May, so they can concentrate on putting together their portfolio in June.

For the final formal evaluation we use the Writing Assessment Form (see Appendix A8–3). The children are given a special writing assignment, which I tell them about a few days ahead of time so they can organize their ongoing work and think about what they want to write.

They write on lined paper, but are free to add illustrations on the back or on another piece of paper.

Over the next week I confer with the children about their work and record on an End of the Year Writing Assessment form (see Figure 8–7). The column previously labeled "Future Focus" now reads "Student Observation." The assessments are sent home to share with parents, and the children bring them back with their parent's comments.

June

In June I work with about five children at a time at the rug area to help them organize their portfolios for the year. After clearing their June file and writing folder, they spread out all the work, sorting it according to months, and discarding (throwing away, taking home, or giving to me) any pieces they don't want. We talk about keeping pieces that they like, that they remember, that indicate what they could do at different times throughout the year, and that demonstrate changes and growth. Some children keep all of their work, while others are very selective. As they sort, I hear many evaluative comments and exclamations of surprise in their conversations (see Photo 8–3).

"I can't believe that I didn't use spaces."
"I can't even read my writing."
"I just wrote letters."
"Look at this. I just wrote one word."
"I kept drawing houses, over and over again."

First, the children select five or six pieces that represent their work throughout the year for the portfolio that is required by the school system. They will take these pieces to their next year's teacher the last day of school. The remaining pieces make up their special portfolio of first-grade work.

After everyone has completed this process, which takes about a week, the children design covers for their portfolios (see Figure 8–8). I try to get large sturdy paper that is big enough when folded to make a file folder pocket to hold a variety of sizes of papers. One year I found some large silver paper at a recycling center, and we used ribbon to fasten the portfolio. Another year we used Velcro. About two days before the end of

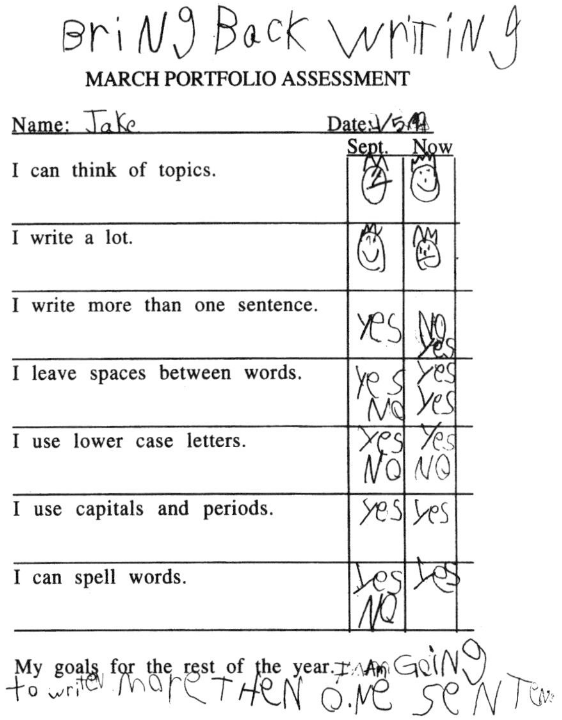

BriNg Back WriTiNg

MARCH PORTFOLIO ASSESSMENT

Name: Jake   Date: 1/5/14

	Sept.	Now
I can think of topics.		
I write a lot.		
I write more than one sentence.	YES	NO yes
I leave spaces between words.	yes No	yes yes
I use lower case letters.	yes No	yes No
I use capitals and periods.	yes	yes
I can spell words.	yes No	yes

My goals for the rest of the year. I AM GoiNg to write MoreTHeN o.Me SeNTce.

FIGURE 8-6 *March portfolio assessment*

school, on the last Visitor's Day of the year, the children share their work and the visitors take the portfolios home (see Appendix B8-3).

For the final portfolio evaluation, the children write about their writing on a piece of lined paper. As a guide I write the following suggestions on the easel:

1. What I wrote about
2. How my writing changed
3. What I like about writing

The children had come a very long way. They were able to write their own evaluations, whereas previously I had to act as their scribe (see Figure 8-9). Their observations were perceptive and would remain

the TRIP to mione

It Wabr on a trip to miane is Fun it Has a
connovor that across the road from my
room. it is only opin at night. We go there.
At night we sleip in are room sat
night. and in the morning we go
swimng my hol famole coms.
we have a lot of fun.
We go down there avre fun.
We stac there for five days.
we have fun down there but
we will be going down
there natst fun. we go
down there whit my Grama
and are papa and cosin.
whan we got there the first
tings we go is go for a swim.

End of the Year Writing Assessment

Student: Danielle   Date: May 23

	Teacher Observation	Student Observation
Writing		
Content		
Writes more than one sentence	Wow	yes
~~Picture~~ Vocabulary	"right across the road"	We always go there
Conventions:		
Spaces between words	yes ✓	yes ✓
Appropriate spacing in words	✓	yes
Capitals and periods		
Handwriting and legibility		
Uses some lower case letters	many	yes
Formation of letters	✓	
Size of letters	always	
Effort	✓	
Spelling		
Spelling	many many	
Standard spelling	yes	
Standard spelling patterns	Writing more	yes
Uses Have-a-go paper		
Teacher comments Your writing gives me a picture of your vacation.		
Student comments		Correct my own words.
Parent comments		

FIGURE 8-7 *End of the year writing assessment*

Photo 8-3 *Organizing portfolios in June*

useful as they continued to write. They were thinking and learning about themselves as writers.

> Sarah wrote, "I have better Lower case Letters."
> Andrew wrote, "I noticed I could not spell bird. I would not put in spaces! Now I put in spaces and can spell bird."
> Curtis wrote, "I noticed at the beginning of the year I only wrote one sentence and I spelled dinosaur and I had to look at a book to figure out the word."

QUESTIONS TEACHERS ASK

1. My district is beginning to mandate portfolio assessment and to tell teachers what to put in them and how to assess them.

FIGURE 8–8 *Portfolio cover*

What does your system do, and what is your opinion of this?

My school system has a very uncomplicated portfolio procedure, which is managed by the classroom teacher and the children. In kindergarten the children are given a fifteen-by-eight-inch portfolio envelope. With the teacher, they select four or five pieces of writing at the end of each year to add to the envelope. It is kept in school and as they move from grade to grade, they take the folder with them. When they leave elementary school, they take the portfolio home.

I like this simple procedure because it keeps the control of portfolios with the children and the classroom teacher and doesn't take time away from the kinds of evaluation I want to create with the children. It gives me the freedom each year to make changes in the ways that the children and I organize, sort, and choose pieces and the ways that we use them for learning.

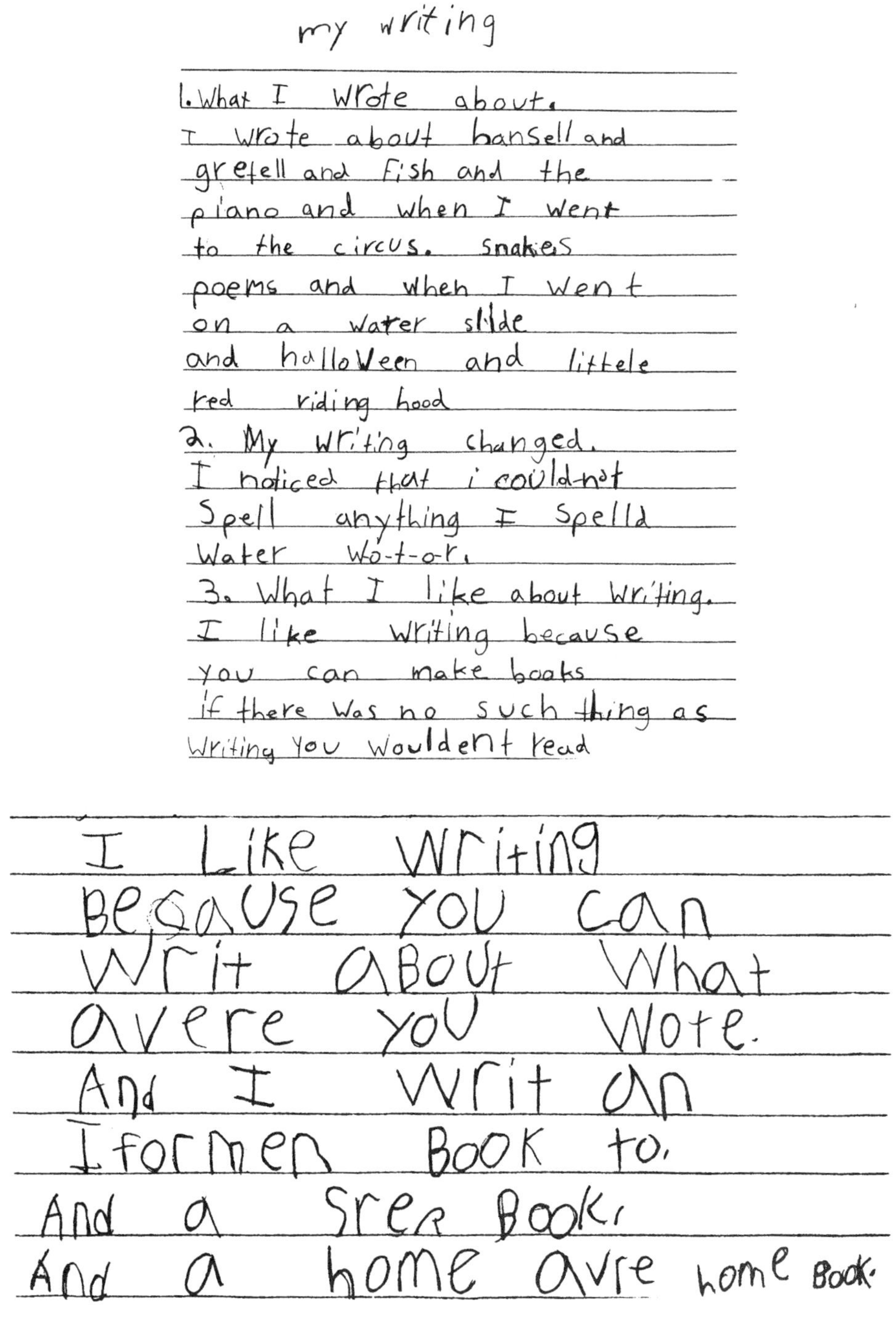

my writing

1. What I wrote about.
I wrote about hansell and
grefell and fish and the
piano and when I went
to the circus. snakies
poems and when I went
on a water slide
and halloveen and littele
red riding hood
2. My writing changed.
I noticed that i could not
Spell anything I spelld
Water wo-t-or.
3. What I like about Writing.
I like writing because
you can make books
if there Was no such thing as
Writing you wouldent read

I Like Writing
Because You can
Writ about What
avere you Wote.
And I Writ an
I former Book to.
And a Srer Book.
And a home avre home Book.

FIGURE 8-9 *Children writing their own evaluations*

I am concerned when portfolio assessment is taken over by administrators who want to use it to standardize writing and evaluate teachers and students. When any kind of assessment becomes formalized, its primary purpose, which is to directly support the student, becomes secondary or lost entirely. As long as the classroom teacher is in control of portfolios, the process will continue to develop, change, and directly effect the children.

FOR FURTHER READING

Cambourne, Brian, and Jan Turbill, eds. 1994. *Responsive Evaluation: Making Valid Judgments about Student Literacy.* Portsmouth, NH: Heinemann.

Clemmons, Joan, Lois Laase, DonnaLynn Cooper, Nancy Areglado, and Mary Dill. 1993. *Portfolios in the Classroom: A Teacher's Sourcebook.* New York: Scholastic.

Graves, Donald, and Bonnie Sunstein. 1992. *Portfolio Portraits.* Portsmouth, NH: Heinemann.

Harp, Bill, ed. 1991. *Assessment and Evaluation in Whole Language Programs.* Norwood, MA: Christopher-Gordon.

Johnston, Peter H. 1991. *Constructive Evaluation of Literate Activity.* New York: Longman.

Rhodes, Lynn K., ed. 1993. *Literacy Assessment: A Handbook of Instruments.* Portsmouth, NH: Heinemann.

9

Spelling

"**B**ut I can't spell," says Roy.

"Just write some letters. Write any letters you think could be in the word," I respond on the first day of writing. Another goal in September is to help the children feel successful in inventing spelling as they write, because in order for spelling to develop, children have to be willing to take risks, approximate, and self-correct over time.

I know that at the beginning of the year the children are learning what I expect of them as writers, specifically regarding spelling. They have come from language-rich kindergartens in my school's system. Their teachers have immersed them in shared literacy and writing process throughout the year, and they are familiar with invented spelling. But sometimes I have a student new to the school, or a child who still wants to be right at all costs. Also, each child has her style regarding fluency, quantity of writing, neatness, and need for accuracy.

Spelling is important as one of the language systems that supports communication, specifically reading and writing, and is best learned through use in authentic literacy situations. "The goal of [a spelling and punctuation] curriculum and instruction is to produce competent and independent spellers and users of punctuation and that a developmental perspective is a crucial part of attaining that goal" (Wilde 1991, 8). Spelling is first learned globally and then becomes more specific, a process that takes many years of reading and writing and is certainly not fully accomplished in the first few years of school.

SPELLING AS A DEVELOPMENTAL PROCESS

When I think of spelling with young children, I think of it within the context of the learner. Learning spelling requires thinking. It is not a random guessing game or an isolated memorizing activity, but based on what the child knows. Learning spelling involves risk taking; a word often isn't spelled correctly the first time. Learning spelling requires a positive attitude. We need authentic reasons in order to work toward accuracy.

Conditions of Natural Learning

If we can notice some developmental patterns in the ways children learn to spell (Reed 1971; Buchanan 1989, 1994; Wilde 1991), then we can conclude that children learn spelling in much the same way they learn to talk and read. Therefore, the conditions of natural learning (Cambourne 1988) can provide a sound theoretical framework for learning spelling in our classrooms.

The children are *immersed* in a rich print environment, and are involved in *demonstrations* of spelling-related strategies, such as phonetics, invented spelling, phonics rules, word families, rhyming words, and root words, all within the context of a whole text. Through active participation during shared reading, children are *engaged* in a playful dialogue about spelling. Because their reading and writing is meaningful to them, they take the *responsibility* to attend to spelling. I have the *expectation* that their spelling will become more conventional over time and I convey that to them. I know that this will happen as children feel free to *approximate* and are given *feedback* and opportunities to *use* what they are learning about spelling in authentic situations.

Invented Spelling

Spelling development can be observed through children's invented spellings (Chomsky 1971; Reed 1971)—the spellings they create from their knowledge about spelling and from their increasing use of conventional patterns. In observing children learning to spell over time, we notice that, "Invention is not a failure to achieve convention but a step on the road to reaching it" (Wilde 1991, 3). Other terms used for invented spelling are functional or temporary spelling, and in my class the terms ear spelling and eye spelling are helpful to the children.

At the beginning of the year I encourage invented spelling as the most important spelling strategy because I want the children to feel confident in their ability to get their ideas down on paper. I send home "Getting Parents Involved," a letter to parents from the Whole Language Teachers Association Newsletter (see Appendix B9-1). I support spelling development in different ways throughout the year. During shared reading the children are exposed to conventional spelling through extensive reading of enlarged texts and intensive discussion of individual words. The children focus individually on spelling patterns, rules, and conventions as their spelling becomes more conventional.

Spelling Continuum

If we observe children's spelling over time, we can notice that it develops along a continuum as it moves toward conventional spelling. For example, in looking at a piece of a child's writing I notice that most of the characteristics of the spelling cluster within a specific level. Over time, the characteristics change and the spelling shifts. However, it is important to be aware that these stages are not exclusive or isolated from each other. For within a piece of writing, several spelling stages are often evident. This is especially apparent when invented spellings and conventional spellings occur in the same piece, an indication that a child is moving away from invented spelling as her only strategy (see Figure 9-1).

Buchanan (1994), in using the word stage, explains that "it indicates that there are periods during which students use only one specific technique to spell all the words they are using. Many things are happening, but it becomes clear from an analytic examination of numerous misspellings that threads or patterns of misspellings emerge; that these patterns follow a sequence; and that as children develop as spellers, the predominant pattern of their misspellings changes, and the power to remember and to predict standard spellings grows" (184).

Me and My frands fawnd a blue brd fliying in The sciy

FIGURE 9–1 *Invented and conventional spelling in same piece*

The spelling stages, described by Buchanan (1989) helped me understand spelling development better. After summarizing her descriptions of the characteristics of spelling at different stages, I examined the writing of the children in my class. In general I found that children's spelling proceeded in the following general sequence: from scribble writing, to letter-like forms, to random letters, to beginning consonants, to adding ending and middle consonants, to including vowels, to conventional patterns, and finally to conventional spelling.

Summary of Developmental Spelling Stages (adapted from Buchanan 1989, 1994)

1. Pre-Phonetic Stage

Things can be represented on paper by symbols that are not pictures. Examples: scribbles, drawings, and symbols

2. Phonetic Stage

There is a connection between the physical aspects of producing a word and the spelling of the word.

Early Phonetic Stage

The number of letters you need to spell a word is equal to the number of syllables in the word (Syllabic Hypothesis). Consonants predominate. Examples: HS = house; RNB = rainbow

Advanced Phonetic Speller

Each element of sound-production in the pronunciation of a word has its own graphic representation. Vowels appear. Examples: HOWS = house; Ranbo = rainbow

3. Phonic Stage

Sound is the key to spelling. Generalizations or rules about sound-symbol relationships are made. Examples: HOUS = house; RANEBO or RAINBO = rainbow

4. Syntactic-Semantic Stage

Meaning and syntax provide important cues which in many cases take precedence over sound cues. Correct vowels, conventional spelling. Examples: MEAT and MEET

SUPPORTING SPELLERS

I continually evaluate the children's spelling so I will know what they need to develop toward accuracy. There are specific strategies that help spellers at different levels that I address during mini lessons and as I work with children individually. I am guided by the following assumptions about how children learn to spell.

- As children spell they are creating their own understandings, hypothesis, rule systems, and strategies for the way words are spelled. Their individual discoveries are part of the process.

Early in the year Danielle wrote a story about her family. She was using what she knew about phonetics, and spelled *my* "MI." I didn't correct her as she read her piece to me. Rather, I commented that I noticed she was using vowels in her words and had spaces between the words. A few days later I picked *my* to feature during shared reading. The class generated a list of words in the *my* family, noting other spellings for the *i* sound (*pie, die*). I commented that although the last sound we hear when we say *my* is *i*, we are spelling it with a *y*. I saw a look of recognition from Danielle, "I got it. I just learned something." That day she spelled *my* correctly in her writing. It was then that I talked to her about the spelling, asking her to tell me what she had discovered as we looked at her two spellings of *my*.

- Children learn spelling by predicting, approximating, disconfirming, self-correcting, and confirming. This doesn't happen all at once, but over time, as they integrate what they know and internalize correct spelling.

Laura was writing *bed*. First she wrote "BD," and then added "*A*" in between the two consonants. She had predicted, written an approximation, realized something was not right, and then self-corrected by adding "A." Although her correction was not accurate, the procedure she used allowed her to try the best hypothesis she knew at the time. She is an advanced phonetic speller, able to show what she knows about vowels in words. The process will lead her toward accuracy.

- Demonstrations about spelling and calling children's awareness to it is essential if we want all children to develop as spellers.

Buchanan (1994) states that "The great bonus that comes out of understanding something about the developmental aspects of learning to spell is the connection we now can make between spelling instruction and the real world of what children know and are practicing in their attempts to spell" (185).

- Extensive reading and writing supports spelling. Visual knowledge, gained from reading and exposure to print plays an important role in spelling (Wilde 1991). The have-a-go paper described on page 178 asks children to write a word they want to spell to see if it looks right (Parry & Hornsby 1985).

170

Auditory and visual knowledge gained from writing and hearing words spelled also plays an important role in spelling. I ask the children to try their ear spelling to hear the sounds in a word, and their eye spelling to visualize the letters in it.

- A few children will become proficient spellers without specific attention called to spelling.

Ian was very interested in spelling in kindergarten. When he came to a word he couldn't read, he would spell it and then be able to read it. Ian could spell all the states and capitals and was one of those children who would continue to learn to spell confidently on his own.

STRATEGIES FOR WHOLE CLASS INSTRUCTION

Some strategies and procedures during shared reading focus explicitly on spelling. Although I realize that some are particularly relevant for individual children at specific stages of spelling, I know that during shared literacy each child is learning at her or his developmental level (Holdaway 1979), and active participation, at whatever level, makes everyone a member of the spelling club (Smith 1989). As I demonstrate and the children participate, they are individually relating what they know about spelling to predict, test their hypothesis, confirm, or miscue, disconfirm, self-correct, and come to a new meaning that makes the most sense to them at the time. They are making sense of spelling through their own discoveries.

Sometimes I focus on these strategies as part of a specific spelling mini lesson, but there are many times during shared literacy when the children are independently focusing on spelling, or I am incidentally mentioning spelling patterns or rules. These ancillary opportunities are crucial because they incorporate spelling as part of the writing/reading process, not as an isolated skill.

Morning Message

Every morning I write the daily schedule and a message on a large piece of lined newsprint and hang it on the easel in the rug area for the class to discuss at morning meeting (see Figure 9–2). At the beginning of the year I write the full text, but by October I write it with minimal cues. I leave out the vowels because children need lots of experiences with them and this procedure gives us the opportunity to discuss vowels along with many other aspects of spelling, such as consonants, blends, prefixes, suffixes, common letter combinations, and a few generally predictable rules.

Schedule

Fr-d-y, J-n—r- 15, 1993

1. Gr—p   (blends, sounds of *ou*)
2. Wr-t-ng   (silent w and e, short i, ing)
3. W-rkshop   (spellings of er, sh, short o)
4. R-c-ess   (short and long e)
5. G-m   (sounds of g, y as a vowel)
6. M-th   (short a, th)
7. L-nch   (short u, ch)
8. R—d-ng   (long e)
9. Sch—l m—t-ng   (sounds of oo, long e, short i, ing)
10. H-m-   (long o, silent e)

Usually we read the schedule together, and then either volunteers or the entire class spell each word as I write in the vowels. Spelling the whole word provides the children with an auditory and visual link and the opportunity "to articulate spelling as a complete string of letters, rather than dealing with only one sound and one letter at a time. . . ." (Wilde 1992, 6). It develops automaticity in spelling through memorization.

This procedure guarantees about twenty school days to focus on how to spell the month, weekly practice spelling the days of the week, and daily practice throughout the year on a few key words. I liken this intense focus to the rereading of favorite stories, which supports emergent readers in becoming independent.

Aside from learning to spell individual words, the children begin to generalize and form hypotheses about spelling. The column with

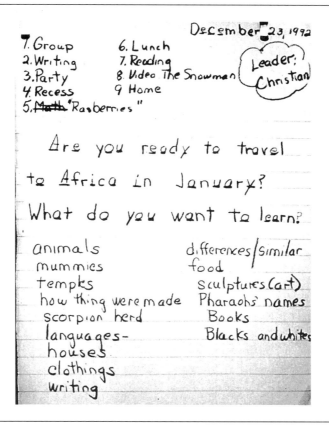

FIGURE 9-2 *Morning message*

parentheses suggests the range of spelling features found in just a few words. We talk about the number of vowels in the words, whether the vowels are the same or different, which vowels are silent, spelling patterns we notice, and rules (and exceptions).

Throughout the day we often make connections with our familiar schedule words and other words we read. For example, if we read *wren* in a story, we might connect the silent *w* to writing. When we read the word *out* we might talk about the fact that the word has the same vowel spelling as *group* but a different sound. When we discuss the different *ch* sound in *lunch* versus *school*, we link it to the names Chris versus Chuck. The value of this repeated focus on the same words is to give the

173

children the opportunity over time to select for themselves what they notice about these words.

Daily Message

Beneath the schedule I write a daily message, usually one or two sentences long, which is often in the form of a question. I sometimes write these sentences with minimal cues, using only beginning consonants, or writing the words without vowels or suffixes. We read the message together as I point and then follow the same spelling procedure as with the schedule. These messages usually relate to something happening in school that I want us to talk about, such as:

- Preparation for an event that day
  "What African animals do you think Christian's parents will show us in their slide show today?"
- Ways to give information
  "Did you know that Africa is the second largest continent? What is the largest continent?"
- Leads to a mini lesson
  "How does writing with lined paper help your writing?"

Establishing this predictable routine assures that we will discuss spelling and graphophonemic cues daily, and that over time the children will have opportunities to develop as spellers and readers and practice what they are learning individually in the safe context of the large group. It connects spelling with authentic, meaningful experiences in the school day.

Sometimes I write the daily message in the form of a *Haiku*. For example, after a snow day I wrote,

> Snow day, cozy day,
> Reading, writing, and napping,
> Shoveling, scraping.

as a lead to discussing what everyone did on the day off. We checked the poem to see if it had seventeen syllables, with five on the first and third lines and seven on the middle line, and if each word had a vowel.

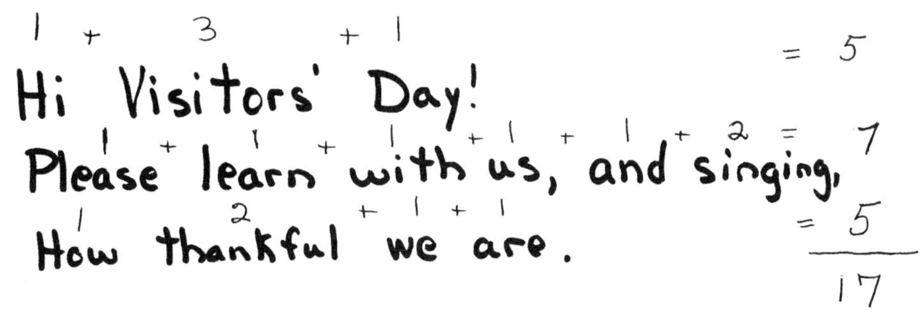

$$1 + 3 + 1 = 5$$

Hi Visitors' Day!

Please learn with us, and singing, $= 7$

How thankful we are. $= 5$
$$\overline{17}$$

FIGURE 9-3 *Haiku*

Over each word, I wrote the number of syllables and we added them across. Then we added the totals down to get the final total of seventeen (see Figure 9-3).

There is space for me to write on the morning message paper during mini lessons and class discussions. Some mini lessons are specific to spelling: we might brainstorm words that begin with *gr*, list all the two letter words on a chart, or write words that have the prefix *tri*. Other mini lessons relate to modeling writing, focusing on good leads for stories, or conventions, such as using spaces between words. Sometimes I write the children's ideas about a social studies topic.

Word Families

We do a lot of play with word families in my class. I define a word family as a group of words having common spelling and common sounds. Related families have one characteristic in common. For example, *pie, die,* and *lie* are a word family, and *sky, my,* and *cry* are related to that family because they end in the same sound but have a different spelling.

Sometimes we generate a word family list during shared literacy. A word is picked from a text we have been reading, or from a common spelling pattern that I've noticed in the children's writing. The song "Alligator Pie" got us talking about rhyming words, and someone noticed that all the words that rhymed didn't have the same letters at the end.

Photo 9-1 *Word family bulletin board*

On the morning message paper I wrote a word to start each column and our list began.

pie   *sky*
die   my
lie   cry

Debbie Gilmore, a second-grade teacher in my school, gave me the following idea: on a bulletin board in the reading area I hang strips of adding machine paper with a spelling pattern written at the top and a small white envelope thumbtacked at the bottom (see Photo 9-1). The children write their initials and a word that fits the pattern on a piece of scrap paper, and put it in the appropriate envelope. During shared literacy I take the word out of the envelope and we talk about it. After this discussion, I write it on the strip, and we reread our growing list. As a variation, *I* write a word that fits the pattern and give it to the children to put in the right envelope.

176

High Frequency Words

Throughout the year we focus on high frequency words that the children use in reading and writing. Several times a week I select a word that I notice in children's writing, that is prominent in a shared literacy text, or that relates to a current science or social studies topic. For example, I picked the word *that* because we had been reading "And that was the end of that," in *Greedy Cat* (Cowley).

I write the word on several pieces of paper, which I put on the writing tables. The children add the word to their have-a-go dictionary (described on page 180). I also write the word on a three-by-five-inch piece of cardboard so we can use it during shared literacy. We discuss the meaning and spelling of the word, find it in different texts, and match it next to the word in a text. As the number of cards grows we line them up on the chalkboard and refer to them during shared literacy. For example, we might:

- find as many of the words as we can in a single text.
- find any words that are used more than once in single text.
- put the words in alphabetical order.
- sort the words according to number of letters, beginning letter, ending letter, vowels, meaning, and so on.

STRATEGIES FOR INDIVIDUAL LEARNING

Most of the individual spelling help that the children receive occurs during writing and workshop and comes from the teacher, peers, or the child's own resources. All are important in strengthening the children's self-motivating, self-monitoring, and self-correcting system for spelling as they engage in learning.

Teacher Support

In order to support individual children in spelling I am continually assessing their spelling, deciding when and how to help them and when to leave their spelling alone. For example, Andrea had been asking me how to spell lots of words, so whenever she was satisfied with her invented spelling, we focused on the meaning of her story during a conference. On the other hand, Kathy, whose writing was fluent and full of meaning, was putting *e*'s at the end of many words. I took the opportunity to work within the zone of proximal development (Vygotsky 1978) and discuss *e*'s at the end of words, helping her learn what she was not yet ready to learn on her own.

As a teacher, I need to know when to capitalize upon a teaching moment and work within the zone of proximal development. I don't use this explicit teaching every time I notice an opportunity, because I value how important and powerful it is when a child discovers something on his own. It's a delicate balance and I don't want to take that opportunity away from a child.

The Writing Conference

During a writing conference, spelling is one of the things we might talk about. We discuss words that are important to that particular child's writing. The discussion varies with the individual. For example, I might focus by:

- commenting on a correct spelling.
- asking if there are any words that are misspelled.
- talking about a word that I think the child could spell correctly.
- relating a word to a previous conference or a shared reading discussion.

Have-a-Go Paper

In October, as many children start asking me how to spell words, I give everyone a have-a-go paper (Parry & Hornsby 1985) to keep in their writing folder (see Appendix A9–1). In a mini lesson I briefly demonstrate the procedure for using it, explaining to the children that during writing time, when they come to a word they are not certain how to spell, they can use the have-a-go paper to help them. The paper has four columns. In the first two columns they should have-a-go at spelling the

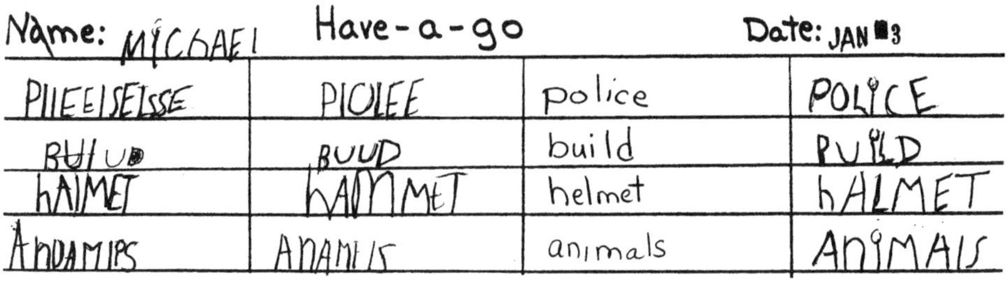

Name: MICHAEL	Have-a-go		Date: JAN 13
PIIEEISEISSE	PIOLEE	police	POLICE
BUIUP	BUUD	build	PUILD
hAIMET	hAMMET	helmet	hALMET
AhuAMIPS	ANANIIS	animals	ANIMAIS

FIGURE 9–4 *Have-a-go spelling paper*

word the best they can. In the third column I will write the correct spelling, and in the fourth column they write it correctly (see Figure 9–4). I mention this paper in a parent newsletter, and then explain the procedure in a letter about spelling to parents that I send home in January (see Appendix B8–2).

The purpose of the have-a-go paper is to help the children spell words *as* they are writing. Have-a-go is an Australian concept. It gives permission to "Give it a try," "Do your best," and conveys to the learner that "You can do it." It allows for risk taking, hypotheses making, approximating, self-correcting, and confirming.

A have-a-go conference takes no more than twenty seconds and can take place as I move about the room or as I sit at a table conducting writing conferences or working on my own writing. The child has already written the word the best she can in the first two columns. I acknowledge the parts of the word that are written correctly and then write the correct spelling, commenting on a variety of strategies that I know are familiar to the child, such as ear and eye spelling, patterns, rules, commonalties with other words on the paper, class spelling words, and words in familiar titles of books.

The value of the have-a-go paper is in the way it's used. First of all, we teachers know that it is essential that "have-a-go" words are words that the children are using in their writing, and *want* to know how to spell. Second, the conversation that I have with the children as I write the word must support them in their spelling development. Third, this strategy should support the writer in communicating with the reader and not take precedence over meaning and content or inhibit the fluency of the writing.

I've noticed that within a given class there is a great range in the use of the have-a-go paper. This has to do with individual spelling development, particular interest in spelling, and children's varying attention to detail and precision. For example, Lauren asked for a have-a-go word when she was aware of a word she couldn't spell, but this didn't stop her from inventing spelling and keeping up her fluency as a writer. Andrea was not a risk taker with spelling and was just beginning to write on her own. She asked for many have-a-go words and began using invented spelling at the end of the school year. Larry didn't find this tool helpful. He was a natural speller and hardly ever asked for a have-a-go word.

Have-a-Go Dictionary

The children also have a personal dictionary made out of six-by-nine-inch composition books. Each letter of the alphabet is assigned about two pages and I write the upper and lower case letter at the top of the page. One year Eric's mom volunteered to write them in at home, and another year a student teacher worked with small groups of children and helped them write the letters.

About twice a week I ask the children to add the high frequency words that we will be discussing during shared literacy. Also, at various times children might transfer some of their have-a-go words to their dictionaries, take a print walk around the room, and add words from charts, write in words from favorite books, or take a mini field trip around the school to obtain new words. However, I offer these dictionaries as only one of the ways they can take ownership of their spelling. As with the have-a-go paper, their use varies with the interest and development of the individual children (see Photo 9–2).

Small Group Spelling Practice

During small group spelling practice the children use their ear and eye spelling in context as they write words from a big book. At the beginning of writing, I ask for six volunteers to join me at the easel with a clipboard, Small Group Spelling Practice form (see Appendix A9–2), and a pencil. I read the first page of a familiar big book and ask someone to choose a word for everyone to practice. On their paper the children write the word once. Next we say the word very slowly. The children

PHOTO 9–2 *Children writing in have-a-go dictionaries*

apply their ear spelling as they write the word in the second column. Finally, we find the word in the text, and they copy it correctly in the third column, concentrating on eye spelling (see Figure 9–5).

Although this procedure could be carried out with the entire class, working with a small group allows everyone to pick a word to practice, and gives me the opportunity to observe and interact with each child more personally. It doesn't matter that some in the group are writing only beginning consonants, while others are spelling many words conventionally, because although they are learning in community, each child is working at her developmental level.

For example, one day we worked with the big book, *Dig a Dinosaur* (Gentner). The first spellings for *dinosaur* ranged from "DS," to "DINSR," to the conventional spelling. However, everyone had it spelled correctly in the third column. As they wrote the word *meat*, we discussed the two different spellings. Several children contributed what they knew about homophones and were beginning to be aware of the relationship between the meaning of words and their spelling.

	Name	DATE	
	SMALL GROUP SPELLING PRACTICE		
	("ear" and "eye" spelling)		
	Practice	Practice	Word
1.	Dr	DYR	DINOSAUR
2.	MT	MEt	MEAT
3.	MOR	MOR	MORE
4.			
5.			
6.			

FIGURE 9-5 *Small group spelling practice form*

Individual Spelling Practice

Toward the end of the school year, I initiate a procedure to encourage the children to practice some words they want to learn to spell individually. They work on a special spelling practice form (see Appendix A9–3), which has a column with space for ten different words and two columns to practice writing them. The children either write their own words and I check them over, or we work together to select words, which I record. Since they are practicing their spelling, it is important that the words are spelled correctly.

They take the paper home and write the words again in the remaining two columns. Usually we pick just five words at school, and the children and their parents have the option to add more. When they are ready, the children return the paper, which has a space for their parent's signature and comments, and they write the words. In a letter to the parents (see Appendix B9–1) I stress that the value of this procedure lies in the children's enthusiasm, willingness, and opportunity to observe progress, not in complete accuracy. Some children pick very challenging words, others choose words they are quite sure they already know, and some don't participate at all.

182

Peer Support

Children learn a lot about spelling informally from each other as they sit at the writing table. Wilde states that, "Children using *each other* as spelling resources is, however, much more productive because instead of an expert providing the right answer, equals are collaborating" (1991, 101).

I hear conversations about spelling as two children work on their individual pieces. Jill is not confident about spelling, but Mary is willing to spell words for her. "Does *come* start with a *c* or *k*?" asks Andrea. I observe intense conversations about spelling when children write books together. Daniel and Billy read and reread each other's writing and edit their spelling as they write a book about soccer.

Individual Resources

My goal is for the children to take the initiative and draw on their own resources for spelling. This is most likely to happen as they become motivated by the need to communicate and be understood by those reading their work. One way to get them thinking about resources to acquire spelling is through a mini lesson. I asked the question, "What are some ways that you find out how to spell words you need?", and the class generated a list, which I wrote on a chart for referral. The list included the following: ask someone, do your ear spelling, do your eye spelling, and look around the room for the word. Although many of the suggestions included teacher and peer support, whenever the children decided to use one of the strategies, they were drawing upon their own resources.

PUNCTUATION

Punctuation is another tool writers use to express their ideas clearly. "Like spelling, therefore, punctuation seems to develop from an early awareness through a period of exploration and gradual refinement and increasing conventionality. Although it involves fewer characters than spelling, it appears to be somewhat more difficult to learn since it's less clearly defined" (Wilde 1991, 32).

Children develop as users of punctuation through exposure during shared literacy and through practice while reading and writing. Applying Holdaway's Natural Learning Classroom Model, during shared reading teachers *demonstrate* and the children *participate* in a discussion of the uses of punctuation. During reading, writing, and workshop they *practice* as they read and write independently or in small groups. Whenever they read to someone else or share their writing they are *performing*.

I find that focus on inflection and oral language is the most powerful way to help children learn about punctuation. During shared literacy we talk about periods, ellipses, exclamation marks, question marks, commas, quotation marks, and apostrophes as we read big books. I explicitly point out how and why these marks are used and we experiment with their uses, always relating to the meaning of the text.

Playing with Punctuation
- We take a deep breath at the end of a sentence and note that the next word will be the beginning of a new sentence and therefore warrants a capital.
- We take a deeper breath and prolong the last word after an ellipses, which is a series of marks (. . . or ***) to indicate the omission of a word or phrase.
- We read with exaggerated expression to feel the impact of exclamation marks.
- We read with exaggerated intonation to ask a question.
- We slow our pace between each word in a list to call attention to commas.
- We conduct readers' theater to experience quotation marks.
- We act out a text, focusing on different marks of punctuation.
- We discuss apostrophes for possessives and contractions.
- We read *without* considering punctuation to notice its importance.

When I work with children individually I refer to these shared literacy demonstrations. As they read to me I notice which marks they are trying to use and which ones I think they are ready to start applying.

184

When I lead children in proofreading, I mention punctuation, especially capitals and periods.

EVALUATION

Much of the spelling evaluation I conduct is ongoing and imbedded in everyday interactions with the children. I am continually assessing and responding both to individual children and to the class as a whole. The Writing and Spelling Assessment form (see Appendix A8–4) described in Chapter 8, which I send home to parents once or twice a year, includes a spelling assessment segment. However, I also use several formal evaluation procedures that help me to evaluate the children's progress over time for my own teaching and to demonstrate this progress to parents—the Spelling Assessment Profile, a formal test administered individually three times a year and a list of first-grade core spelling words developed by the teachers in my school system.

Spelling Assessment Profile

The Spelling Profile (see Appendix A9–4), which along with a reading and writing profile make up the Individual Assessment Profile described in Chapter 6 (see Appendix A6–5), is a procedure for recording the children's growth as spellers. The class profile provides spaces to record the developing spelling elements being used by each child, as well as to indicate their interest in spelling. At the beginning of the year I start to fill in the profile by evaluating the children's writing and analyzing the formal spelling test I administer (see Figure 9–6). As the year goes on, I continue to update the profile.

Formal Spelling Test

Three times a year, in September, January, and May, I administer a Word Awareness Writing Activity, adapted from the work of Richard Gentry (1985). This spelling assessment consists of twelve words that contain

Spelling September		Interest in spelling	Phonetic	Consonants	Vowels	Phonic to semantic	Correct vowels	Conventional patters	Conventional spellings	Spelling stage							
Pam	3	Yes	no							EP							
Peter	3	Yes	no							EP							
Sam	2	Yes	sure			some	some			P							

FIGURE 9–6 *Spelling profile at beginning of year*

common phonetic elements and spelling patterns. I explain to the children that I will be asking them to write some words so I can know how to help them with their spelling. I tell them that I know that they are just learning about spelling and the important thing is for them to write down any letters that they think might be in the word. I administer the test to about three children at a time, letting each child work at his own pace. I say each word, use it in a sentence, and encourage them to write it the best they can.

I give the test again in January and compare the two tests to observe growth over time and to update the assessment profile. On the May test I write some specific comments to the parents about the spelling patterns and conventions over which their child has control. I make copies of all three (see Figure 9–7) and send them home to the parents along with a letter explaining the end of the year spelling evaluation (see Appendix B9–3).

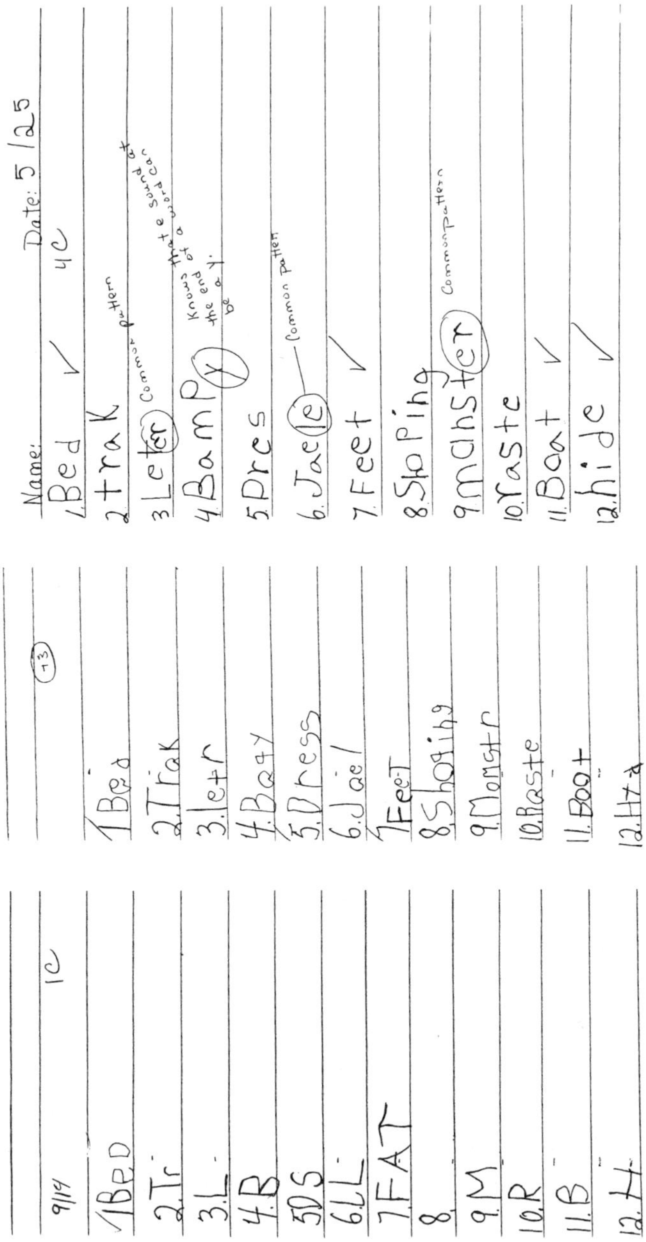

Name: _____ Date: 5/25

4C

1. Bed ✓
2. traK
3. Leter (Common pattern)
4. BamPy — Knows that e sound at end of a word can be a y.
5. Prcs
6. Jae(e) — common pattern
7. Feet ✓
8. Sloping
9. mahster (Common pattern)
10. Taste
11. Boat ✓
12. hide ✓

(+3)

1. Bed
2. Trak
3. letr
4. Bay
5. Dress
6. Joel
7. Feet
8. shoping
9. Momstr
10. Raste
11. Boot
12. Hta

9/14

1C

1. BED
2. Tr
3. L
4. B
5. DS
6. LL
7. FAT
8.
9. M
10. R
11. B
12. H

FIGURE 9-7 *Assessment test three times a year*

QUESTIONS TEACHERS ASK

1. Do you give a Friday test?

No. First, I do not believe that a spelling test meets the developmental needs of children, especially first graders, most of whom are just developing towards independence in reading.

In fact, the typical Friday spelling test, which is usually preceded by a pretest and related exercises throughout the week, probably hinders spelling development and is a waste of time for the children who can already spell the words. Although many spelling programs (whether from a published spelling book or teacher created) focus on spelling patterns, families and rules, and memorizing a list of words to spell on a test, they do not support children in creating their own strategies or in learning to apply spelling patterns or rules to new words they are reading and writing. Wilde claims that, "Spelling books have many drawbacks. They are decontextualized, treat learning as accumulative rather than evolving, and don't draw on learners' prior knowledge" (1991, 72).

Second, an adult-created spelling list for the entire class rarely meets the needs of individual children. It may be too easy for some and too hard for others. The challenge for good spellers will likely be too low and without rigor, while for the poor speller it may be unrealistically high and encourage acceptance of failure. Even if lists for spelling groups are created to meet individual needs, the children would have to be grouped by ability and thus weaken the collaborative learning community essential for developmental learning. Finally, the Friday spelling list can be a source of weekly tension in the families of children who have difficulty spelling, and some children can not get the home support necessary to be successful on the test.

Wilde, in an article entitled "A Proposal for a New Spelling Curriculum" noted that some teachers are teaching spelling as part of writing process where they comfortably encourage invented spelling, but at the same time follow the traditional procedure of the weekly spelling list. "Although teachers may feel that these two ways of using spelling complement each other, they actually represent philosophies of language and learning that are not only different but potentially contradictory. They grow out of divergent views of what it means to learn to be a good

188

speller. Teachers who use both approaches are aware that invented spelling helps writing but do not see it as a way of learning spelling itself; their views of spelling pedagogy remain largely traditional and unquestioned" (276).

FOR FURTHER READING

BOLTON, FAYE, AND DIANE SNOWBALL. 1993A. *IDEAS FOR SPELLING.* PORTSMOUTH, NH: HEINEMANN.

———. 1993B. *TEACHING SPELLING: A PRACTICAL RESOURCE.* PORTSMOUTH, NH: HEINEMANN.

BUCHANAN, ETHEL. 1989. *SPELLING FOR WHOLE LANGUAGE CLASSROOMS.* KATONAH, NY: RICHARD C. OWEN.

———. 1994. "SPELLING FOR THE WHOLE LANGUAGE CLASSROOM." IN *UNDER THE WHOLE LANGUAGE UMBRELLA: MANY CULTURES, MANY VOICES,* EDITED BY ALAN D. FLURKEY AND RICHARD J. MEYER. URBANA, IL: NATIONAL COUNCIL OF TEACHERS OF ENGLISH.

GENTRY, RICHARD, AND JEAN WALLACE GILLET. 1992. *TEACHING KIDS TO SPELL.* PORTSMOUTH, NH: HEINEMANN.

POWELL, DEBBIE, AND DAVID HORNSBY. 1993. *LEARNING PHONICS AND SPELLING IN A WHOLE LANGUAGE CLASSROOM.* NEW YORK: SCHOLASTIC.

WILDE, SANDRA. 1991. *YOU KAN RED THIS! SPELLING AND PUNCTUATION FOR WHOLE LANGUAGE CLASSROOMS, K-6.* PORTSMOUTH, NH: HEINEMANN.

10

Math

Although math is integrated throughout the curriculum, we have a separate math time each day for about forty-five minutes. During this time, we address the following main topics: counting, number, the four processes (addition, subtraction, multiplication, division), classification, patterns, place value, fractions, estimation, geometry, and measurement. The children use manipulatives, play games, write their own equations, problems, and solutions, and use calculators as they experiment with numbers, learn number facts, and discover math concepts. They practice writing numerals and number facts, which they use during games and projects and as they create their own equations and work on class projects.

It is widely acknowledged that children construct their own mathematical knowledge. To do this, children need opportunities to explore materials through free play, to participate in lessons directed by teachers, and to work independently and collaboratively on guided lessons introduced by teachers.

Free exploration with various math manipulatives gives children the best opportunity to learn and construct their own knowledge and hypothesize about various math concepts. When they use these manipulatives in specific activities during directed lessons, they have already developed some of their own understandings of the materials and are better able to concentrate on the game or activity.

Directed lessons occur when I work with the children in a large or small group or individually on a specific skill, strategy, or concept. At this time I do a lot of explicit teaching and work within the "zone of proximal development" (Vygotsky 1978), helping children make connections that at the time they would not be able to make on their own. Guided lessons include the times when children practice these directed lessons without me. Sometimes I give them an assignment and other times they choose one of the games or activities on their own. Since I am not with them to direct the procedure, they often create many of their own rules and strategies.

Applying Holdaway's Natural Learning Classroom Model, I consider that *demonstration* and *participation* take place during directed lessons, *practice/role-play* during free and guided exploration, and *performance* when the children show me what they are learning and when they take over and lead a game as teacher. These provide authentic opportunities for me to evaluate their abilities and to plan new teaching and learning situations.

There are three organizational structures that I use for math: math groups, whole class lessons, and special ongoing math activities.

MATH GROUPS

These are heterogeneous groups (the same as the committee groups described in Chapter 2), which allow five or six children to work together on a common concept. Each day the groups rotate to a different activity, which include a teacher-directed lesson and three projects that don't need my explicit instruction. Often a teacher-directed lesson becomes a guided activity the next week. Typical group projects include the following:

- Teacher-directed lesson
- Exploratory and/or guided activities
- Unit blocks project

Typical activities include:

- Dice game
- Unit blocks
- Math diaries
- 2 Independent projects

191

Getting Math Groups Started

On the first day of school I put out five different sets of manipulatives on tables or floor areas around the room. The children are free to move from space to space to build. For example, I might put out pattern blocks, Cuisenaire Rods, Unifix Cubes, number bars, dice, and calculators. I move about the classroom observing the children and recording what I notice on the Class Math Assessment Profile (see Figure 10-1). For example, Sandy builds a design with pattern blocks and tells me that two red (a trapezoid) ones are the same as a yellow (hexagon) one. Beth rolls two dice and adds them on a calculator.

After a few days of free exploration, I start the math group rotation. I play a banking game with one group, assign another committee to build with the unit blocks, and ask the other groups to continue with free exploration. After each committee has played the dice game and built with the unit blocks, we start a new set of projects. I record the schedule of the projects on a chart so the children and I can keep track of the group rotation (see Figure 10-2).

Dice Games

My principal, Chet Delani, who has provided me with a great deal of guidance in the area of math, introduced me to various dice games. I find that dice games, which we call banking games, are one of the most effective ways to help children develop a sense of number and place value and learn number facts. There are many variations, but they all follow the same general procedure: the children roll a die or dice, receive a corresponding number of pieces (chips, blocks, or coins) from the banker, and trade these counting pieces for an equivalent piece. For example, when using coins, the children trade in five pennies for a nickel, two nickels for a dime, two dimes and a nickel for a quarter, and so on. I am usually the banker and continually question, comment, and observe as we play.

I use several cooperative learning strategies to encourage the children to work together and focus on problem solving rather than competing to see who has the most. One technique has children working in pairs, taking turns rolling the dice and talking over their math problem

	Interest in math	Counts to ___	Recognizes numbers	Writes numbers	Conserves number	Dice	Understands four processes	Place value	Math diary	Creates patterns	Sorts/classifies	Reads graphs	Estimates	Problem solves	Uses math vocabulary
Nicole	✗	30⁺	1-29	✓	✓	✗	+-		hot it PB	I	✗	✗	✓	✓	
Peter	✗	30	1-29	✓	✓		+-	✓		✓	✓	✓	?	
Sandy	✓	20	teen	✓	?	count	+	✓						some

Math Profile   Sept.

FIGURE 10-1 *Class math assessment profile*

as they ask for the pieces and make their trades. If there is an uneven number of children in the group, one child becomes my banking assistant. At the end of the lesson the pairs pool their winnings and get a group total. For example if the three pairs pool seventy-five cents, eighty-four cents, and ninety-two cents, we arrive at a group total of $2.51, which we write on the teaching easel and share with the class.

There are many variations of this banking game that extend the children's thinking as the year progresses. The game grows in sophistication and complexity as we use two die, add ten to the number rolled or subtract one dice from another. Throughout the year dice games provide me with excellent opportunities to assess children's math development. For example, I am continually observing and recording which children count the dots on the dice, which ones can recognize the configuration and conserve number, and which ones can make trades in their heads.

Math Groups	Math Jacob	Science Paul	Trips Andrew	Writing Tyler
1	Banking with Money	Dot to Dot	Number Count	Diary
2	Diary (20)	Banking with Money	Dot to Dot	Number Count
3	Number Count	Diary (10)	Banking	Dot to Dot
4	Dot to Dot	Number Count	Diary	Banking

FIGURE 10-2 *Math group rotations*

Some of the manipulatives we use for the banking game are:

- Coins
- Cuisenaire Rods
- Ones and tens bars

Variations of dice usage include:

- Use more than one die
- Subtract one die from another
- Multiply two dice
- Double the dice
- Add 10 to the dice
- Use dice with more than six pips (for example, 7 and 12 pips on a die)
- Dice with numbers instead of pips

Cuisenaire Rods

Cuisenaire Rods (Cuisenaire Co. of America, Mt. Vernon, NY 10550) are an important math manipulative in the math program at our school. A set includes 10 different rods, each a different color with a size increment of one centimeter. The 1 rod is white; 2 rod is red; all the way to the 10 rod which is orange. Ten white rods equal one orange rod (see Figure 10–3).

In first grade the children develop an understanding of addition, subtraction, multiplication, and division through the use of the rods. They first learn the concepts by working with the colors and then transfer to the number values. For example:

$r + r + p$ red rod, plus a red rod, equals a purple rod $2 + 2 = 4$

$p - r = r$ purple rod, minus a red rod, equals a red rod $4 - 2 = 2$

$2 \times r = p$ two of the red rods equal a purple rod $2 \times 2 = 4$

$p \div r = r$ purple rod divided by a red equals a red rod $4 \div 2 = 2$

In addition, I often put rods out for free exploration. We play whole class games, which help the children learn the colors and related numbers of each rod, and the children use rods when they record in their math diaries (see Photo 10–1).

Math Diaries*

During math groups or whole class assignments, the children write their own equations in math diaries. I make these little books by stapling together five or more pieces of centimeter graph paper (about six-by-eight inches). By the end of the year, the children have usually completed five or six books.

When the children write in their diaries, they generate their own equations and are free to use manipulatives—such as rods, Unifix Cubes, or calculators—to help them. They usually focus on a number that I assign. For example, in the middle of the year they write equations for numbers eleven through twenty in a diary. Starting on the first page they write the numeral "11" at the top and on each line write an equation using "11,"

*Many thanks to my principal, Chet, and the first grade teachers at my school for showing me the uses of math diaries.

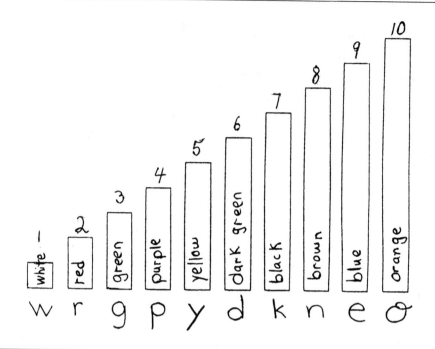

FIGURE 10-3 *Cuisenaire Rods scale*

either as the answer or as part of the equation (see Figure 10-4). I tell the children to write one numeral or sign (+, −, ×, ÷) in each box, which keeps their work organized and easy to read. Another day they will work with "12." When they have finished the book, they take it home.

I put a check beside the correct equations. Sometimes I talk with the children about errors that I believe they can understand and correct. Other times I just focus on what they have done accurately. The children keep a number line in front of them to help them write the numerals correctly. As the year goes on, I underline numerals that are written backwards or otherwise incorrectly and ask the children to rewrite them correctly.

Math diaries provide an excellent way for children to learn together as a community, while working at their developmental level and allowing me to teach them at their instructional level. On a given day, although everyone might be working with the number "15," the following kinds of equations might appear in different diaries:

Photo 10–1 *Using Cuisenaire Rods*

$$7 + 8 = 15$$
$$15 = 15$$
$$9 + 6 - 6 + 6 = 15$$
$$2 \times 7 + 1 = 15$$
$$30 - 15 = 15$$
$$1 + 1 + 1 + 1 + 1 + 1 + 1 + 1 + 1 + 1 + 1 + 1 + 1 + 1 + 1 = 15$$
$$30 \div 2 = 15$$

The children also use the diaries to practice the numbers and concepts that we are working on at a particular time in the year. For example, in my class, diary topics have included:

- Cuisenaire Rods—equations using colors
- Numbers 1 through 10

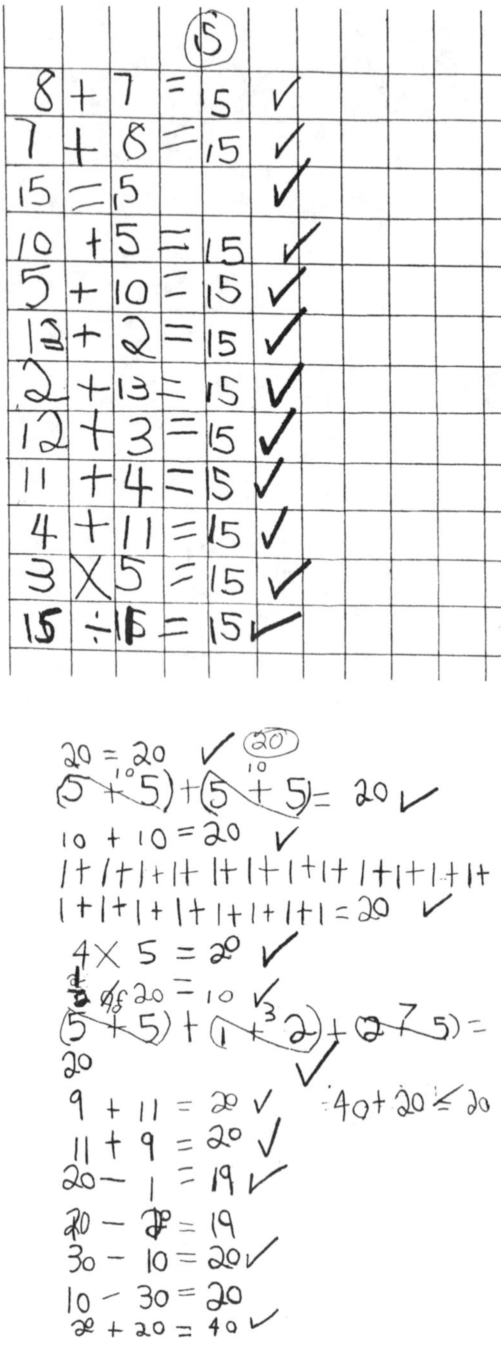

Handwritten worksheet:

Top grid (circled 5):

8 + 7 = 15 ✓
7 + 8 = 15 ✓
15 = 15 ✓
10 + 5 = 15 ✓
5 + 10 = 15 ✓
13 + 2 = 15 ✓
2 + 13 = 15 ✓
12 + 3 = 15 ✓
11 + 4 = 15 ✓
4 + 11 = 15 ✓
3 X 5 = 15 ✓
15 ÷ 1 = 15 ✓

Lower section (circled 20):

20 = 20 ✓
(5 + 5) + (5 + 5) = 20 ✓
10 + 10 = 20 ✓
1+1+1+1 1+1+1+1 1+1+1+1
1+1+1+1+1+1+1 = 20 ✓
4 X 5 = 20 ✓
½ of 20 = 10 ✓
(5 + 5) + (1 + 2) + (2 + 5) = 20 ✓
9 + 11 = 20 ✓   40 + 20 ≠ 20
11 + 9 = 20 ✓
20 − 1 = 19 ✓
20 − 2 = 19 ✓
30 − 10 = 20 ✓
10 − 30 = 20
20 + 20 = 40 ✓

FIGURE 10-4 *Focusing on an assigned number*

- Numbers 11 through 20
- Tens (10 through 100)
- Hundreds (100 through 1000)

Independent Projects

The independent projects that the children work on during math groups cover the different concepts that constitute a balanced math program. There are many resources available to get ideas for projects for small groups. Some of my favorites are listed in the text set on page 211.

For recording projects, I either use the black line masters that the resource provides, create my own form, or ask the children to record on blank pieces of paper. During projects, we work on concepts such as estimating, measuring, patterns, numbers, geometry, and spatial relations. For example:

- Estimating and measuring the height, girth, and weight of a favorite stuffed animal using various measuring units such as Unifix Cubes, color links, and tiles.
- Estimating and measuring the length of pieces of furniture in the room, using the same unit of measure.
- Estimating and measuring the same item, using different units of measure.
- Drawing patterns seen around the room (for example, on windows, shelves, and books)
- Building with patterns (see Photo 10–2). These include copying and extending an existing pattern using pattern block cards. (Children can also make patterns for their peers to copy.)
- Playing a variety of recording games. The simplest game requires the children to roll one die and fill in a graph. An effective way to practice number facts is for the children to roll the dice and record the equation and sum in a box (see Figure 10–5). Many of the variations described for the banking game are applicable for these individual recording games.

PHOTO 10–2 *Building with patterns*

- Creating geometric shapes with geo boards.
- Making matrixes with attribute blocks.

Unit Blocks

During math group time, usually one group is assigned to the unit block area (see Photo 10–3). Sometimes the children choose their own topic, and sometimes I assign a topic or put a parameter on what they will build. For example, when we were studying Africa, the group read *The Village of Round and Square Houses* (Grifalconi) and created their own village. As part of a literature group focus on *Arrow to the Sun* (McDermott) they represented the scenes of the different *kivas* described in the book.

Marge Thurber, a first-grade colleague, assigns two children to work together in the block area to create the story from a book that the

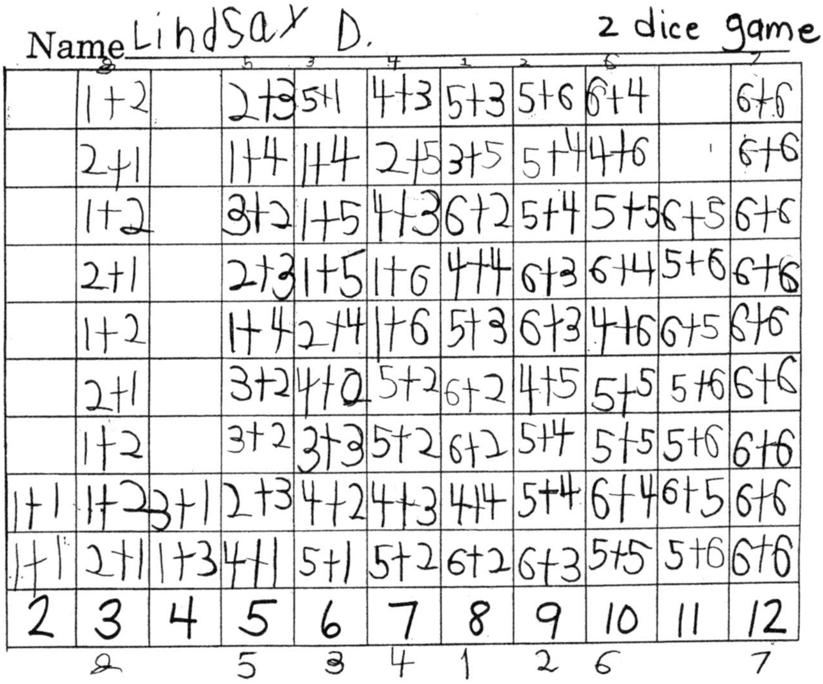

Name Lindsay D.   2 dice game

2	3	4	5	6	7	8	9	10	11	12
	1+2		2+3 5+1	4+3	5+3	5+6	6+4			6+6
	2+1		1+4 1+4	2+5	3+5	5+4	4+6			6+6
	1+2		3+2 1+5	4+3	6+2	5+4	5+5	6+5		6+6
	2+1		2+3 1+5	1+6	4+4	6+3	6+4	5+6		6+6
	1+2		1+4 2+4	1+6	5+3	6+3	4+6	6+5		6+6
	2+1		3+2 4+0	5+2	6+2	4+5	5+5	5+6		6+6
	1+2		3+2 3+3	5+2	6+2	5+4	5+5	5+6		6+6
1+1	1+2 3+1	2+3	4+2 4+3	4+4	5+4	6+4	4+6	6+5		6+6
1+1	2+1 1+3	4+1	5+1 5+2	6+2	6+3	5+5	5+6	6+6		
2	3	4	5	6	7	8	9	10	11	12

2   5   3   4   1   2 6   7

FIGURE 10–5 *Rolling the dice and recording the equation in a box*

class has been reading. They work throughout the morning and then tell the class about their work, taking comments and questions. For example, after reading several versions of *Little Red Ridinghood,* the children created the different scenes in the story, using pattern blocks and other small building figures to represent the characters and furniture.

WHOLE CLASS LESSONS

Most whole class lessons take place at the rug area and are usually teacher directed. Some are short lessons, which are carried out as time allows throughout the day and include practicing number facts or solving word problems. Other whole class lessons are scheduled for the math time and usually involve the use of manipulatives, some form of recording, and follow-up discussion.

PHOTO 10-3 *Group at unit block area*

Short Lessons

There are many short math lessons throughout the day, such as working with the calendar, counting (by one's, two's, five's, ten's, etc.) the number of days we have been in school, and reading counting and number books. There are times during the day, such as when we are waiting to go to lunch, that are perfect for short lessons. At these moments we often practice number facts or solve a word problem. Sometimes I pick up Whisper Bear, a puppet who never speaks out loud but whispers math problems for me to ask the class. After I ask the question, I put Whisper Bear on my lap while the children work on the problem. When I raise him in the air, they whisper their answer. This keeps the children from shouting their responses and competing with each other to be correct. Then, as a group, we discuss the answer.

Long Lessons

Fred Gross, a staff developer in our school system, came to my class once a week for ten weeks to help children work together to construct

202

PHOTO 10–4 *Illustrating solution to math problem*

their own ways of solving math problems. We started at the rug area, where one of us would pose a problem for the children to solve, writing the necessary data on the chalkboard. One of the problems was, "On a farm there were 6 cows and 5 chicks. How many legs and tails did these animals have all together?"

Children then worked throughout the room in teams of two or three to solve the problem. We encouraged them to use manipulatives and asked them to illustrate their solution on a large piece of paper (see Photo 10–4). Fred and I walked around the room, observing, encouraging, and asking questions. At the end of the period we sat in a circle with our work and each team shared what it had done.

The goal of these lessons was to encourage children to think flexibly about math and understand that there are different ways to solve problems. The room was filled with talk as the partners worked together, counting, recounting, discussing, and explaining their ideas. The children demonstrated their solutions in various ways (see Figure 10–6).

6 cow's
5 chickens
45

34 FeeT
11 TaSle

4+4+4+4+4+4 = 24
2+2+2 + 2+2 = 10
1+ 1 + 1 + 1 + 1 + 1 = 6
1+ 1 + 1 + 1+1 +1 = 5

chuckieand Erica.

= 2
= 11 tALS

We did it with mony.

FIGURE 10-6 *Demonstrations of math solutions*

5 Cheks 6 CoWS   Feet

1 2 3 4 5   = 45

I rot DaW evre time
I DeD A groop of Legs
or tel and I DeD the
Chekns. the Cheks wer
and 10 +5. I KowteD By toos
2, 4, 6, 8, 10, 12 14, 15.
thar was oan chep left
awt. I LopnD tha if wes, E, s
I DeD it wet Chep. Kevin
was my partner.

FIGURE 10–6 (continued) *Demonstrations of math solutions*

SPECIAL MATH ACTIVITIES

We undertake special math projects at different times throughout the day and week. These include categorizing, tallying, and graphing the kinds of food the children bring in for the town food pantry every month, keeping an ongoing count of the books we have read as a class, and taking surveys and graphing the results of favorite foods, colors, and sports.

Equation Math

Equation math is an activity that provides the children with daily practice with numbers. Every day a different numeral is written on a special bulletin board and during the morning the children are encouraged to write their own equation about the number and put their initials after their work.

Early in the school year I demonstrate the procedure. For example, I write the number "4" at the top of the board, circle it so we can identify it easily, and ask for volunteers to tell me something about the number. Mac told me his brother was four and I wrote "Mac's brother is four," followed by his initials. Sarah told me that 2 + 2 = 4 and I wrote that for her. After we added some more equations, I asked the class moderator to erase the work and suggest a number between one and ten for to- morrow and write it on the board. I told the children that when they came in the next day they could write something about the new num- ber. The following morning three did, and at the beginning of math time I asked the moderator to call on those people to read their work, erase it, and pick a new number. As the year went on, more children participated, primarily by writing equations.

Box Math

Box math is a weekly activity that helps children practice the different number concepts and processes we work on throughout the year. It is called box math because the children put an answer to an equation in a box on the chalkboard (see Photo 10–5). Each Monday I write an equa- tion for every child in the class (if I have twenty-five students, I write twenty-five different equations). During the week the each child solves it and writes his or her initials on the line following the equation. On Fri- day the children sit on the floor in the area in front of the chalkboard, and as a group we discuss and correct the equations, as they work the problems with rods or other manipulatives. This activity is a useful way for me to teach and reinforce math concepts and procedures and to evaluate the math understanding and development of each child.

Graphs and Charts

There are many types of graph and chart activities for primary children (see Chapter 11). For example, at one of the morning settling-in times I ask the children to estimate the number of chips in a jar. They write their response on a class grid, and later in the day a group of children

Photo 10-5 *Writing answer to equation in box*

count the chips and report to the class. As we begin to work with larger numbers, I show the children how to group the counting materials by tens for easier counting. Although initially I give demonstrations of possibilities for these projects, very soon the children take them over and pursue them on their own.

EVALUATION

I am continually evaluating the children's math understandings as I work with them in groups and individually. I observe what they do with manipulatives, and I listen as they explain what they are doing. I observe what they record in their math diaries and on worksheets, and read what they write about math.

207

Writing About Math

Throughout the year the children write about math. One year the backs of our literature response journals (see Chapter 4) became Math Journals, and the children recorded math experiences there. For example, they wrote what they noticed after coloring in different number patterns on a hundred chart (see Figure 10-7). When they were studying geometry, I asked them to draw and write about triangles (see Figure 10-8).

Math Evaluation Profile

I have developed a math profile similar to the ones for reading, writing, and spelling, and I use many of the same evaluation procedures for recording. I start with a class evaluation form (see Appendix A10-1). As I watch and work with children during different math experiences, I fill

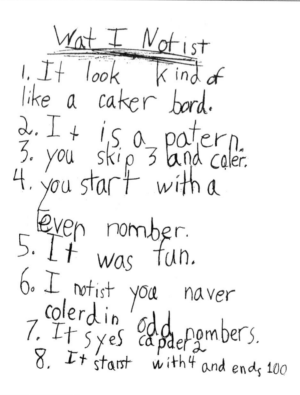

FIGURE 10-7 *What student noticed after coloring in number patterns*

in the profile (see Figure 10–1). Periodically I transfer the information to an Individual Math Evaluation Profile (see Appendix A10–2).

QUESTIONS TEACHERS ASK

1. Do you use math worksheets and workbooks?

The children do complete worksheets on a regular basis so they can practice the conventional written form of mathematics and demonstrate their ability to answer basic math skills in traditional form. I use individual worksheets rather than a single math workbook so I can select and make up my own worksheets that reflect what the children are learning.

A TRIANGLE CAN BE BIG OR FAT OR SMALL.
A TRIANGLE CAN BE A MOUNTIN.
A TRIANG is DIFFRINT THEN A SQUARE.

FIGURE 10–8 *Writing and drawing about triangles*

However, since I believe that primary age children can understand much more about mathematical concepts than worksheets or work-books can provide, I ensure that a lot of their math experiences involve playing games, building and expanding concepts with manipulatives, and discussions.

2. Does your math program reflect the National Council of Teaching Mathematics (NCTM) Standards?

Yes. When the NCTM standards came out in 1989 I was delighted, because they reflected the concepts and outcomes for math that are appropriate for young children and affirmed that hands-on experiences are essential for children in developing an understanding of mathematics.

FOR FURTHER READING:

BAKER, ANN, AND JOHN BAKER. 1990. *MATHEMATICS IN PROCESS.* PORTSMOUTH, NH: HEINEMANN.

BAKER, DAVE, CHERYL SEMPLE, AND TONY STEAD. 1990. *HOW BIG IS THE MOON? WHOLE MATHS IN ACTION.* PORTSMOUTH, NH: HEINEMANN.

BARATTA-LORTON, MARY. 1976. *MATHEMATICS THEIR WAY.* READING, MA: ADDISON-WESLEY.

BURK, DONNA, ALLYN SNIDER, AND PAULA SYMONDS. 1988. *BOX IT OR BAG IT: TEACHERS RESOURCE GUIDE: MATHEMATICS, FIRST-SECOND.* SALEM, OR: THE MATH LEARNING CENTER.

———. 1991. *MATH EXCURSIONS 2: PROJECT-BASED MATHEMATICS FOR SECOND GRADERS.* PORTSMOUTH, NH: HEINEMANN.

———. 1992. *MATH EXCURSIONS 1: PROJECT-BASED MATHEMATICS FOR FIRST GRADERS.* PORTSMOUTH, NH: HEINEMANN.

BURNS, MARILYN. 1992. *ABOUT TEACHING MATHEMATICS: A K-8 RESOURCE.* SAUSALITO, CA: MARILYN BURNS EDUCATION ASSOCIATES.

BURNS, MARILYN, CATHY HUMPHREYS, AND BONNIE TANK. 1988. *A COLLECTION OF MATH LESSONS: FROM GRADES 1 THROUGH 3.* NEW YORK: CUISENAIRE COMPANY.

NATIONAL COUNCIL OF TEACHERS OF MATHEMATICS. 1989. *CURRICULUM AND EVALUATION STANDARDS FOR SCHOOL MATHEMATICS.* RESTON, VA: NCTM.

OHANIAN, SUSAN. 1992. *GARBAGE PIZZA, PATCHWORK QUILTS, AND MATH MAGIC.* PORTSMOUTH, NH: HEINEMANN.

WHITIN, DAVID J., HEIDI MILLS, AND TIMOTHY O'KEEFE. 1990. *LIVING AND LEARNING MATHEMATICS: STORIES AND STRATEGIES FOR SUPPORTING MATHEMATICAL LITERACY.* PORTSMOUTH, NH: HEINEMANN.

WHITIN, DAVID J., AND SANDRA WILDE. 1992. *READ ANY GOOD MATH LATELY? CHILDREN'S BOOKS FOR MATHEMATICAL LEARNING, K-6.* PORTSMOUTH, NH: HEINEMANN.

TEXT SET: MATH BOOKS

AKER, SUZANNE. 1990. *WHAT COMES IN 2'S, 3'S, & 4'S.* NEW YORK: SIMON & SCHUSTER.

ANNO, MITSUMASA. 1977. *ANNO'S COUNTING BOOK.* NEW YORK: THOMAS Y. CROWELL.

———. 1991. *ANNO'S MATH GAMES III.* NEW YORK: PHILOMEL.

ARCHAMBAULT, JOHN. 1989. *COUNTING SHEEP.* NEW YORK: HENRY HOLT.

DUNBAR, JOYCE. 1990. *TEN LITTLE MICE.* NEW YORK: METHUEN BOOKS.

ERNST, LISA. 1986. *UP TO TEN AND DOWN AGAIN.* NEW YORK: LOTHROP, LEE & SHEPARD.

GERSTEIN, MORDICAI. 1984. *ROLL OVER.* NEW YORK: CROWN.

GIGANTI, PAUL JR. 1992. *EACH ORANGE HAD 8 SLICES.* NEW YORK: GREENWILLOW.

GROSSMAN, VIRGINIA, AND SYLVIA LONG. 1991. *TEN LITTLE RABBITS.* LITTLETON, MA: SUNDANCE.

HAYES, SARAH. 1990. *NINE DUCKS NINE.* NEW YORK: LOTHROP.

HOBAN, TANA. 1987. *26 LETTERS AND 99 CENTS.* NEW YORK: GREENWILLOW.

HUTCHINS, PAT. 1971. *CHANGES, CHANGES.* NEW YORK: MACMILLAN.

———. 1986. *THE DOORBELL RANG.* NEW YORK: GREENWILLOW.

LEEDY, LOREEN. 1994. *FRACTION ACTION.* NEW YORK: HOLIDAY HOUSE.

LESIEG, THEO. 1961. *TEN APPLES UP ON TOP.* NEW YORK: RANDOM HOUSE.

MERRIAM, EVE. 1993. *12 WAYS TO GET TO ELEVEN.* NEW YORK: SIMON & SCHUSTER.

PEEK, MERLE. 1969. *ROLL OVER! A COUNTING BOOK.* NEW YORK: CLARION.

———. 1987. *THE BALANCING ACT.* NEW YORK: CLARION.

SIS, PETER. 1989. *GOING UP.* NEW YORK: GREENWILLOW.

SLOAT, TERI. 1991. *FROM ONE TO ONE HUNDRED.* NEW YORK: E. P. DUTTON.

11

Science

We are involved in science all the time in my classroom through the processes of reading, writing, and math, as we listen to literature, when we generate our own topics of inquiry during workshop, and as we pursue social studies topics (see Photo 11–1). This chapter discusses three projects in which the children are engaged in scientific inquiry—the study of properties, children as scientists, and the waterworks.

STUDY OF PROPERTIES

Our system-wide science curriculum distinguishes three major strands for inquiry and discovery for each grade: physical science, life science, and earth science. Physical science for first grade focuses on the senses and properties, and throughout the year the children are involved in an ongoing process of observing and recording the properties of many animate and inanimate objects. This focus on properties and observation enables us to incorporate the life science study of organisms and the earth science study of seasons, sun, and shadows. My goal is for the children to become keen observers and flexible thinkers and to develop vocabulary to describe the world around them, regardless of the topic (see Photo 11–2).

Graphing

Graphing helps us sort, categorize, organize, and count different objects and concepts. Early in the school year, I introduce properties by

Photo 11–1 *Involved in science all the time*

using favorite objects that the children have brought from home. We gather in a circle at the rug area with our object in front of us and a large graph in the middle (Barratta-Lorton 1976). I made the graph out of a window shade, on which I marked a four-by-eight-foot grid with four-inch squares. The grid is big enough for all of us to see and can accommodate a variety of objects. The shade can be rolled up for easy storage.

There are different ways to sort and categorize the objects and once the children get the idea of what we're doing, they come up with many variations. I guide the activity so that we include graphing by color, shape, texture, size, and weight. These main categories and specific attributes are written on a chart, which I begin to refer to as we work (see Photo 11–3). I want the children to become familiar with it since they will be using it when they start recording different observations independently.

The value in this activity lies in the children's conversations about their observations. As they participate in graphing experiences over

Photo 11–2 *Science area*

several days, they continue to construct their own hypotheses. As they place an object on the graph, I ask them to give their reason for placing it where they have.

> "My cat is pink, and doesn't go with the red objects so I made a new row."
> "Part of my doll is round and part is oval."
> "I think my car is smooth because when I touch it, it isn't bumpy."
> "My stuffed elephant is small because real elephants are enormous!"
> "This bird's nest is heavy because it has a lot of mud in it."

For the next week or so I put the graph out in the morning, and as they settle in, some children place different objects they find around the room on the graph. The graph is also available during workshop.

After we have graphed using concrete objects, we move to the pictures and then symbols. I ask the children to find an object around the room that would fit in the four-inch square on the grid. On a piece of

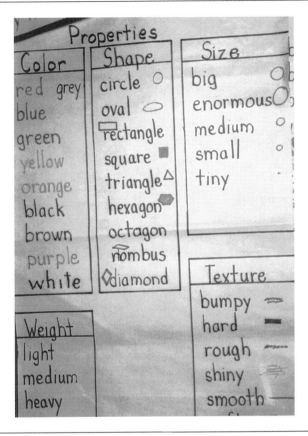

PHOTO 11-3 *Graphing chart*

paper they draw a picture of their object, and then we place the picture on the graph in the same way we did the objects. Next we write the name of the object on a paper and place it on the graph. As we work through this process, I make labels with the main properties (color, shape, texture, size, and weight) so we can use them as graph headings.

Throughout the year we graph different objects in different ways. We move from large differences, such as toys from home, to more subtle differences, such as kinds of apples. We graph artifacts from Africa as part of our social studies topics. We use scientific equipment, such as scales and measuring devices to observe weight and size, and we make rubbings to focus on texture.

215

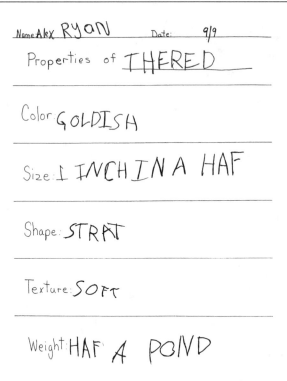

Name Alex RYAN   Date: 9/9

Properties of THERED

Color GOLDISH

Size: 1 INCH IN A HAF

Shape: STRAT

Texture: SOFT

Weight: HAF A POIVD

FIGURE 11-1 *Observation form*

Introducing the Observation Form

Each week the children complete an observation form, which changes
in complexity and focus during the year. The basic form includes a
space for the children's names, the date, the object they are observing,
an illustration, and a list of the properties. I introduce the form (see Appendix A11-1) by using the books of Tana Hoban which contain photographs of items with common or related properties. First I model the
procedure and then assign the children to work in pairs to fill out the
form. I give each team a Tana Hoban book and an object that is pictured
in the book. After they locate the object in the book and put a marker
on the page, they each fill out their own form, talking together about
their drawings and the property words and/or pictures that they want
to include (see Figure 11-1). Later, we gather at the rug to discuss the
objects, books, and forms.

Using Creature Features

Early in the year we read the big book, *Creature Features* (Drew 1988). The book gives clues about the creatures that different children have, and invites the reader to guess what creature is in their box. The clues include the five categories mentioned on our chart: color, shape, texture, size, and weight as well as several body parts of the creatures. Referring to the chart as we read familiarizes the children with it and helps them use the terminology. After reading the book several times, everyone writes a creature feature mystery for a class book.

Completing Weekly Observations

The children know that sometime during the week, usually during settling-in time or workshop, they are responsible for completing an observation. Each Monday I display a new object at the science table, along with copies of the observation form and colored pencils. The chart listing the property words hangs on the wall by the table. There is room for four children to work at one time, and I encourage them to collaborate by talking about the different properties, reading the words to each other, and discussing their meanings. When they are finished, they place the completed form in a folder and check their name off on a class list.

At the end of the week we sit in a circle with our observation forms in front of us, the object in the middle, and discuss our findings (Doris 1992). The children learn that there isn't always one correct answer and that they may disagree about the properties they assign to the same object, as long as they can give a reason for their choice. For example, David thought that since his apple was smaller than all the apples in the row marked "small," we should make a new row marked "tiny."

Sometimes I ask for a show of hands: "How many said that the feather was gray? How many said it was brown? How many said it had more than one color? Who had a different answer?" Finally the children file their observations in their folder in the science observation file box, and we save these throughout the year to put into a book to take home in June. When the children work in pairs and share one observation form, I place a copy in each child's file.

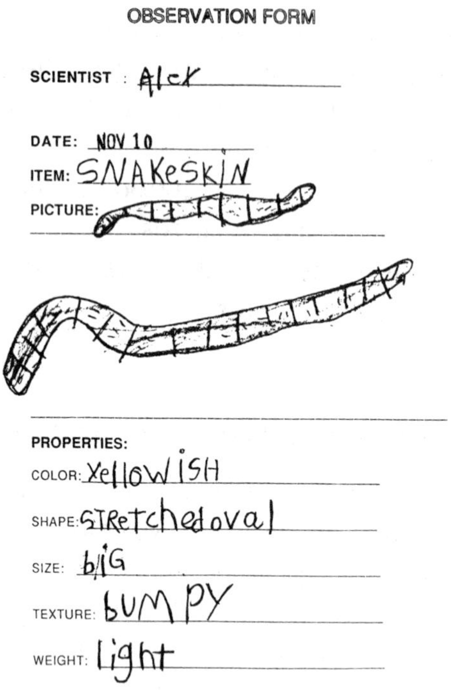

OBSERVATION FORM

SCIENTIST : Alex

DATE: NOV 10

ITEM: SNAKeSKIN

PICTURE:

PROPERTIES:

COLOR: Yellowish

SHAPE: STRetched oval

SIZE: biG

TEXTURE: bUMPY

WEIGHT: light

FIGURE 11-2 *Observation form listing each of the properties*

I change the form from time to time as the children gain observation skills and strategies and control of their reading and writing. One form lists each of the properties (see Figure 11-2 and Appendix A11-2) and another form also provides a space for children to write what they notice (see Appendix A11-3). After I read the big book *Animal, Plant or Mineral?* (Drew) I included a place to check off the material of the object (see Appendix A11-4). One day Renée brought in two shells and suggested that we compare two like objects, so I created a form for recording both (see Figure 11-3 and Appendix A11-5).

Later in the year we observe the changes that occur in an object over time. The children work in teams and decide on something to bring from home that they think will show changes. Most brought in food, such as bread, bananas, and ice cream. We observed one item for

OBSERVATION RECORDING FORM

SCIENTIST _Alex_

DATE _June_

OBJECT OBSERVED _One leaf   two flower_

MY PICTURE

Material: Animal_____ Plant _Plant ✓_ Mineral_____

PROPERTIES	ITEM ONE _leaf_	ITEM TWO _flower_
1. Color	green	purple
2. Shape	oval	star like
3. Texture	soft	soft
4. Size	medium	small
5. Weight	light	light

What I noticed _I notest that thar is a little yellow in the flower And fine-payel is on the bottum._

FIGURE 11-3 *Observation form recording two like objects*

a week (see Appendix A11-6). One year we extended the project over four weeks (see Appendix A11-7).

The object of observation is chosen in many ways. Once I get the procedure started, children start bringing in objects. Some weeks I offer a choice. For a time, one of the jobs of the science committee was to choose the object. When our hamster had twelve babies, we made a series of observations (see Figure 11-4) and wrote a class newspaper on the experience (see Appendix B11-1). Pets of the children that visited for a day were often the focal point of class observations.

The examples described here only tap the surface. There are many possibilities of the projects and activities that could generate from this one general procedure. For example, during the observation of changes, children wanted to observe the changes that would occur when they added water to their object.

219

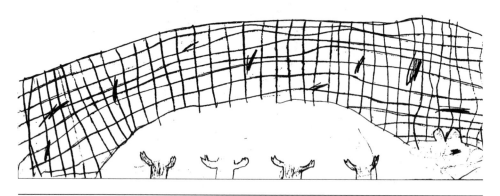

FIGURE 11-4 *Hamster babies observations*

CHILDREN AS SCIENTISTS

Children love to be scientists. But planning and setting up experiments can take a lot of time and be difficult to implement successfully during class time. By involving the children in the planning and teaching, I have been able to include more science experiments in my classroom. I send a letter home explaining the procedure (see Appendix B11-2), and an Experiment Recording Form (see Appendix A11-8) for the children to fill out with the help of their parents. The children plan an experiment, bring in the materials, set it up, and carry it out with small groups during workshop.

For ideas, they take experiment books home from the classroom, get books from the school library, use books from home, or create experiments on their own. Examples of experiments include sink and float, oil and water, and air pressure. The children are truly scientists and teachers. They wear lab coats, which were donated by a parent who worked in a hospital, set up the experiments, plan the number of children they want in a group, have the children check off after they have participated, and clean up at the end. Unless I'm called upon for help, I don't get involved with these small group projects.

SCHOOL-WIDE THEME ABOUT WATER

Every year for about eight weeks everyone in our school focuses on a school-wide theme. In the past, these have included the Renaissance, Recycling, Westward Ho! and Water. The staff, principal, parents, and children are involved in the planning, and although a theme is for the entire school, each class generates its own direction, emphasis, extent of participation, and specific projects. A school-wide celebration is held at the end.

Getting Started

In anticipation of the school-wide theme about water, every child in the school took home a letter before February vacation requesting that they bring in a white T-shirt and $1. The money would cover expenses of having a water logo printed on the shirts. At that time, I briefly told the children about the forthcoming study and we talked about what we might learn.

The First Day

When the children arrived in the classroom on the Monday, they put on their T-shirts and found a folder at newly-assigned study group seats. The study groups were named after rivers: the Amazon, Ganges, Nile, and Mississippi. The folder contained a world map showing which group each child was in and the continent on which the river they were assigned was located. Each river was labeled and the river for the child's group was highlighted on their maps. A plastic file box with the name of the group and its members was on each table. These were placed on a

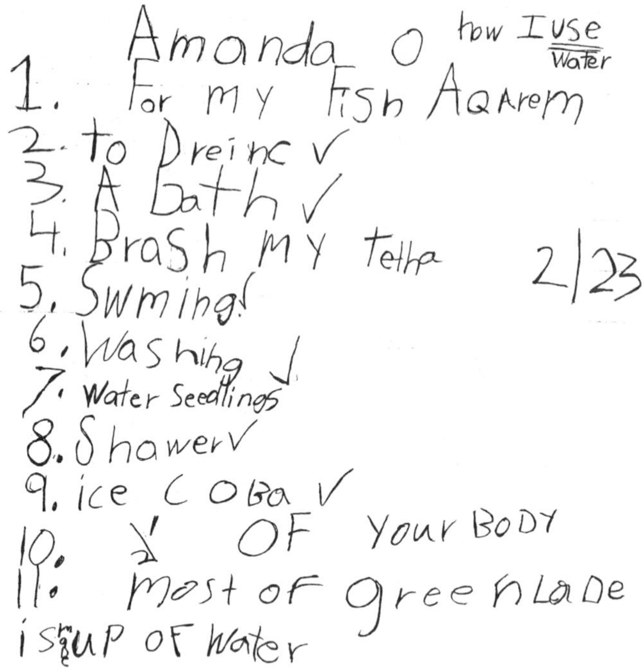

Amanda O how I use ~~Water~~
1. For my fish AqArem
2. to Dreinc ✓
3. A bath ✓
4. Brash my tetha   2/23
5. Swming✓
6. Washing ✓
7. Water Seedlings
8. Shower ✓
9. ice Coba ✓
10. ✓ OF Your BoDY
11. most of green LaDe
is ⁂uP oF Water

FIGURE 11–5 *"How I Use Water"*

shelf when not in use. The children kept their paper in the folders throughout the study and took them home at the end of the study.

All the children and every staff member, including secretaries, custodians, and cafeteria workers, wore their T-shirts to the Monday morning school meeting. Judy Blatt, a third-grade teacher, led the staff in a short rap about water. Then Lee Jones, portraying a science professor and Terri Redfern, taking the role of a duck, performed a short skit to introduce the school-wide "question of the week" about water and an accompanying project. They opened an envelope containing the question and read it to the children, motivating them for the classroom discussion.

Each Monday a new theme for the week was introduced. Some of the questions were, "How do we use water?"; "How do we have fun with water?"; "How can water be helpful and how can it be destructive?" This coming together every week to share and join classroom projects helped develop a sense of school community.

Back in class the children wrote and drew pictures of the different ways they could think of to use water. Some worked alone, some worked together, but they each had their own paper (see Figure 11–5). Then we sat at the rug, and I wrote their suggestions on chart paper as the children referred to their lists, checked off items, and added new ones. They put their individual lists in their folder and we hung the class list in the school craft center along with lists generated by the other classes. At the following Monday school meeting, Lee and Terri showed a big book they had made from all the lists.

Developing a Focus

Reading Books

The initial school meeting and follow-up activities created enthusiasm in my class for the water theme. However, before we would identify specific areas of interest to pursue, I wanted to provide the children with more information and research more resources about water.

I spent the next three days reading aloud different kinds of books about water, and after each reading we discussed its general category—storybook, information book, or information storybook (Leal 1993)—and the general topic it addressed. *Where the River Begins* (Locker) and *Follow the Water from Brook to Ocean* (Dorros) got us thinking about different bodies of water and the water cycle. *The Boy Who Held Back the Sea* (Locker) introduced us to the positive and negative effects of water. *The Magic School Bus at the Waterworks* (Cole) helped us focus on our dependence on water and issues of pollution. *Big Al* (Clements) opened up the world of fish to us, and *Beaver at Long Pond* (Lindsay) got us thinking about freshwater animals. We made a chart with this information and added to it as we read new books (see Photo 11–4).

Sorting Books

During February vacation I had gathered thirty books about water from the library and my personal collection. On Thursday we spent time as a class exploring and sorting them. First, I held up a book, read the title, and handed it to one of the children who indicated an interest in it. After each child had a book to start browsing, I put the remaining books in a

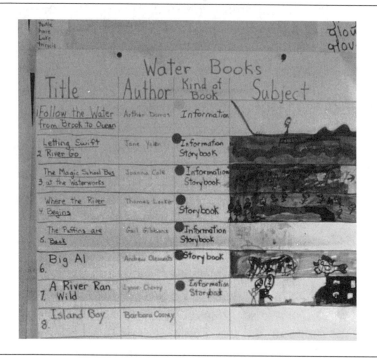

PHOTO 11–4 *Chart of books about water*

pile on the floor. I then asked the children to look at several, pick one that particularly interested them to share with the class, and decide whether it was a storybook, information book, or information storybook. During the next half hour we explored many books, talking, looking, and reading together, as well as working alone. Then we gathered together with our chosen book. After the children told in which category they thought it fit, and the rest of the class agreed, they put a colored circle sticker on the book (red circle for storybooks, green for information books, and yellow for information storybooks) and placed it on a shelf designated for books about water.

Webbing

On Friday we all sat on the rug with a piece of paper and clipboard and made a list of some of the things we would like to learn and study about water. I made a list, too. As the children offered their ideas, we made a web on a large piece of paper. I circled some of the big categories and

224

asked for a general show of hands to indicate particular interest. We decided on three main categories—water cycle, waterworks, and animals. We also decided that pollution would be included in each category.

Planning Structures

Since the kick off for water was launched at a school-wide level, I waited until we had been involved for a week before spending time on in-depth planning for my own class. Keeping in mind the school activities, classroom reading, and webbing, I started filling in Planning Structures that I use for every major area of study we undertake. (It continued to change and expand as the study went on.) The final plan was as follows:

1. Big idea
Water is one of the three basic elements needed for life. Without it we cannot live, and yet water can kill us. Water as a life force and life destroyer.

2. Binary opposite: Survival/destruction. We will focus on the positive and negative effects of water, especially when I read books to the class. For example, when we read *Where the River Begins* by Thomas Locker, we talked about the benefits of rain for crops and reservoirs, but the inconvenience and potential danger of the rainstorm for the boys and their grandfather in the story.

3. Geography: Rivers. Each study group will learn and present something about their river to the rest of the class.

4. Natural Learning Model: Opportunities for demonstration, participation, practice/role-play, and performance.

Projects

Throughout the eight weeks, we were engaged in several water projects, usually during workshop time. Some were whole-class endeavors and others were pursued by individuals or small groups. The projects generated from a variety of sources: the children's interests; my planning; projects from Ethel Kantor, the school art specialist; topics from Monday

PHOTO 11–5 *"I Like the Rivers"*

school meetings; school-wide assemblies; and experiments presented by parents. Each topic related to a focus book.

Rivers

"I like the Amazon," "I like the Ganges," "I like the Mississippi," "I like the Nile," were the first lines to the verses of a song each group made up about their river (see Photo 11–5). The tune and words were an innovation on "I like the Rain" by Claude Belanger.

I worked with each group during workshop time. We looked through information books about rivers, locating the name of the river in the index and putting markers at each page where it was mentioned. I helped them skim and read for information to include in their song. After we selected a few facts and concepts about the river, I wrote them on a chart, and the children illustrated them with markers (see Photo 11–6). Later, each group taught the class their verse and explained the

PHOTO 11-6 *Children illustrating facts about rivers*

information in the song. As a class we followed the same procedure to write the chorus, I like the River."

Writing this song provided extensive opportunities for vocabulary development. I guided each group so that the key word in each stanza would offer important information. Sometimes the children didn't know what the words meant, but were motivated to learn. For example, one group discovered that the Amazon River has more than a thousand tributaries, and wanted to give that information in their song.

This project offered clear examples of the Natural Learning Model in action. The children were engaged in an authentic and meaningful project of writing and illustrating a song to share with others. I *demonstrated* the skills of using an index and skimming for specific information, and the children *participated* in the experience. During the rest of the year I noticed the children *practicing* these skills for other authentic and meaningful purposes. They shared or *performed* the skill when they told me about it, helped their classmates, or used it for further learning. The children became the demonstrators and users of new knowledge.

PHOTO 11–7 *Freshwater and saltwater fish bulletin board*

Fish

At the start of the project many children had indicated an interest in fish. This didn't surprise me, since throughout the year much of our curriculum had generated from the children's expressed interest in animals. The science coordinator had agreed to set up a fish tank in my classroom, but our hamster had babies and we needed the tank. Also, I felt that I could only manage one kind of living animal at this time.

Therefore, the focal point for this interest was the creation of a bulletin board about freshwater and saltwater fish. Children would make fish from collage materials (paper, fabric, glitter, etc.). Markers, pens, or pencils were used to write a label for the fish. Since the fish would represent real fish, the children would use information books for models.

The children mounted their fish and labels on the bulletin board outside the classroom; freshwater fish on dark blue paper and saltwater fish on a lighter color (see Photo 11–7). Crayon-resist paintings, depicting fish in the deep sea which the children made in art class formed the border. Tissue paper fish, also made in art class, decorated the wave outside the room. (The wave, made by a parent group out of blue craft paper, extended down both sides of the two corridors.)

Simple Water Projects

One of my room mothers organized parents to come to the room and present simple water experiments to small groups of children during workshop. They planned the activity and brought the materials. Experiments included creating a model of H_2O, water imbibing through celery stalks and flowers, and watching colored water absorbed by different kinds of paper (see Photo 11–8).

OUR OWN MAGIC SCHOOL BUS AND WATERWORKS

The class's intense enjoyment and interest in *The Magic School Bus Goes to the Waterworks* (Cole), which I read to them generated this project. We had four copies of the book and it was always chosen for silent reading. I presented the idea of making a model of the waterworks similar to the model in the book, through which the children could crawl, just as the children in the book had floated in a water bubble from reservoir to sink. We would invite our families and other classrooms to visit the waterworks as part of Visitors' Day, which is a time when we invite family and friends to school (Chapter 14).

Planning Our Waterworks

As the children sat at the rug with clipboards, paper, and pencils and took notes, I reread the key book. They wrote or drew pictures of materials we might need, and some drew plans of the model and wrote down things they wanted to be certain to include (see Figure 11–6). As we talked, I wrote my notes at the easel. Some of the children copied my list, others added their own, and a few primarily drew pictures. The session

PHOTO 11-8 *Simple water experiments*

was interactive: I'd comment as I wrote, the children would tell the group what they were including, and discuss with the people sitting near them what they were writing and drawing. I collected their papers and after school I consolidated their ideas into two lists. I hung the list that specified possible projects in the room, and I printed the other list, detailing materials we might need for each child to take home.

Constructing the Waterworks

The children started drawing plans. Within a week they had brought in materials and the parents had supplied us with enough big boxes to start construction (see Photo 11-9).

We divided the waterworks into four main sections: the reservoir, cleaning tank, sand and gravel tank, and holding tank. Each group was assigned a section and with the help of parents, everyone began decorating

FIGURE 11–6 *Waterworks notes*

the insides of the boxes. The children referred to the book as they drew pictures and decorated the inside walls with recycled materials to distinguish their section. I did not define or structure this initial construction because I wanted to see what ideas the children would come up with and I felt that they needed to plunge in and have-a-go in order to develop a clearer idea of what we were doing. Clearer definition evolved as the project progressed. For example, one group made pictures and taped them to the sides of their boxes, another spent most of the time decorating the inside, and one group pasted cotton balls inside to represent the globs of alum mentioned in the book.

At the end of the construction session we got together as a class, revisited the book, and looked at the construction as each group explained what it had done. Then we set up the boxes and everyone crawled through (see Photo 11–10). From this first preliminary crawlthrough many important decisions were made. We decided that to help the visitors

PHOTO 11–9 *Constructing the waterworks*

understand how water gets from the reservoir to the kitchen sink we needed more pictures and written descriptions on the outside of the boxes to describe what was happening on the inside.

We covered each box with craft paper. Some children measured the length and width of the boxes with Unifix Cubes and transferred the measurement to inches with a yardstick. Others helped glue the paper.

For the next few days the groups started making the pictures and additional signs for the outside of their section. We had spent a lot of time looking at the border illustrations in *A River Runs Wild* (Cherry), so we decided that our drawings would have a border (Giacobbe 1992). We looked at several other books with borders and listed lots of possibilities, which included borders with pictures and borders with patterns. When the four sections of the waterworks were complete we attached them together.

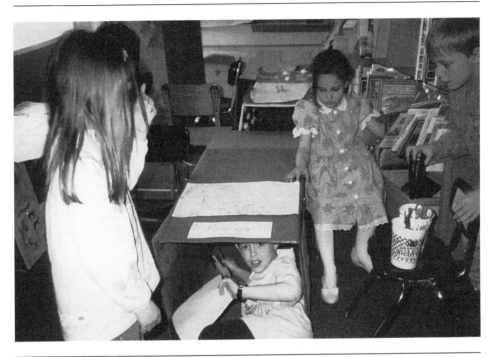

PHOTO 11-10 *Crawling through the waterworks*

Journeying Through the Waterworks

Readers' Theater

We decided to perform Readers' Theater to explain the waterworks on Visitors' Day. We adapted a section from *The Magic School Bus at the Waterworks* and described the four sections of the waterworks. I enlarged the text on the computer and pasted it on two big pieces of cardboard so the children could easily read their part. Each child chose a sentence to read, and the group read the title, main headings, and extra lines. The group monitor held up the page in the book that described the section we were reading.

The School Bus

We made a school bus from a long cardboard box that we covered with yellow craft paper and decorated with water motifs. This became the entrance into the waterworks.

PHOTO 11–11 *Waterworks*

Bubbles

"I'm going to draw myself jumping," said David. Dawn told me that she drew little bubbles in her big bubble.

In *The Magic Schoolbus at the Waterworks,* as the children leave the bus, they float in bubbles to join the reservoir on their journey through the waterworks. I asked the class to draw themselves inside a bubble that I had outlined for each one on eight-by-eleven-inch white construction paper. Mrs. Schreiner, my aide, demonstrated ways to draw figures in action that would fill the space. She used children as models and related some of the shapes she drew to the shapes of letters. For example, she commented that the shape of Erica's arms when she crossed them reminded her of a *w.* The children went to work, sketching with a pencil and then filling in with magic markers, colored pencils, or crayons. They cut out the bubbles and we hung them across the room to welcome people into our classroom and to the waterworks.

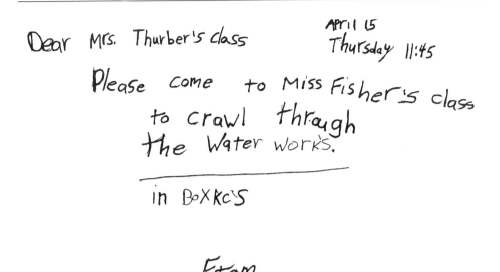

Dear Mrs. Thurber's class   April 15
                                   Thursday 11:45

Please come to Miss Fisher's class
to crawl through
the Water works.

in BoXkc'S

From
Miss Fisher's class

FIGURE 11-7 *Invitation to waterworks*

Sharing the Projects with Visitors and the School

The children wrote invitations and asked their visitors to come at 11:45 AM. As the visitors arrived, the children showed them around the room, and at noon, I started the tape, *This Pretty Planet: Songs for the Earth* (Amidon), which was the signal for the children to bring their visitors to the rug. We sang the first two songs, "This Pretty Planet," and "Water, Water Everywhere," both written on charts so the children and visitors could follow along. I took a few minutes to welcome everyone, thank the visitors for their continued support, and tell them about this wonderful class, which now called itself, "The Thinking Class, The Learning Class, The Singing Class, and The Caring Class." Next we performed the Readers' Theater and ended by singing our song, "I Like the Rivers." The visitors then had the opportunity to go through the waterworks.

Class enthusiasm was high to share the waterworks with the school. However, I decided we could not invite every class to see the project. The construction was not sturdy enough for 400 children to go through, and I knew that the class would not be able to sustain too many performances of Readers' Theater successfully. So we invited the other first grades and each classroom that had a sibling in my class. Some of the children wrote invitations, which they delivered, and I arranged the times with the teachers (see Figure 11–7).

We gave four performances all together, two on Thursday and two on Friday, accommodating eight classes in all. First we sang the two songs from the tape, then performed Readers' Theater, and finally invited the children to imagine they were water bubbles getting purified as they flowed from the reservoir to the kitchen sink.

FOR FURTHER READING

BARATTA-LORTON, MARY. 1976. *MATHEMATICS THEIR WAY.* READING, MA: ADDISON-WESLEY.

BUTZOW, CAROL M. & JOHN W. 1989. *SCIENCE THROUGH CHILDREN'S LITERATURE: AN INTEGRATED APPROACH.* ENGLEWOOD, CO: TEACHER IDEAS PRESS.

DORIS, ELLEN. 1991. *DOING WHAT SCIENTISTS DO: CHILDREN LEARN TO INVESTIGATE THEIR WORLD.* PORTSMOUTH, NH: HEINEMANN.

ELLEMAN, BARBARA. 1992. "WATER AND WATERWAYS." *BOOK LINKS* (NOVEMBER): 7–15.

PHELAN, CAROLYN. 1994. "JOANNA COLE AND BRUCE DEGEN'S MAGIC SCHOOL BUS." *BOOK LINKS* (SEPTEMBER): 44–47.

SAUL, WENDY, ET AL. 1993. *SCIENCE WORKSHOP: A WHOLE LANGUAGE APPROACH.* PORTSMOUTH, NH: HEINEMANN.

SAUL, WENDY, AND SYBILLE A. JAGUSCH, EDS. 1991. *VITAL CONNECTIONS: CHILDREN, SCIENCE, AND BOOKS.* PORTSMOUTH, NH: HEINEMANN.

TEXT SET: FAVORITE SCIENCE BIG BOOKS

BIDDULPH, FRED AND JEANNE. 1992. *EARTH AND MOON.* BOTHELL, WA: THE WRIGHT GROUP.

CUTTING, BRIAN AND JILIAN. 1992. *ANTS, ANTS, ANTS.* BOTHELL, WA: THE WRIGHT GROUP.

DREW, DAVID. 1988A. *CREATURE FEATURES.* CRYSTAL LAKE, IL: RIGBY.

———. 1988B. *SOMEWHERE IN THE UNIVERSE.* CRYSTAL LAKE, IL: RIGBY.

GENTNER, NORMA. 1993A. *BEAR FACTS.* BOTHELL, WA: THE WRIGHT GROUP.

———. 1993B. *Dig a Dinosaur*. Bothell, WA: The Wright Group.

Jenkins, Heather. 1993. *The Survival of Fish*. Bothell, WA: The Wright Group.

Valley, Jim. 1993. *Rain Forest*. Bothell, WA: The Wright Group.

Van Bramer, Joan. 1992 *Whale Rap*. Crystal Lake, IL: Rigby.

Walker, Colins. 1992. *Plants and Seeds*. Bothell, WA: The Wright Group.

TEXT SET: WATER BOOKS

Clements, Andrew. 1988. *Big Al*. New York: Picture Book Studio.

Cole, Joanna. 1986. *The Magic School Bus at the Waterworks*. New York: Scholastic.

———. 1992. *The Magic School Bus on the Ocean Floor*. New York: Scholastic.

Dineen, Jacqueline. 1986. *The Face of the Earth: Rivers and Lakes*. Lexington, MA: Schoolhouse Press.

Dorros, Arthur. 1991. *Follow the Water from Brook to Ocean*. New York: Harper & Row.

Gibbons, Gail. 1988. *Sunken Treasure*. New York: Thomas Y. Crowell.

Jenkins, Heather. 1993. *The Survival of Fish*. Bothell, WA: The Wright Group.

Johnston, Tom. 1988. *Science in Action: Water! Water!* Milwaukee, WI: Gareth Stevens.

Jonas, Ann. 1987. *Reflections*. New York: Greenwillow.

Locker, Thomas. 1984. *Where the River Begins*. New York: Dial.

———. 1986. *Sailing with the Wind*. New York: Dial.

Martin, Bill Jr., and John Archambault. 1988. *Listen to the Rain*. New York: Holt.

Morris, Dean. 1988. *Underwater Life: the Oceans*. Milwaukee, WI: Raintree Children's Books.

Pallotta, Jerry. 1991. *The Underwater Alphabet Book*. Watertown, MA: Charlesbridge.

Rauzon, Mark, and Cynthia Overbeck Bix. 1994. *Water, Water Everywhere*. San Francisco: Sierra Club Books for Children.

Royston, Angela. 1992. *Eye Openers: Sea Animals*. New York: Macmillan.

Steig, William. 1971. *Amos and Boris*. New York: Farrar, Straus, & Giroux.

Van Bramer, Joan. 1992. *Whale Rap*. Crystal Lake, IL: Rigby.

Waters, John. 1973. *Seal Harbor: The Life of the Harbor Seal*. New York: Frederick Warne.

Williams, Lawrence. 1990. *Last Frontiers for Mankind: Oceans*. New York: Marshall Cavendish.

TEXT SET: BOOKS WITH BORDERS

—————

Aylesworth, Jim. 1992. *The Folks in the Valley.* New York: Harper.

Brett, Jan. 1989. *The Mitten.* New York: G. P. Putnam.

———. 1991. *Berlioz the Bear.* New York: G. P. Putnam.

Brett, Jan, and Edward Lear. 1991. *The Owl and the Pussycat.* New York: G. P. Putnam.

Browne, Anthony. 1989. *The Tunnel.* New York: Knopf.

Cherry, Lynne. 1992. *The River Ran Wild.* New York: Harcourt Brace.

Christensen, Bonnie. 1994. *An Edible Alphabet.* New York: Dial.

Fox, Mem. 1989. *Night Noises.* New York: Harcourt.

Lindbergh, Reeve. 1990. *Johnny Appleseed.* Boston, MA: Little, Brown.

McDermott, Gerald. 1974. *Arrow to the Sun.* New York: Viking.

Ringgold, Faith. 1991. *Tar Beach.* New York: Crown.

Williams, Vera B. 1984. *Music, Music for Everyone.* New York: Greenwillow.

TEXT SET: TANA HOBAN

—————

Hoban, Tana. 1971. *Look Again!* New York: Greenwillow.

———. 1974. *Circles, Triangles and Squares.* New York: Macmillan.

———. 1983. *Round & Round & Round.* New York: Greenwillow.

———. 1984a. *Is it Rough? Is it Smooth? Is it Shiny?* New York: Greenwillow.

———. 1984b. *I Walk and Read.* New York: Greenwillow.

———. 1986. *Shapes, Shapes, Shapes.* New York: Greenwillow.

———. 1987. *26 Letters and 99 Cents.* New York: Greenwillow.

———. 1988. *Look! Look! Look!* New York: Greenwillow.

———. 1989. *Of Colors and Things.* New York: Greenwillow.

———. 1990. *Exactly the Opposite.* New York: Greenwillow.

12

Social Studies

ocial studies is explored throughout the day in my classroom through different strands of learning: incidental learning, mini topics and Whole Class topics. For example, opportunities for incidental learning occur every day when my principal, Chet Delani, starts the morning announcement in Spanish and then poses a geography trivia question (see Photo 12–1) such as, "We are now traveling to South America. Can you find the country of Bolivia?"

Many mini topics develop during workshop as the children generate their own topics or when we focus on topics within the required curriculum. Every year I spend a month or more exploring a few Whole Class topics in social studies and science. Here I describe two social studies topics that the entire class studied together. "My Family Now and Long Ago," a study of our ancestors, immigration, and early settlement in this country, developed primarily from my interests. The study of Africa was part of the prescribed social studies curriculum in my school system.

PLANNING STRUCTURES

There are several structures that support a generative curriculum and direct the planning and ongoing implementation of whole class studies in social studies: the Natural Learning Classroom Model, storytelling, and big ideas.

PHOTO 12–1 *Geography trivia*

The Natural Learning Classroom Model

Since becoming familiar with Holdaway's work (1986), I have applied his Natural Learning Classroom Model in planning and guiding the social studies curriculum in my classroom (Fisher 1991). Whenever I map out the content, strategies, and skills that seem important to include in a topic study, I consider some of the following specific examples from the four conditions of the model:

- *Demonstration.* Children gain new information and expand their schema from various demonstrations. They go on field trips; listen to speakers; observe artifacts; see filmstrips, movies, and videos; work with computer programs; read books, magazines, and newspapers; and hear stories, songs, poems, and chants.

- *Participation.* Children interact with the demonstration in a variety of ways. They ask questions, participate in discussions, explore and investigate artifacts, and discuss, extend, and innovate on texts.
- *Practice role-play.* Children need time to practice what they have learned through the demonstrations and participation. These include art projects, dramatic play, math application, music, reading, writing, and science investigations.
- *Performance.* Children need to share what they know. Sometimes this is as simple as showing a friend what they have done. More formal ways include creating a museum in the classroom and inviting people to visit; displaying art work in the room, around the school, and in town buildings such as the library; publishing books, pamphlets, or newspapers; giving demonstrations to other classes; putting on plays; and creating a video show.

This initial planning produces a quasi-traditional lesson plan, but working within a generative curriculum transforms these plans into a dynamic learning journey for both the children and me. We all become demonstrators and participators at different times and with different people. The children come up with ideas and ways of doing things that I could never imagine. For example, once when they set up a homestead, the children took the role of different animals, and not just homesteaders as I had suggested. The original lesson plan gets left behind and although new plans are continually created, they usually don't get written down because no one has the time or need to do so. Everyone is too busy learning.

Stories

I wanted our studies to be alive with stories. Kieran Egan (1986) suggests that stories focus on the affective issues that are at the center of our lives. They draw us into a subject by posing questions, conflicts, and problems. Stories also offer ways for us to come to some understanding of human motivation, interaction, and dynamics, and gain information and knowledge on the subject.

241

Stories, which add context to our studies, are told by the children, me, and other adults, or are experienced through books and other media. Oral or written, they include personal narratives, retellings from fiction and nonfiction, fairy tales, folk tales, and realistic fiction.

WESTWARD HO!

Every year we study about our ancestors and their immigration to this country. Referred to as "the ancestor study," this study embodies the democratic principles of community that I try to foster in the classroom. I want the children to appreciate themselves and others both from the position of difference and from the position of identity. This study opens their awareness to the differences among the people they will meet throughout their lives and to the value of the rich diversity of nationalities, customs, and ethnic groups among the inhabitants of this country.

We start by focusing on our own roots—where our ancestors came from, how they immigrated, why they came, where they settled, and what work they did when they got here. By sharing our own roots and comparing stories with each other, we begin to expand our awareness of the differences and similarities of the individuals and ethnic groups that make up a democracy.

Although much of the general format of this ancestor study has remained the same, each year it has taken on a life of its own. My understanding and appreciation of the multicultural history of our country changes as I continue to learn. New adult and children's books reflecting current perspectives of political theory and American history are published, and each year there is a different group of children in my class with uniquely different ancestral stories.

The year that "Westward Ho!" was the school-wide theme my class concentrated on the settlement of homesteads east of the Mississippi. We approached the study by comparing our own daily lives with what everyday life may have been like for our immigrant ancestors. We gained information by surveying and interviewing our parents and relatives, by examining artifacts and pictures, and by reading books (demonstration and participation). The children integrated what they were learning through developing a homestead in the classroom (*practice/role-play*). They became the demonstrators and guided visitors through the museum and homestead on Visitors' Day (*performance*).

Introducing My Roots

I began our class study by introducing my Scottish roots from my mother's side of the family, drawing the children into the study with story. The children entered the classroom after lunch to the sound of Scottish bagpipe music. Wearing my Ross kilt, I handed out Scottish shortbread for them to eat while I read *Wee Gilles* (Leaf), a storybook about a boy who has to decide whether to live with his father's family in the highlands and stalk stags, or chase steers with his mother's family in the lowlands. He finally decides to be a bagpiper and to travel both to the lowlands and the highlands. I drew a picture map of the setting, and the children got clipboards and drew their version as I read. Our pictures showed Wee Gilles, the high mountains and low hills, a dotted line indicating where he went, and a key to describe in words what the drawings on the picture map represented.

Next, I located Scotland on the map and globe and in several books, so that the children would get used to finding the same place on various maps. We talked about the pictures of Scotland I had put up during lunch: castles; archeological digs; Mary Queen of Scots; sheep; lochs; a picture of my grandfather, Donald Ross, and the modern city of Glasgow from which he had emigrated. I showed artifacts I had brought from a recent trip to Scotland: tartan fabric; a Scottish doll; peat from a peat bog; wool; and a model and pictures of the Loch Ness Monster. I mentioned that there were information and storybooks relating to Scotland on the display shelf. We ended the session singing "Loch Lohman."

Surveys, Artifacts, and Books

In this study the children primarily gained information through discussions with family members and with each other, from observing artifacts, and by listening to stories, and looking at books. Their first source of information came from interviews and discussions with family members. They filled out a questionnaire and survey and gathered artifacts at home. The second source came from each other as they took turns sharing what they had discovered at home. Throughout the study I read aloud a variety of story and information books, and the children also read and examined pictures in the books.

We started gathering information by looking at the living conditions of our current lives. The children filled out a Home Questionnaire, on which they recorded specific information about their present homes, families, food, clothing, and modes of transportation. We graphed the results and referred to them throughout the study as we set up the homestead and learned about early settlement life (see Appendix A12–1).

The final question on the questionnaire, "Why did you or your ancestors leave your homeland and come to this country?" led us to the time when our ancestors came to this country, as American Indians, eastern or western Europeans, African Americans, or Asians, and led us into the next survey, entitled "My Family Now and Long Ago." This survey, which the children also completed at home with their families, focused on their present family traditions, birth information about themselves and their parents, and their ancestors' country of origin (see Appendix A12–2). An accompanying letter told about the museum we would be creating in our classroom and asked the families to help gather artifacts for it (see Appendix B12–1).

Throughout the next two weeks all the children had the opportunity to read their surveys to the class and to show and tell about their artifacts, which included family heirlooms, such as dishes, dolls, jewelry, clothing, old family photographs, postcards, and pictures in books. Most of the artifacts became part of the children's display for the museum, and a few were used as props for the homestead.

I read many storybooks, information books, information storybooks, and biographies to the class, and these literature and text sets were kept on the library display shelf and in a box nearby. Throughout the month, as the homestead developed, we read and discussed a few pages a day of *Log Cabin in the Woods: A True Story About a Pioneer Boy* (Henry), a picture storybook about the life of a family in Indiana in

1832. I also read many other related storybooks and we spent time looking at photographs and illustrations in information books.

The Homestead

The focal point of our Westward Ho! study was the dramatic play environment of a homestead created by the children in the classroom. To get it started, I chose a group of five children to begin setting it up in the block area. I gave very little direction, but by the end of the workshop time they had created a homestead with a kitchen and sleeping area, using big blocks, unit blocks, and some of the artifacts brought from home. They demonstrated to the rest of the class what they had done, and this procedure of play and sharing was repeated daily throughout the study.

The generative nature of learning was very apparent as the homestead developed. Children added to and changed the environment left by the previous group. More artifacts were brought from home, especially pieces of kitchen equipment, including a butter churn, bowls, and popcorn to grind. As I continued to read aloud, the children's concept of a homestead grew. Their growing knowledge was evident in the details they added to the environment and in the increased sophistication and complexity of their play. One group expanded the environment to the reading area where they created a garden and barn. Although it had to be taken down every day because we needed the space for group time, it became an integral part of the environment and each group included it in its play.

Rachel summed up the value of the homestead environment in an article she wrote for our end-of-the-year of the newspaper (Fisher & Cordeiro 1994):

"When We Went West" by Rachel

When we studied "Westward Ho" my class set up a homestead. Some people brought in things from home to put in our homestead. When people were going west people built houses out of logs. Some people lived with other families. We played as if we were a family in the olden days.

Our class is divided in different groups. There are four groups. The different groups are called A, B, C, and D. Each group played in the homestead for a little while during workshop time. When my group played in the homestead we had an ox, a mother, a father, two sons, and a daughter. We pretended to be a family.

It was a very hard life for them. I liked it and learned.

The Museum and Visitors' Show

Although children are performing and sharing all the time in a generative curriculum, most large group topic studies culminate with a formal sharing project. Our Westward Ho! study concluded with a Visitors' Day that featured a museum, the homestead, and a group presentation.

We started creating the museum as the children brought in their family surveys and artifacts. At first, a single display shelf was sufficient, but as more and more family memorabilia arrived, the museum began to take over all the flat surfaces and bulletin boards in the room. Every day the children took on the role of museum curators and kept these display areas organized. For Visitors' Day, some children displayed their artifacts at their work tables in order to alleviate the crowding.

Visitors were invited to arrive at 11:30 AM. As each visitor arrived, they were greeted, given a program (see Figure 12–1), and showed to a seat for the class performance by the child who invited them. The presentation opened with the Pledge of Allegiance and "America the Beautiful." All the children had a part to announce and a line to recite from one of the two texts, "Where We Live," and "Our Ancestors," which we had written.

Where We Live

1. We all live in the town of Sudbury.
2. Sudbury is in the state of Massachusetts.
3. Massachusetts is part of the country, the United States.
4. The United States is on the continent of North America.
5. North America is part of the planet Earth.
6. The earth is in the Milky Way Galaxy.
7. The Milky Way is in the Universe.
8. We are glad our ancestors and relatives came to this country.

246

CELEBRATING THE COUNTRIES OF OUR
ANCESTORS

Mrs. Fisher's First Grade
Josiah Haynes School, Sudbury, Massachusetts
Thursday, December 19
11:45 to 12:45

1. WELCOME	Ellie
	Chelsea
2. SALUTE TO THE FLAG	Heather
3. "AMERICA THE BEAUTIFUL"	Junior
4. OUR ANCESTOR STUDY	Julianna
5. OUR ANCESTORS	James
6. OUR CIVIL RIGHTS	Stevie
7. "LOCH LOCHMAN"	Jennifer
8. OUR NAMES AND OUR ANCESTORS	Jenna
	Ian
9. "COCKLES AND MUSSELS"	Rachel
10. "THIS LAND IS YOUR LAND"	Aaron
	Lindsay
11. WHERE WE LIVE	Laura
12. "WE ALL LIVE TOGETHER	Amy
13. CLOSING	Stacey
13. INVITATION	Tony
	Andy
	A.J.
	Ryan
	Victor

FIGURE 12-1 *Program of ancestors*

9. We are glad we are all together in this classroom together.

10. How did it ever happen?

Our Ancestors

1. Ancestors are relatives who lived long ago.

2. Ancestors are not living now.

3. Many of our ancestors and relatives came to this country from Europe.

4. Some came from South America, Asia, Africa, and Australia.

5. A few of us have American Indian ancestors.

6. Some people came here to get better jobs.

7. Some came here for food and warmer clothes and houses.

8. Some came here to go to their own church or temple.

9. Some came here so they could vote.

10. Some came for adventure.

11. They came for their civil rights.

The children also introduced themselves and spoke about the countries of their ancestors. As a group we recited a poem about our civil rights and sang five songs.

After the presentation, the visitors were invited to join their host or hostess for an individual tour of the displays and homestead. The next day we took the museum down.

This topic study is a good example of the generative nature of the Natural Learning Model. There was a continuous interplay between demonstration, participation, role-play, and performance. Everyone became a demonstrator at some time, when showing artifacts, reading to a friend, telling someone an idea for the homestead, or guiding visitors through the museum. It was often difficult to tell the difference between demonstration and performance, for when the children were demonstrating, they were performing and when they were performing, they were demonstrating.

IMMIGRATION STUDY

Another year we focused on the immigration of our ancestors. The children obtained information from interviews with their family members, artifacts were brought in, and we read many books about the immigration movement to this country.

I read a chapter a day from *The Long Way to a New Land* and *The Long Way Westward* (Sandin 1981; 1989). These are information storybooks about a family leaving Sweden and arriving in New York City and traveling by train to join relatives on a farm in Minnesota. We discussed each chapter in detail as I offered background information and the children asked questions and told their stories. We also read *Ellis Island: Gateway to the New World* (Fisher), an information book with pho-

**INTERVIEW
MY IMMIGRANT ANCESTORS**

1. Who were my ancestors that immigrated into this country?
Carl Erik, Jonas,

2. Where did they come from?
Sweeden

3. When did they come?
1900

4. How did they get here?
by boat

5. Where did they enter this country?
New York

6. Where did they settle?
Minnesota

7. What did they do to make a living?
farming

8. Why did they immigrate?
drought They had no food

Name of person interviewed: Mr. B
Interviewer: Mrs. Fisher   Date 11/10

FIGURE 12-2 *Interview using characters as ancestors*

tographs showing immigrants on the voyage across the Atlantic, arriving at Ellis Island and starting out in New York City.

When we finished reading these books, I demonstrated the procedure for the interview, My Immigrant Ancestors (see Appendix A12-3), that they would be conducting at home. First, I interviewed my student teacher, Paul Berardi, and we filled out the form as if Carl Krik and Jonas, the two children in *The Long Way to a New Land,* were our ancestors (see Figure 12-2). Then, Paul and I interviewed each other and showed the artifacts we had brought from home.

The interview included the following eight questions:

1. Who were my ancestors that immigrated into this country?
2. Where did they come from?

3. When did they come?

4. How did they get here?

5. Where did they enter this country?

6. Where did they settle?

7. What did they do to make a living?

8. Why did they immigrate?

The children took home two blank forms, so they could get information from both sides of their family, and a letter to parents explaining the project (see Appendix B12–2). As the children returned their interview papers, they shared the information and artifacts with the class. Paul and I transferred the information onto a chart, which we referred to throughout the study in discussing differences and similarities among ancestors' histories. We discovered that most of our ancestors came by boat to New York City, but that Marina's parents arrived by airplane from Greece, and Daniel's mother and father flew from Korea to San Francisco. Laura's parents came to North America via Canada. Brandon's mom came from Canada too, but his father traced his ancestors back to the early settlement of the pilgrims in Massachusetts.

As we talked about the reasons that our ancestors had immigrated, we realized that many came here for freedom and a better life. This generated an interest in the slaves, who didn't come by choice and who didn't gain freedom and a better life and resulted in a mini study about black people's struggle for freedom. We read many storybooks and biographies about Harriet Tubman, Martin Luther King, Jr., and Rosa Parks.

On Visitors' Day, as part of the class presentation, each child talked about some of the important information that he or she had learned about the countries of their ancestors.

AFRICA STUDY

Although the study of Africa was part of a school-required curriculum, the children had generated interest in the topic before we began the study. For example, at the beginning of the year, when I asked them to write to me about places they would like to visit, several mentioned Africa. Many also indicated an interest in animals that I knew would be included in our African study.

On the day before December vacation, as we finished a student-generated study of animal classification, I told the children that we would be studying Africa when we returned to school in January. I introduced the topic before vacation so that they could anticipate what we would be studying in the new year and so that the planning I'd be doing during vacation would be generated from their interests. We brainstormed the following list of what we might like to study (Fisher 1995):

- Animals
- Mummies
- Temples
- How the people make things
- Scorpion herd
- Languages
- Houses
- Clothing
- Writing
- How is it different and similar to us
- Food
- Sculpture and art
- Pharaohs' names
- Books
- Black and white people

Initial Planning

During the vacation I used the brainstorming list to identify topics for six committees that would form the organizational framework for our study: animals, clothing, the arts, food, houses, and languages. I purposely made the topics concrete because I wanted us to be able to find information and create projects easily (Fisher 1995). (Language didn't fit this criteria, but throughout the year several children had expressed interest in learning about languages, and I wanted to honor and encourage that interest.)

Big Ideas and Binary Opposites

Pat Cordeiro (1992a) introduced me to the concept of Big Ideas as a way of organizing curriculum. Big Ideas are broad topics or concepts, such as "infinity," "justice," "systems," and "changes" that reach across the curriculum. I chose diversity as a Big Idea and the binary opposites, similarities and differences, to guide my planning. In order to understand and appreciate differences between ourselves and others, we need to be aware of similarities. One way to start, especially for primary age children, is to relate new information, skills, and attitudes to existing experiences. Discussing and understanding similarities and differences fosters multicultural understanding and encourages celebration of diversity.

A focus on diversity seemed to capture the drama and story of the questions that I asked the children and myself throughout the study:

1. How is life in Africa today similar and different than our life?
2. How is life in Africa similar and different in different parts of the continent?

Introducing with Story

On Monday, the first day back from vacation, I introduced the study through story, by stepping into the role of a nervous teacher about to take a trip to Africa; nervous because she didn't know much about the continent to which she was traveling. I focused my monologue on the six committee topics by expressing my concerns about the food I would be eating, the clothing I should take, where I would be living, and whether I would be able to communicate with the people since I only spoke English. I shared my enthusiasm at the possibility of watching animals in their natural habitat and seeing the variety of arts, which I had observed in books and magazines.

252

It went something like this:

Boys and girls, I need your help. I'm so excited because I have a chance to go to Africa, but I'm *soooo* nervous because I don't know much about the country. I'm going to go by plane, but how will I travel once I get there? On a camel? Do they have automobiles? What clothes should I take? I know it is hot in the desert, but what should I wear when I go into the rain forest? And food, what if I don't like any of the food? What foods do they have that are like what I eat? Oh, there is so much to learn before I go. Hey, maybe you could help me, in fact, would you like to go along? I feel less nervous already.

After I invited the children to go on the trip with me, they entered into the conversation. We brainstormed what we knew about Africa, and I wrote the ideas on six pieces of chart paper, each headed with one of the committee topics. I told the children to think about the committee they would like to be on to help plan the travel for the rest of the class. Our story had begun. Books would be our main guide as we traveled through Africa. We would step into the roles of the characters and dramatize what we were learning. We would create scenery for our trip in the form of murals—a game reserve, villages and cities—and we would create a museum of artifacts. We would also prepare food to eat on our trip.

Obtaining Initial Information

During the first two days, as a way of preparing the children to choose a committee, I read several books about Africa: *The Day of Ahmed's Secret* (Heide), a story set in modern day Cairo; *Osa's Pride* (Grifalconi), a story about a girl in an village in Ghana; *How the Guinea Fowl Got Her Spots* (Knutson), a folk tale set in the African Plains; *Who's in Rabbit's House?* (Aardema), a story in the form of a play; and the first chapter of *A New True Book: Africa* (Georges). We talked about what we noticed and could learn about Africa from these different kinds of books.

Establishing the Committees

On Wednesday I discussed the letter they would be taking home to their parents about our African study and specifically about choosing a committee. The children were to discuss the committee choices with their parents and by Friday bring back a paper listing their first and second choices (see Appendix B12–3).

On Friday we discussed the choices and formed the committees. I made a graph with the six choices and wrote everyone's name on Post-it notes so we could move them around easily. Since no one had chosen languages and only one person had selected clothing, we decided to eliminate those as choices and just work with four. I also felt that four would be easier for me to facilitate, and I wanted the children to be on the committee they really wanted. At first the remaining four committees were uneven, but several children were willing to change. Finally I asked if everyone was satisfied, because once the committees got started, it would be hard to change. A few more switches were made, and the class agreed that having three committees of six, and one of four was manageable.

Applying the Natural Learning Model

I started an Environmental Play Planning Guide that I developed for kindergarten (Fisher 1991, 185), for the African study and continued to add to it as the theme study developed.

Demonstration and Participation

Arranging materials   Each first grade in our school is supplied with a box of artifacts, pictures, books, and filmstrips about Africa. During the first week of the study, the children and I unpacked the box and sorted the materials. We put a blue circle sticker on the books and added them to a special shelf with other books about Africa. We arranged the artifacts (a mask, carved wooden animals, cloth) on a display table, and hung up the maps and pictures.

Reading Books and Notetaking   One of the main ways the children gained new information about Africa was from the stories I read to them and the accompanying discussions. Since I wanted the committee members to be actively involved in the process of obtaining information on which to plan the projects for the class, I introduced a notetaking procedure. Each time I read a book about Africa, a member from

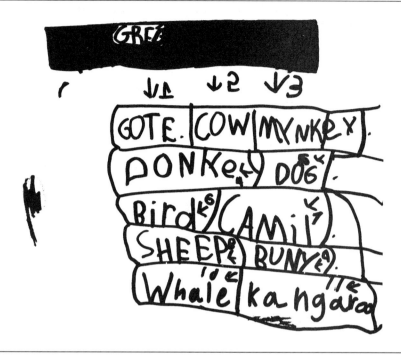

FIGURE 12-3 *Notetaking*

each committee took notes on their topic. Each child did this at least once, and some also volunteered to take notes on transportation, language, and clothing (Fisher 1995).

Before I started reading, they wrote their name, committee name, and book title on a piece of paper on a clipboard. As I read, they wrote and drew pictures of anything they noticed or heard about their subject. Classmates and I made suggestions, we discussed possible entries, and committee members helped each other. There was a lively interplay between demonstration and participation by all the children, but especially by the designated notetakers for the day (see Figure 12-3).

Another time all the children sketched in their notebooks, which they had brought from home and kept in their writing folders, in preparation for making masks. As I read *Who's in Rabbit's House?* (Aardema) and as we looked at information books depicting African art, the children sketched animals and spirits that they might represent in their

255

mask and drew shapes and colors they might want to include. Later, they referred to these notebooks at the art table while making their masks.
Artifacts Several children brought in African artifacts from home. David told us about the baskets his dad bought in Egypt. Lea contributed a blanket, which we used to cover the display table. Alan brought in two carved elephants and many books with African animals.

Marianne Hatton, a parent who was born and brought up in South Africa, brought in artifacts to share with the class. The children sat in a circle and in turn each one picked an artifact from her bag. She told them about it and passed it around the circle for the children to touch and examine closely. Then they were placed on a table and later the children sketched one.

Practice/Role-Play

After about two weeks of reading and notetaking, I met with each committee to discuss possible projects for the class. We referred to our notes and looked at books we might use. The committees chose the following projects and I added some activities, too.

> *Animals*: Making animals with clay (the art teacher took this over); animals in murals.
>
> *Arts*: Making masks; acting out some of the stories; making an adinkra cloth with parents at the school craft center; decorative border for a mural; decorations in the mural.
>
> *Food*: We looked at cook books and decided on four recipes.
>
> *Houses*: A mural of *The Village of Round and Square Houses* (Grifalconi); and *The Day of Ahmed's Secret* (Heide); making a diorama of a village on a large table (Fisher 1995).

For the next few weeks, most of the activity during workshop centered around committee projects. Since committee members were responsible for the planning and directing, the projects reflected the children's interests and development, not teacher directed ideas and activities. I was primarily a facilitator and resource during this practice time.

The committees made a list of the supplies they needed and an outline of their project. They used the notes they had taken during group

256

time, which were kept in manila folders in a file box, and referred to the various books we had about Africa. Although I met with every committee for initial planning, I left them alone as much as possible, and when they asked for help, I tried to respond with a question or comment that would turn the decision making back to them. For example, when the houses committee asked me if they should use paint or crayon on their mural, I told them to talk it over and decide for themselves.

The animals committee made a mural depicting animals in the diverse geographical regions of Africa. The arts committee organized the class in small groups to make animal masks and offered advice for a decorative border for the mural. The food committee used their notes and cookbooks to decide upon four different recipes that parents would prepare with the class. The houses committee planned a diorama showing houses in the city and country and taught the class how to make round and square houses out of paper.

Performance

Performance and sharing happened incidentally and informally throughout this study, especially since the committees acted as the experts on their topics. Children were sharing information, looking at books, reading their notes, and collaborating as they worked on the projects together. Using the masks they made, they acted out the play *Who's in Rabbit's House?* as I narrated the story. The projects became one of the highlights during Visitors' Day.

FOR FURTHER READING

CORDEIRO, PAT. 1995. *ENDLESS POSSIBILITIES: GENERATING CURRICULUM IN SOCIAL STUDIES AND LITERACY.* PORTSMOUTH, NH: HEINEMANN.

DERMAN-SPARKS, LOUISE, AND THE A.B.C. TASK FORCE. 1989. *ANTI-BIAS CURRICULUM: TOOLS FOR EMPOWERING YOUNG CHILDREN.* WASHINGTON, DC: NATIONAL ASSOCIATION FOR THE EDUCATION OF YOUNG CHILDREN.

FISHER, BOBBI. 1995. "THINGS TAKE OFF." IN *ENDLESS POSSIBILITIES: GENERATING CURRICULUM IN SOCIAL STUDIES AND LITERACY,* EDITED BY PAT CORDEIRO. PORTSMOUTH, NH: HEINEMANN.

FISHER, BOBBI, AND PAT CORDEIRO, EDS. 1994. "GENERATING CURRICULUM: BUILDING A SHARED CURRICULUM." *PRIMARY VOICES K-6* 2(3).

JORGENSEN, KAREN. 1993. *HISTORY WORKSHOP: RECONSTRUCTING THE PAST WITH ELEMENTARY STUDENTS.* PORTSMOUTH, NH: HEINEMANN.

MANNING, GARY, MARYANN MANNING, AND ROBERTA LONG. 1994. *THEME IMMERSION: INQUIRY-BASED CURRICULUM IN ELEMENTARY AND MIDDLE SCHOOLS.* PORTSMOUTH, NH: HEINEMANN.

TAKAKI, RONALD. 1993. *A DIFFERENT MIRROR: A HISTORY OF MULTICULTURAL AMERICA.* BOSTON, MA: LITTLE, BROWN.

TUNNELL, MICHAEL O., AND RICHARD AMMON. 1993. *THE STORY OF OURSELVES: TEACHING HISTORY THROUGH CHILDREN'S LITERATURE.* PORTSMOUTH, NH: HEINEMANN.

WEAVER, CONSTANCE, JOEL CHASTON, AND SCOTT PETERSON. 1993. *THEME EXPLORATION: A VOYAGE OF DISCOVERY.* PORTSMOUTH, NH: HEINEMANN.

TEXT SET: WESTWARD HO!

ADLER, DAVID. 1992. *A PICTURE BOOK OF HARRIET TUBMAN.* NEW YORK: HOLIDAY HOUSE.

AYLESWORTH, JIM. 1992. *THE FOLKS IN THE VALLEY.* NEW YORK: HARPER.

AZARIAN, MARY. 1981. *A FARMER'S ALPHABET.* BOSTON, MA: DAVID R. GODINE.

BURTON, VIRGINIA LEE. 1942. *THE LITTLE HOUSE.* BOSTON, MA: HOUGHTON MIFFLIN.

CHERRY, LYNNE. 1992. *THE RIVER RAN WILD.* NEW YORK: HARCOURT BRACE.

COERR, ELEANOR. 1986. *THE JOSEFINA STORY QUILT.* NEW YORK: HARPER.

COONEY, BARBARA. 1988. ISLAND BOY. NEW YORK: VIKING.

———. 1994. *ONLY OPAL: THE DIARY OF A YOUNG GIRL.* NEW YORK: PHILOMEL.

DRAGONWAGON, CRESCENT. 1990. *HOME PLACE.* NEW YORK: MACMILLAN.

GORSLINE, DOUGLAS. 1978. *THE PIONEERS.* NEW YORK: RANDOM HOUSE.

HALL, DONALD. 1979. *OX-CART MAN.* NEW YORK: VIKING.

HENRY, JOANNE LANDERS. 1988. *LOG CABIN IN THE WOODS: A TRUE STORY ABOUT A PIONEER BOY.* NEW YORK: MACMILLAN.

HOUSTON, GLORIA. 1992. *MY GREAT AUNT ARIZONA.* NEW YORK: HARPER.

JOHNSTON, TONY. 1985. *THE QUILT STORY.* NEW YORK: G. P. PUTNAM.

———. 1988. *YONDER.* NEW YORK: DIAL.

KELLOGG, STEVEN. 1988. *JOHNNY APPLESEED.* NEW YORK: MORROW.

KLINSEY-WARNOCK, NATALIE. 1994. *WILDERNESS CAT.* NEW YORK: COBBLEHILL.

KNIGHT, AMELIA S. 1993. *THE WAY WEST: JOURNAL OF A PIONEER WOMAN.* NEW YORK: SIMON & SCHUSTER.

KNIGHT, JAMES E. 1982. *THE FARM: LIFE IN COLONIAL PENNSYLVANIA.* MAHWAH, NJ: TROLL.

KURELEK, WILLIAM. 1985. *THEY SOUGHT A NEW WORLD.* PLATTSBURGH, NY: TUNDRA BOOKS.

LYON, GEORGE ELLA. 1992. *WHO CAME DOWN THAT ROAD?* NEW YORK: ORCHARD.

MCCURDY, MICHAEL. 1988. *HANNAH'S FARM.* NEW YORK: HOLIDAY HOUSE.

PRYOR, BONNIE. 1987. *THE HOUSE ON MAPLE STREET.* NEW YORK: WILLIAM MORROW.

SANDIN, JOAN. 1989. *THE LONG WAY WESTWARD.* NEW YORK: HARPER.

WHEATLEY, NADIA, AND DONNA RAWLINS. 1992. *MY PLACE.* BROOKLYN, NY: KANE/MILLER.

YOLEN, JANE. 1992. *LETTING SWIFT RIVER GO.* BOSTON, MA: LITTLE, BROWN.

TEXT SET: IMMIGRATION

CAZET, DENYSE. 1993. *BORN IN THE GRAVEY.* NEW YORK: ORCHARD BOOKS.

CHMIELARZ, SHARON. 1994. *DOWN AT ANGEL'S.* NEW YORK: TICKNOR & FIELDS.

FISHER, LEONARD EVERETT. 1986. *ELLIS ISLAND: GATEWAY TO THE NEW WORLD.* NEW YORK: HOLIDAY HOUSE.

FREEDMAN, RUSSELL. 1980. *IMMIGRANT KIDS.* NEW YORK: E. P. DUTTON.

KURELEK, WILLIAM. 1985. *THEY SOUGHT A NEW WORLD.* PLATTSBURGH, NY: TUNDRA BOOKS.

LEVINE, ELLEN. 1989. *I HATE ENGLISH!* NEW YORK: SCHOLASTIC.

——. 1993. *. . . IF YOUR NAME WAS CHANGED.* NEW YORK: SCHOLASTIC.

MOCHIZUKI, KEN. 1993. *BASEBALL SAVED US.* NEW YORK: LEE & LOW.

POLACCO, PATRICIA. 1988. *THE KEEPING QUILT.* NEW YORK: SIMON & SCHUSTER.

ROSENBERG, MAXINE B. 1986. *MAKING A NEW HOME IN AMERICA.* NEW YORK: LOTHROP, LEE & SHEPARD.

SANDIN, JOAN. 1981. *THE LONG WAY TO A NEW LAND.* NEW YORK: HARPER.

——. 1989. *THE LONG WAY WESTWARD.* NEW YORK: HARPER.

SAY, ALAN. 1993. *GRANDFATHER'S JOURNEY.* BOSTON, MA: HOUGHTON MIFFLIN.

WILLIAMS, SHERLEY ANN. 1992. *WORKING COTTON.* NEW YORK: HARCOURT BRACE.

YEE, PAUL. 1991. *ROSES SING ON NEW SNOW.* NEW YORK: MACMILLAN.

TEXT SET: AFRICAN STORIES

AARDEMA, VERNA. 1977. *WHO'S IN RABBIT'S HOUSE?* NEW YORK: DIAL.

——. 1981. *BRINGING THE RAIN TO KAPITI PLAIN.* NEW YORK: SCHOLASTIC.

——. 1992. *ANANSI FINDS A FOOL.* NEW YORK: DIAL.

BASH, BARBARA. 1989. *TREE OF LIFE: THE WORLD OF THE AFRICAN BAOBAB.* BOSTON, MA: LITTLE, BROWN.

CHAISSON, JOHN. 1987. *AFRICAN JOURNEY.* NEW YORK: BRADBURY.

CLIMO, SHIRLEY. 1989. *THE EGYPTIAN CINDERELLA.* NEW YORK: HARPERCOLLINS.

FEELINGS, MURIEL. 1974. *JAMBO MEANS HELLO.* NEW YORK: DIAL.

GRIFALCONI, ANN. 1986. *THE VILLAGE OF ROUND AND SQUARE HOUSES.* BOSTON, MA: LITTLE, BROWN.

——. 1990. *OSA'S PRIDE.* BOSTON, MA: LITTLE, BROWN.

HALEY, GAIL. 1970. *A STORY A STORY.* NEW YORK: ATHENEUM.

HEIDE, FLORENCE, AND JUDITH GILLILAND. 1990. *THE DAY OF AHMED'S SECRET.* NEW YORK: LOTHROP.

KNUTSON, BARBARA. 1990. *HOW THE GUINEA FOWL GOT HER SPOTS.* MINNEAPOLIS: CAROLRHODA BOOKS.

KROLL, VIRGINA. 1992. *MASAI AND I.* NEW YORK: FOUR WINDS.

——. 1993. *AFRICAN BROTHERS AND SISTERS.* NEW YORK: FOUR WINDS.

McDERMOTT, GERALD. 1972. *ANANSI THE SPIDER.* NEW YORK: HOLT.

——. 1992. *ZOMO THE RABBIT.* NEW YORK: HARCOURT BRACE.

WILLIAMS, KAREN LYNN. 1990. *GALIMOTO.* NEW YORK: MULLBURY BOOKS.

13

Communicating with Parents

I've always believed that other than the children, parents are a teacher's best advocate. When we get comments like the following, we know that we're on the right track.

> "Kyle is very proud of his accomplishments in school—he has made such progress this year!"
>
> "Maggie is really enjoying first grade. I want to thank you for giving her a classroom where she feels confident in herself to express what she is learning."
>
> "We are thrilled with Dawn's enthusiasm for first grade. Thank you for all of your involvement and dedication. We are so amazed with everything that she has going on."
>
> "The nurturing and caring you showed the children as individuals has reinforced to Alice how important it is to be kind to one another."

There are two important messages in these comments: recognition and celebration of the children's learning, enthusiasm, engagement and developing sense of caring, and validation of my work. Teachers need occasional recognition for their hard work and commitment, and an out-and-out thank you is always appreciated from time to time. When parents tell me, either orally or in writing, that they notice their child's effort, progress, and interest in learning, I know that they are understanding what I am trying to accomplish in my classroom.

The thinking and learning environment that we offer children is enhanced by positive, ongoing, and varied communication with their parents or the primary caregivers in their lives. The more all the adults in the children's lives know and understand each other, the better they can support them as self-confident, productive lifelong learners.

From my experiences, I've concluded that parents want assurance from their child's teacher in four areas. First, they want to know that the teacher will do whatever is necessary to create and sustain an environment that is emotionally, socially, intellectually, and physically safe for their children. Next, they want to know that the teacher has a sound theoretical base for her teaching, and can explain it. This implies that the teacher is keeping up with current pedagogy by conversing with other educators, reading professional books, and attending workshops and conferences. Parents also want to know that their children are learning, which means that both the teacher and the children must be able to demonstrate this on an ongoing basis. Finally, parents want to know that they will be included as partners in their child's school experience.

Different parents respond to different methods of communication. Therefore, I have developed a variety of communication methods to meet all of our needs; these include: newsletters and progress reports, parent conferences and phone calls, and communication through the children, such as portfolio evaluation and Visitors' Day. If we take the time to create trust and develop open communication at the start of school, it is easier to sustain a positive, open relationship throughout the year.

SEPTEMBER

I start communicating before the first day of school, when I send the children an introductory newsletter (see Appendix B2–1) telling them about the year and describing what to do when they come to the classroom on the first day. I purposely address this first communication to the children, because I want them to know that they are most important to me. However, since I know that they will be discussing it with their parents, I am also communicating to the parents through their children (see Chapter 1).

On the first day of school I send home an information packet to the parents. It includes a letter from me, a parent information form, a handout about learning, and various forms from the office and the school parent organization. I staple these together and write each child's name on the front to be certain that everyone gets one.

My Letter

The purpose of the letter is to make the parents feel included in their children's new classroom, to let them know about some of the things that they will be learning during the year, to explain the parent information form, and to note any other details that will help our year start out successfully (see Appendix B13-1).

Parent Information Form

The Parent Information form that parents fill out at the beginning of the year, (see Appendix 13A-1) gives parents the opportunity to tell me what they think is important about their children both socially and intellectually, and what expectations they have for them in these areas in the upcoming year. It lets parents know that I value their observations and expectations and suggests that I will include their input as I work with their children, and as we communicate throughout the year. The following are typical comments I have received on this form.

> "Just have a great year."
> "Continue to love learning."
> "Be challenged."
> "Learn a little more about give and take. He always wants his own way."
> "She knows how to read, so I don't want her to be bored."
> "Learn to read and add and subtract."
> "Learn not to write the letters backwards."
> "Has a great interest in space travel."
> "Seems to prefer to play alone. I'd like him to be more social and invite friends home."

The simplicity of the form invites parents to respond in a way that is comfortable for them. Some write a few phrases or sentences, others list important points, a few write detailed paragraphs, and a small number don't send it back at all. The form gives me the opportunity to understand the children from the parents' point of view and to respond accordingly. It is especially helpful in providing a common area of understanding as I plan for parent conferences and write progress reports.

WRITTEN COMMUNICATION WITH PARENTS

The written communications described in this section are between me and the parents, and include newsletters, progress reports, and letters that I send home.

Newsletters for Parents

Throughout most of my teaching career I have sent home newsletters. Their purpose is to inform parents about what is going on in the class and to explain the theoretical basis for what I'm doing. This communication is primarily between the parents and me, although sometimes the children suggest what I ought to include. I tell them what's in the newsletter before giving it to them to take home. Then these newsletters often become catalysts for conversation between the children and parents.

I have used two different newsletter formats for first grade. At first I wrote a one-page weekly newsletter, which was an ongoing account of what was happening in the class. As I became more involved in a generative curriculum, I changed to writing a monthly newsletter, about four pages long, which explained projects and learning procedures in more depth.

Weekly Newsletter

One of the main benefits of the weekly newsletter (see Appendix A13-2) was that families received an ongoing report of what was happening in the class. Its printed form included sections for reading, writing, literature, math, social studies, science, and general notices. Due to the limited space allotted for each area, the newsletter didn't take long to write, and the format lent itself to listing important points rather than long sentences. I wrote it in long hand and usually added to it every day after school or as we completed a particular project.

The weekly newsletter had limitations, however. Because the categories were confining, because the project or strategy that I wanted to describe often fit into more than one subject area, the format didn't lend itself to describing the rich, interactive nature of a generative curriculum. I shifted to a newspaper format, similar to the one that I had created for the classroom newspaper.

Monthly Parent Newsletter

The monthly newsletter gives a much more complete description than the weekly newsletter of what is going on in the class. In the first article I usually describe how the group is developing as a classroom community. Then I update what we are currently addressing in reading, writing, and math and discuss ways that we are integrating social studies, science, and literature. Finally, I explain special projects, highlight upcoming events and provide any specific information for parents. I send the newsletter home once a month, interspersing it whenever possible with parent letters and Visitors' Days, so that families will be receiving something important about their children's school experiences about twice a month (see Appendix B13–2, 13–3, and 13–4).

Letters

Throughout the year I send various letters to parents explaining reading, writing, and spelling theory as it applies to practice in the classroom, describing various social studies and science projects, and asking for parental involvement in their children's school year (see Appendix B13–5). Other letters are discussed in appropriate chapters throughout the book and copies of many of them are found in Appendix B.

Home/School Journals

One of the ways that parents and I communicate is by writing back and forth in home/school journals, which I usually start at the end of September, after back-to-school night. On the cover of a eight-and-a-half-by seven-inch composition book, I write the child's name and put a letter inside to parents that explains the uses of the journals (see Appendix B13–6). To introduce the procedure, on the first page I record the date and write five or six lines about the child. For example, "Chad really seems to enjoy drawing and writing. The other day he started writing a book about snails. He numbered the pages and made a cover, and now other children have picked up on the idea. Does he like to write at home?"

There are several kinds of parent responses:

"Joel will be going to the hospital to have his tonsils out next week. Do you have any books we could read on the subject?" (reporting absences)

"Mandy's grandfather died last night, and needless to say, she is very upset. I will be away for a few days, and my mother-in-law will be staying with the children. Thanks for your understanding." (describing a home incident)

"Yesterday Faith came home very upset about some hitting that was going on in the playground at recess. Would you look into it and give me a call? Thanks." (requesting clarification about a social issue)

"Kathy is so excited about writing a different math equation on the board every day. She's up and dressed for school every morning by 7." (validating something in school)

"Peter insists that he read before turning out the light every night. He is certainly excited about reading." (sharing something the child has done at home that is school related)

"Ted is still writing his numerals backward. Is that typical? Should I be worried? (asking for clarification about an academic issue)

"Do you need chaperones for the trip to Drumlin Farm? I'd love to help out." (volunteering to help)

Parents keep the journals at home and when they have something to tell me, they send them back with the children, who put them in a special basket for parent notes. I usually write a quick response during the day and return the journal to the child at the end of the day. Once in a while, when I feel that the comment warrants a longer and more reflective response, I send the journal home the next day.

Some parents keep the journals going all year, others write in them once in a while, and some never send them in. Sometimes parents and I just send notes back and forth, and sometimes I check in periodically on the phone with certain parents.

Progress Reports

In my school system teachers send home three written progress reports a year. These are written in narrative form and provide between two and five lines for teacher comments on social/emotional growth, academic progress in reading, writing, and math, the child's strengths, areas of concern, and a space for parent comments (see Appendix A13–3). One of the benefits of this kind of narrative report is that it encourages teachers to focus on what the children can do and how they are progressing in their own learning. Unlike a check list or rubric, it does not require us to compare children.

We give out the first progress report at the November parent conference. Conference participants sign a copy for school records, and parents are given a carbon copy. The second progress report goes home sometime in March, but since all the reports don't have to go home on the same day, we have the flexibility to write them over time, and to hand them out in person if we choose to hold a parent conference. Parents keep one report, sign the other and return it to school. The June report is sent home on the last day of school and no signature is required.

COMMUNICATING THROUGH CHILDREN'S WORK

I communicate best with parents through the children and their work, and throughout this book I have described many of the letters and procedures that I use to inform parents about their children's progress. These include the parents, involvement with envelope books, monthly portfolio assessment, and social studies and science projects. The following projects are other ways that the children include their families in the thinking and learning that goes on in the class.

Mr. Bear

Mr. Bear was an important part of my classroom community in kindergarten and has continued to hold a prominent place in the lives of my first graders. I got the idea for Mr. Bear from "Oscar's Journal," an article by Susan Durst (1988). Since I wrote about it in *Joyful Learning*, teachers from all over the country have told me about the different ways that they have made their bear an important member of their classroom, and I wonder how many Mr. Bears there are in the United States and Canada, going home each night to spend a cozy evening with a nurturing child.

Mr. Bear, along with his journal, travels home in a special bag with a different child each night. The child, usually with the help of family members, writes about Mr. Bear's visit in the journal, and then shares the journal with the class the next morning.

Although periodically Mr. Bear accumulates possessions as he travels from home to home, in my class the focus has remained with the journal and specific projects that I introduce throughout the year. The journal is an eight-and-a-half-by-seven-inch composition book, and we usually complete four of them in a year. I start the procedure by writing the first entry, in the form of a letter written to the class by Mr. Bear, and read it on the first day of school (see Appendix B13–7). I explain where I got Mr. Bear, tell a little about my family, so that the children and their families will get to know me, and describe the general procedure for taking him home. The children take turns by alphabetical order of first names. I usually take him for vacations because I don't want him left at a grandparent's home or lost forever over a long holiday.

At the start of community circle during morning group, we hear Mr. Bear's journal. His current host or hostess either reads the journal or

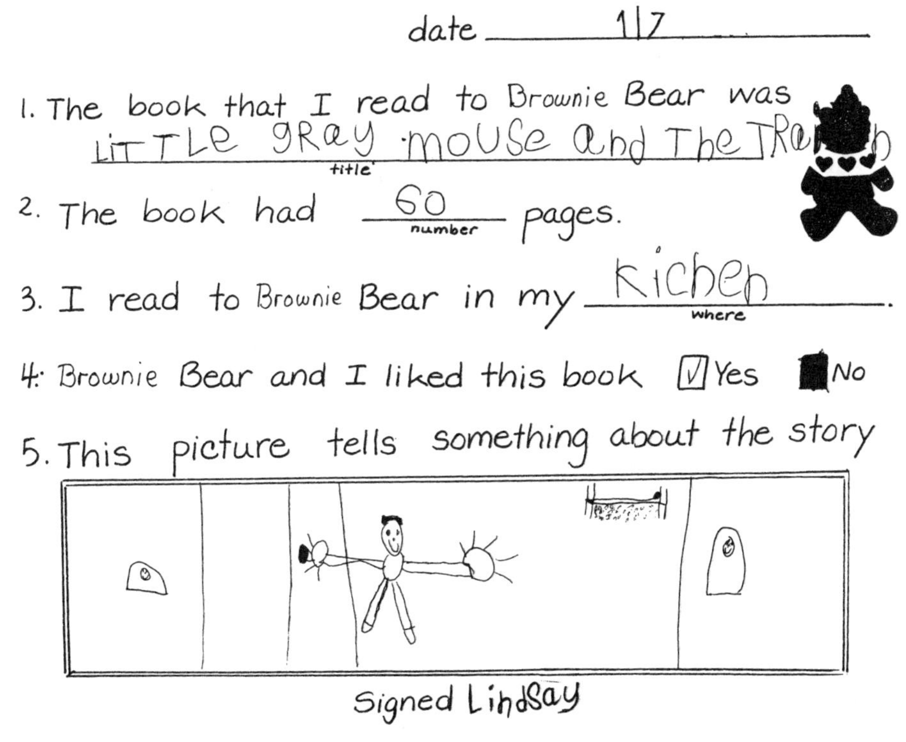

date _____ 1|7 _____

1. The book that I read to Brownie Bear was
LiTTLe gRay mouSe and The TRo̶l̶l̶
   title

2. The book had ___60___ pages.
                 number

3. I read to Brownie Bear in my __Kicheh__.
                                   where

4. Brownie Bear and I liked this book ☑Yes ■No

5. This picture tells something about the story

Signed LihdSay

FIGURE 13-1 *Mr. Bear's bedtime story*

asks me to do it. At the beginning of the year the parents do a lot of the writing, and I do most of the reading, but as the year progresses, the children take over both tasks. The journal entries usually include adventures Mr. Bear has experienced during the visit and other information about family life at the host home. When one journal is completed, we number a new one and add it to the bag. This gives children and their families the opportunity to read what others have written and to review the year through Mr. Bear's eyes. Some parents have told me that they spent most of an evening reading through all of Mr. Bear's journals.

Pat Hartvigsen, a first-grade teacher in Sudbury, shared with me the bedtime story form (see Figure 13-1) that she sends home with Mr.

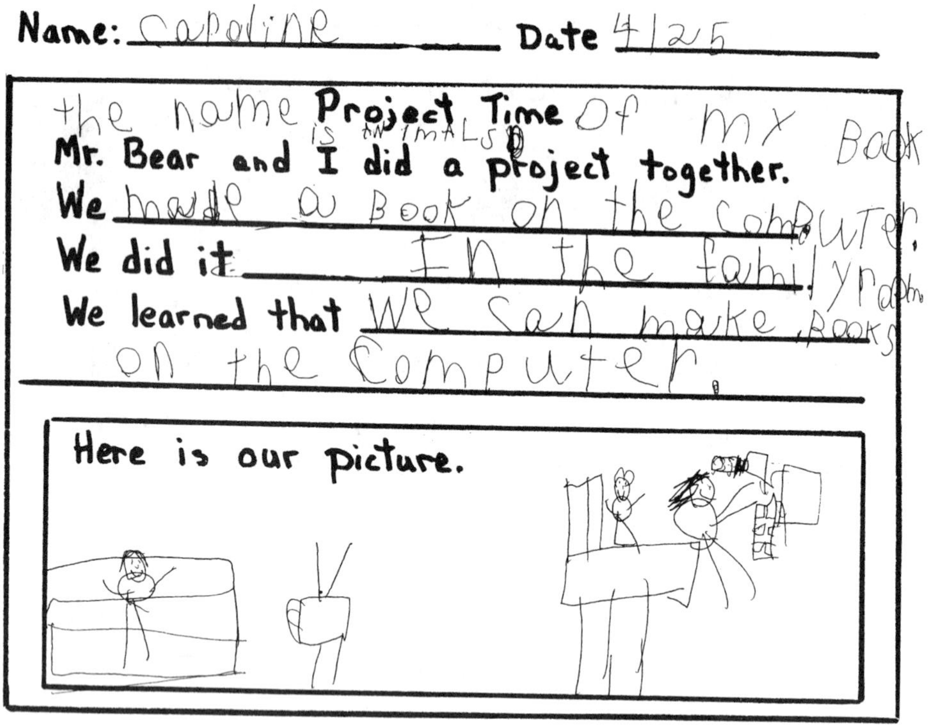

Name: Caroline   Date 4/25

> the name Project Time of my Book
> is animals
> Mr. Bear and I did a project together. Book
> We made a Book on the computer.
> We did it   In the family room
> We learned that We can make Books
> on the computer.
>
> Here is our picture.

FIGURE 13-2 *Mr. Bear's project form*

Bear, which I initiate after Mr. Bear has gone home two times with each child. To introduce the procedure, I take Mr. Bear home, write in his journal and fill out the form and share it with the class. A folder with copies of the form for each child is added to the bag. As the year goes on I introduce a project form and a math project form for Mr. Bear (see Figures 13-2 and 13-3 and see Appendixes A13-4–A13-6).

Each summer I get a new bear for the upcoming year and the old bear sits with its predecessors in a basket in my classroom. I get a new bear because I don't want any bear to get so old that it would fall apart. Also, children from previous years sometimes come back to the class and invite their bear to visit them for an evening. I always get small

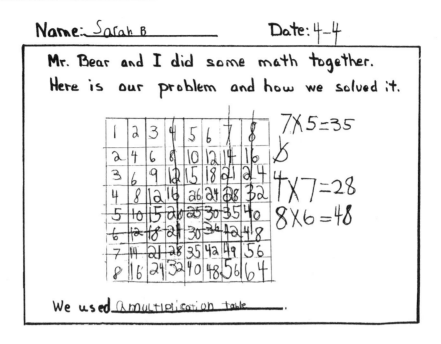

Name: Sarah B   Date: 4-4

Mr. Bear and I did some math together.
Here is our problem and how we solved it.

7X5=35

7X7=28

8X6=48

We used a multiplication table.

FIGURE 13-3 *Mr. Bear's math problem*

bears, no more than about eight inches tall, so that they can be taken home easily. One year I used a bear that Linda Erdmann, a teacher friend, made for me. Last year, Mr. Bear was a cuddly puppet.

Helping in the Classroom

One of the most productive ways for parents to understand what is happening in the classroom is for them to come in and help. I try to get at least one adult (parent, grandparent or other relative, or important family friend) from each of the children's families to spend part of a morning in the class so they can get a sense of what the day is like for their child and get to know the other children as they enjoy a special time together.

During back to school night and also through a letter to parents, I explain the procedure for helping in the classroom. We schedule the

271

date in advance, so I can be certain that they will see a typical morning routine without interruptions such as a school meeting or specialist, and so that we only have one visitor a day in the room.

I encourage the parents to come at the beginning of the day, so they can see how the children settle in and get their work ready, and to be there for shared literacy. This is an optimal time for the children and I to demonstrate the teaching and learning that goes on. Parents can see firsthand how skills and strategies are experienced in context as we read a Big Book, hear the children's rich conversation about a wonderful storybook I read, feel our sense of community as we sing together, and understand the caring atmosphere we are developing as they participate in passing the rock with us.

During writing and workshop time, they help in some way. Some work with small groups on a science, art, or cooking project that they have planned or help children at the computer. Sometimes the child of the visiting parent asks his classmates to sign up if they would like to read with that parent. While the rest of the class is writing, the children go one by one to a special place in the reading areas and share a favorite book. Sometimes the children read and sometimes the parent reads.

There are many other ways that parents work in the class. A group of parents helped us create the waterworks. Chris' father brought his mountain climbing gear and slides of his climb up Mt. McKinley (see Photo 13–1). Sarah's mom and dad brought special viewing devices so the children could observe the eclipse of the sun, Brandon's mom helped the children write words for a song about Japan, and Kristen's parents brought in new baby rabbits and puppies.

Parents who can't come into the class are often willing to work at home. For example, they send in food for class parties, cut out materials for art projects, sew puppets, and pick up recycled materials on the weekend.

Ongoing Communication

In addition to talking with parents face to face during parent conferences and Visitors' Day, I also value our brief conversations when they help in the classroom, come to a school-wide event, and pick their chil-

PHOTO 13–1 *Parent presentation*

dren up from school. When I realize that we haven't communicated in a while, I'm apt to write parents a note describing something positive about their child or give them a call on the telephone.

VISITORS' DAYS

Visitors' Day is a celebration day. The children invite the important people in their lives to visit the classroom to participate in a group time and to see what they have been learning. Visitors include family members, such as parents, siblings (not attending the school), aunts, uncles and grandparents, as well as foster parents, other caregivers, and friends.

We usually have four Visitors' Days a year, in October, December, March, and in June. Although each day follows the same general format, each one emphasizes something special. The one held in early October gives the children a chance to introduce their visitors to the daily

273

classroom routine, and gives me a chance to show them what the children learn during shared reading. The two held during the middle of the year are planned at the end of a class study so we can share what we have learned, and demonstrate progress made in reading, writing, and math. The last Visitors' Day brings the year to closure through celebration, and gives me an opportunity to thank parents for their support.

I have found that the best time is from 11:45 AM–12:45 PM, which is right after recess and before the children go to lunch. This gives us time to get ready in the morning, and allows the visitors to use their lunch hour from work to come to school.

As the visitors arrive, the children show them around the room until I start singing, a signal for everyone to come to the rug area for group time. Group time starts at noon and lasts about twenty-five minutes, giving time at the end for the visitors to continue to explore the room and leave at their own pace (see Photo 13-2).

Getting Ready

We start talking about Visitors' Day several weeks ahead of the date, and I send the date and time home at least ten days in advance so the visitors can arrange their schedules. We plan the group time and practice the songs and readings we will present, deciding on projects we want to share, and ongoing work, such as writing folders and math journals that we want the visitors to see.

On the day before each Visitors' Day, the children take clipboards, pencils, and paper and list the things in the room they want to be sure to show their visitors (see Figure 13-4). (As with all notetaking and list making, children can draw pictures as well as write words. This includes children who aren't writing yet, or who like to express themselves through drawing.) Then we share as a group at the rug and I write their ideas on chart paper. The children are encouraged to add ideas and make corrections on their clipboard papers (see Photo 13-3).

On Visitors' Day the clipboards, along with other work such as projects and writing folders are at the children's places, ready to show the visitors.

PHOTO 13-2 *Parents on visitors' day*

The October Visitors' Day

I plan the first Visitors' Day of the year four to six weeks after school starts. I announce it at parent open house in September and we send home an invitation the following week. The main focus is to show how teaching and learning happen in the classroom, demonstrating the reading, writing, and math materials used by the children, as well as the classroom routines involving their use. The children list many of the materials on their individual clipboard lists, and I ask them to be sure to include writing folders and science observation papers. Since we use Cuisenaire Rods extensively throughout the year, I put them out on a table (see Photo 13-4).

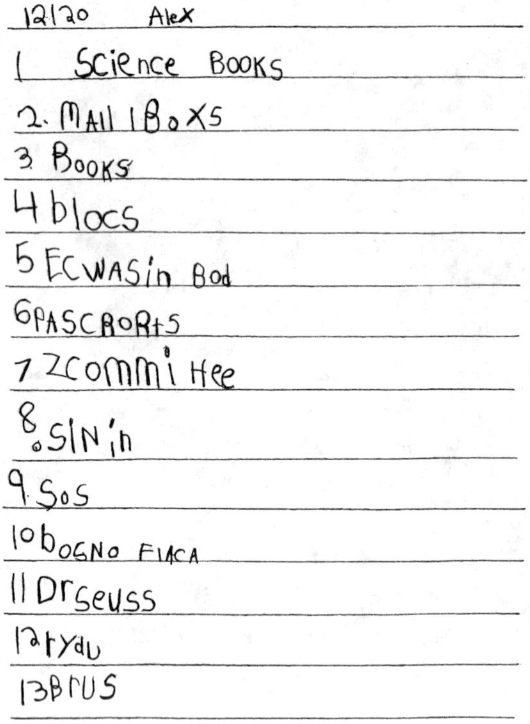

```
12/20    Alex
1  Science Books
2. MAil I BoXS
3 Books
4 blocs
5 ECWASin Bod
6PASCRORtS
7 ZComm'i Hee
8. SIN'in
9 SoS
10 boGNo FilACA
11 Drseuss
12 fydu
13 BrUS
```

FIGURE 13–4 *List of things to show visitors*

At group time we have a shared reading lesson. We sing several songs and as I point, we read a Big Book that the children have picked. A favorite at this time of year is *The Little Yellow Chicken* (Cowley). I ask the children what they notice. Perhaps they find letters, mark off spaces between words, or suggest other words that would make sense in text. We might reread a sentence to help figure out an unknown word or predict and discuss what might come next in a story. We fill in the vowels in the morning schedule and message, by spelling the words as I write in the letters.

This demonstration of shared literacy is very important because it gives the visitors a chance to see the merit and opportunities of learning in community. It also gives me the chance to demonstrate how children learn reading and writing skills and strategies in the context of whole texts and shows the value and procedure of the explicit teaching

276

PHOTO 13-3 *Writing the list on clipboards*

I employ. During this time I also give announcements, validate the class, and thank the parents for their classroom support.

During the tour of the room, the visitors see the classroom materials and the children's work (see Photo 13-5). This is especially important at the beginning of the year since papers are not sent home daily (see Photo 13-6). Visitors learn that they can come to the classroom at other times to look at the writing and science files, and that all the children's work will be sent home at the end of the year. Since the core of the math program involves manipulatives and small- and large-group problem solving, visitors can become familiar with some of the materials we will be using throughout the year (see Photo 13-7).

Visitors are also interested in learning the daily classroom routine. They want to picture what their children do throughout the day in school. Understanding emerges as they sign in (just as the children do when they first enter the classroom), participate in shared reading and discuss the morning message, and complete their individual tour of the room.

PHOTO 13–4 *Cuisenaire rods are left on tables*

December and March Visitors' Days

These two Visitors' Days are each scheduled as part of the culmination of a class study and give an authentic opportunity to focus on sharing, the fourth component of Holdaway's Natural Learning Classroom Model. Since December is a high energy month for children, I always plan a class project to channel this energy, which culminates in a Visitors' Day a few days before vacation. The other Visitors' Day is usually before spring vacation, as we finish up another study which is often part of a school-wide theme (see Chapters 11 and 12).

During group time, some of the focus is on the topic that we have been studying, and includes songs and choral readings. I demonstrate skills and strategies that I want the visitors to know we are presently learning. The children's clipboard lists include many of the items from previous Visitors' Days, as well as new ones. For example, have-a-go dictionaries and

PHOTO 13-5 *Reading to a Parent*

papers, math diaries, expanded observation forms, and reader response journals are now an important part of the learning routine.

June Visitors' Day

The focus of the last Visitors' Day is to celebrate our year together through song, review the work we have done all year, and to say goodbye in a formal way. I schedule it about a week before the last day of school. This day requires a lot of preparation because we have to complete our main projects (writing portfolios, reader response journals, math diaries, science folders) before then. However, we then have the last few days to relax and be together, to finish saying good bye, and to begin to put things away in the room.

Photo 13–6 *Sharing writing with parents*

During the group time we sing some favorite songs, focusing on songs of peace, such as "Teaching Peace" by Red and Kathy Grammer, as a way of expressing our classroom community. The children read the article they wrote for the end-of-the-year newspaper, and they tell one thing that they learned in first grade. I thank the parents for their support, and tell them what readers, writers, and mathematicians their children have become.

At their places the children put their clipboard lists, writing portfolios, math journals, science observation booklets, special learning projects, and copies of the class learning list and end-of-the-year newsletter (see Appendix B14–8). The visitors take these with them when they leave.

These Visitors' Days are beneficial to the children, the visitors, and to me. They enable and encourage the visitors to be involved in the children's life in school and to be kept abreast of their progress throughout

280

PHOTO 13-7 *Visitors learning about manipulatives*

the year. As the children prepare for and participate in these days, they become increasingly engaged in the process and content of their learning, and I learn what the children value most in the classroom. I receive the opportunity to inform the visitors about the classroom and to speak individually with each of them. We all benefit from the closer communication that develops among us.

Epilogue

This is an exciting time in education for classroom teachers. We are with the children day in and day out, and thus have the best opportunity to know what they need to grow as learners. We know that when children, both individually and collectively, are truly engaged in their own reading, writing, and math pursuits, learning is limitless. We know that children have an unbounded curiosity about social studies and science.

Therefore, it is up to us, the classroom teachers, to become the leaders in education as we move into the twenty-first century. We are ready and are taking the lead by ensuring that we have a major say in decisions concerning the children. We insist that the children are at the forefront of all our discussions regarding education.

We read widely and become teacher-researchers in our classrooms; we talk with colleagues and try out new ideas; we attend conferences and reorganize our classrooms with the help of the children; and we join teacher support groups and advocate what is best for the children.

My goal as a teacher has always been to support the children I teach as lifelong learners for a variety of meaningful purposes in their lives, and, as *I* continue as a lifelong learner, my educational philosophy continues to develop. In this book I have described my latest experiences as a teacher, and in the future, I will continue to build upon what I have done, trying new ideas and generating new ways that we can think and learn together.

FOR FURTHER READING

BISSEX, GLENDA, AND RICHARD H. BULLOCK. 1987. *SEEING FOR OURSELVES: CASE-STUDY RESEARCH BY TEACHERS OF WRITING.* PORTSMOUTH, NH: HEINEMANN.

BROWN, REXFORD G. 1991. *SCHOOLS OF THOUGHT: HOW THE POLITICS OF LITERACY SHAPE THINKING IN THE CLASSROOM.* SAN FRANCISCO: JOSSEY-BASS.

DAHL, KARIN L. 1992. *TEACHER AS WRITER: ENTERING THE PROFESSIONAL CONVERSATION.* URBANA, IL: NATIONAL COUNCIL OF TEACHERS OF ENGLISH.

FLURKEY, ALAN D., AND RICHARD J. MEYER. 1994. *UNDER THE WHOLE LANGUAGE UMBRELLA: MANY CULTURES, MANY VOICES.* URBANA, IL: NATIONAL COUNCIL OF TEACHERS OF ENGLISH.

GARDNER, HOWARD. 1991. *THE UNSCHOOLED MIND: HOW CHILDREN THINK; AND HOW SCHOOLS SHOULD TEACH.* NEW YORK: BASIC BOOKS.

——. 1993. *CREATING MINDS.* NEW YORK: BASIC BOOKS.

GIROUX, HENRY A. 1988. *TEACHERS AS INTELLECTUALS: TOWARD A CRITICAL PEDAGOGY OF LEARNING.* NEW YORK: BERGIN & GARVEY.

GOODMAN, KENNETH. 1992. "I DIDNT FOUND WHOLE LANGUAGE." *THE READING TEACHER* 46: 188–99.

GRAVES, DONALD. 1989. *DISCOVER YOUR OWN LITERACY.* PORTSMOUTH, NH: HEINEMANN.

HEALY, JANE. 1990. *ENDANGERED MINDS: WHY CHILDREN DON'T THINK AND WHAT WE CAN DO ABOUT IT.* NEW YORK: SIMON & SCHUSTER.

HUBBARD, RUTH S., AND BRENDA M. POWER. 1993. *THE ART OF CLASSROOM INQUIRY: A HANDBOOK FOR TEACHER-RESEARCHERS.* PORTSMOUTH, NH: HEINEMANN.

MOFFETT, JAMES. 1994. *THE UNIVERSAL SCHOOLHOUSE: SPIRITUAL AWAKENING THROUGH EDUCATION.* SAN FRANCISCO: JOSSEY-BASS.

NEWMAN, JUDITH M. 1991. *INTERWOVEN CONVERSATIONS: LEARNING AND TEACHING THROUGH CRITICAL REFLECTION.* PORTSMOUTH, NH: HEINEMANN.

NODDINGS, NEL. 1992. *THE CHALLENGE TO CARE IN SCHOOLS.* NEW YORK: TEACHERS COLLEGE PRESS.

PERRONI, VITO. 1991. *A LETTER TO TEACHERS: REFLECTIONS ON SCHOOLING AND THE ART OF TEACHING.* SAN FRANCISCO: JOSSEY-BASS.

SCHON, DONALD A. 1983. *THE REFLECTIVE PRACTITIONER.* NEW YORK: BASIC BOOKS.

SHANNON, KATHLEEN. 1995. *AT HOME AT SCHOOL: A CHILD'S TRANSITION.* BOTHELL, WA: THE WRIGHT GROUP.

TOUSDALE, ANN M., SUE A. WOESTEHOFF, AND MARNI SCHWARTZ, EDS. 1994. *GIVE A LISTEN: STORIES OF STORYTELLING IN SCHOOL.* URBANA, IL: NATIONAL COUNCIL OF TEACHERS OF ENGLISH.

Appendix A
Reproducible Forms

NAME: _____ DATE: _____

Committee choices:

1. _____

2. _____

Three people I would like to work with:

1. _____

2. _____

3. _____

What helps my learning in school:

1. _____

2. _____

3. _____

4. _____

5. _____

6. _____

APPENDIX A1–1 *Blank Committee Choices Form*

DAILY REPORT

	Tally	Total
BOOKS		
COUNTING		
KINDNESS		
MENTAL MATH		
PHONICS		
POEMS		
SPELLING		
SONGS		
WRITING		

© 1995 by Bobbi Fisher. For classroom use only.

APPENDIX A1–2 *Moderator's Daily Report*

TALKING THE PROBLEM

1. What is the problem?

2. What do we want to have happen?

3. What are some ways to solve it?

4. What way shall we try?

5. Try our solution for two days.

6. Was the solution a good one?

7. Do we need to talk about the problem some more?

Date:

APPENDIX A1–3 *Seven Signs of Talking the Problem*

INQUIRY INTERVIEW

NAME: _____   **DATE:** _____

Interest questions

1. What do you know a lot about?

2. What are you interested in learning about?

3. What can you do well?

4. What would you like to be able to do better?

5. What do you do at home when you have free time?

6. What do you collect?

7. What countries are you interested in?

8. What are you interested in about long ago?

9. What famous people are you interested in?

10. What science topics are you interested in?

11. What kinds of stories and books to you like to hear?

12. What kinds of things do you notice?

13. What kinds of things do you wonder about?

APPENDIX A2–1 *Inquiry Interview*

Process questions

1. Do you learn best working alone, with someone, or both?

2. How do you feel about noise when you are working?

   • Does it bother you?

   • Do you like it quiet?

3. How does talking help you as you work?

4. When you learn something new do you like to:

   • write about it?

   • draw about it?

   • tell someone about it?

   • make up an experiment about it?

   • make up a play, puppet show or song about it?

   • use blocks to tell about it?

APPENDIX A2–1 (continued) *Inquiry Interview*

DAILY PLANS

DATE: _____ **SPECIALS:** _____

SETTLING-IN
_____

MORNING GROUP
_____

WRITING MINI LESSON
_____

WORKSHOP
_____

MATH
_____

SHARED LITERACY
_____

OTHER
_____

APPENDIX A3–1 *Daily Lesson Plans*

PLANS FOR THE WEEK OF ——————————

DAY:

SETTLING-IN	SHARED LITERACY
WRITING	WORKSHOP
MATH	READING
WRAP-UP	

Evaluation and preparation for tomorrow

Story

APPENDIX A3–2 *Plans for the Week (One Day)*

PLANS FOR THE WEEK OF _____

GENERATIVE TOPICS _____

MONDAY _____

Group Focus

Teacher Focus

Math

TUESDAY _____

Group Focus

Teacher Focus

Math

WEDNESDAY _____

Group Focus

Teacher Focus

Math

THURSDAY _____

Group Focus

Teacher Focus

Math

FRIDAY _____

Group Focus

Teacher Focus

Math

APPENDIX A3–3 *Plans for the Week (One Week)*

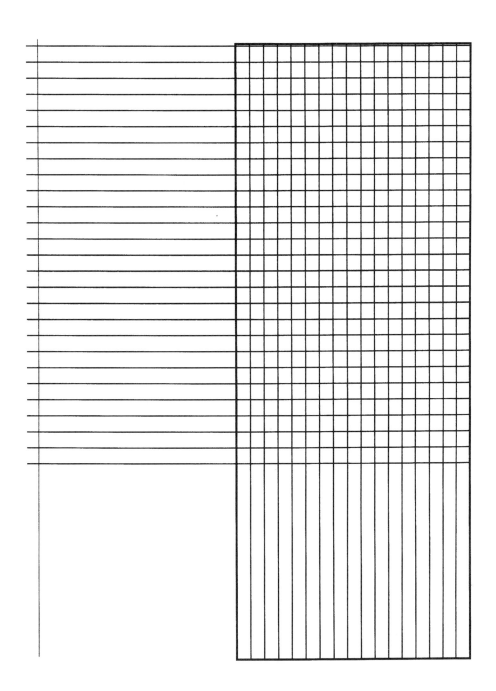

APPENDIX A3–4 *Blank Grid to Fill in Plans*

NAME: _____ DATE: _____

STORYBOOK PLAN

TITLE
_____

CHARACTERS
_____

PLACE
_____

TIME
_____

MOOD
_____

APPENDIX A4–1 *Storybook Plan Form*

EXPLICIT INSTRUCTION
PLANNING AND EVALUATION FORM

Date				
TEXT				
CLASSROOM CONTEXT				
CATEGORIES OF LEARNING				
Strategies				
Skills				
Content				
SOURCES				
Teacher knowledge				
Teacher observations				
Children's questions				
TYPES OF EXPLICIT INSTRUCTION				
Physical demonstration				
Questioning				
Making statements				
Eliciting practice				
Validating				

APPENDIX A5–1 *Explicit Instruction Planning and Evaluation Form*

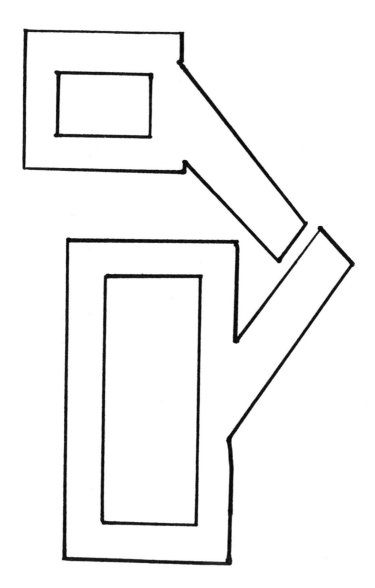

APPENDIX A5–2 *Masks*

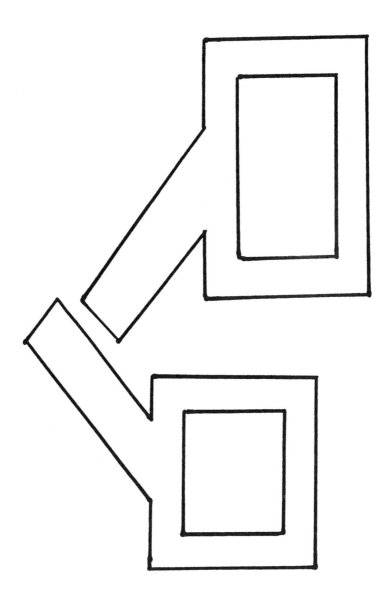

APPENDIX A5–2 (continued) *Masks*

READING CONFERENCE RECORDING FORM   Name: _____

DATE	TITLE	STRATEGIES	MISCUES	TEACHING OPPORTUNITIES	COMMENTS

APPENDIX A6-1 *Reading Conference Recording Form*

Name:

MISCUE RECORDING FORM

DATE	MISCUE MATCH	MEANING MATCH	SYNTATIC MATCH	VISUAL MATCH	AUDITORY	INTONATION	PUNCTUATION	COMMENTS

Adapted from *Reading Miscue Inventory*, by *Goodman*, Watson & Burke.

APPENDIX A6-2 *Miscue Recording Form*

BOOKS I CAN READ   Name: _____

DATE	TITLE	Practice Level*	PARENT/TEACHER COMMENT

* Practice level

E = Easy; R = Just Right; Ch = Challenge; H = Too Hard

APPENDIX A6-3 *Parent Recording Form: Books I Can Read*

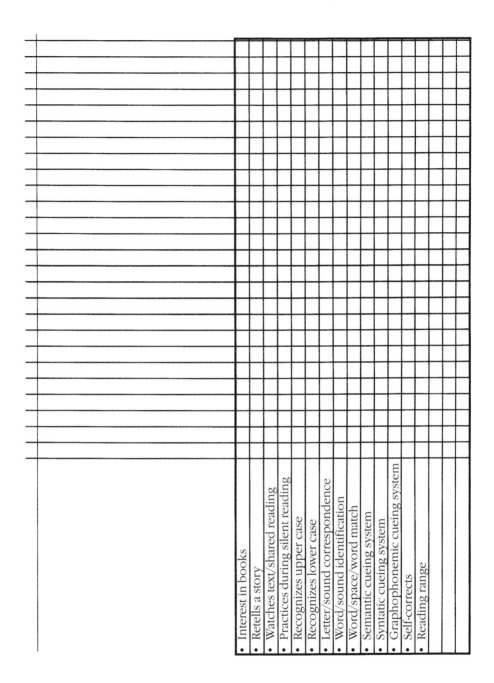

- Interest in books
- Retells a story
- Watches text/shared reading
- Practices during silent reading
- Recognizes upper case
- Recognizes lower case
- Letter/sound correspondence
- Word/sound identification
- Word/space/word match
- Semantic cueing system
- Syntatic cueing system
- Graphophonemic cueing system
- Self-corrects
- Reading range

APPENDIX A6–4 *Class Reading Evaluation*

NAME _____ TEACHER _____ GRADE _____

Key: 1 = Most of the time   2 = Some of the time   3 = Not noticed yet
        * = Has full command   + = In control   o = Needs time

READING ASSESSMENT Date				
• Interest in books				
• Retells a story				
• Watches text/shared reading				
• Practices during silent reading				
• Recognizes upper case				
• Recognizes lower case				
• Letter/sound correspondence				
• Word/sound identification				
• Word/space/word match				
• Semantic cueing system				
• Syntatic cueing system				
• Graphophonemic cueing system				
• Self-corrects				
• Reading range				

WRITING ASSESSMENT				
• Interest in writing				
• Drawing tells a story				
• Drawing predominates				
• Writing tells a story				
• Writing predominates				
• Reads back own writing				
• Spaces between words				
• Writes a sentence				
• Uses capitals and periods				
• Writes first/last name				
• Uses lower case letters				
• Pencil grip and direction				
• Handwriting/legibility				

SPELLING ASSESSMENT				
• Interest in spelling				
• Phonetic				
• Consonants				
• Vowels				
• Phonic to semantic				
• Correct vowels				
• Conventional patterns				
• Conventional spellings				
• Spelling stage				

APPENDIX A6–5 *Individual Assessment Profile Chart*

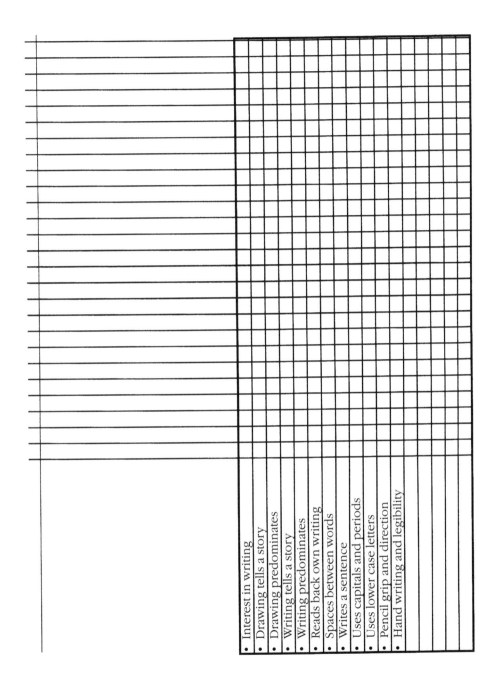

- Interest in writing
- Drawing tells a story
- Drawing predominates
- Writing tells a story
- Writing predominates
- Reads back own writing
- Spaces between words
- Writes a sentence
- Uses capitals and periods
- Uses lower case letters
- Pencil grip and direction
- Hand writing and legibility

APPENDIX A7-1 *Class Writing Evaluation Profile*

NAME: _____ **DATE:** _____

HOME/ADVENTURE/HOME

HOME

ADVENTURE

HOME

APPENDIX A7-2 *Home/Adventure/Home Plan Form*

APPENDIX A8–1 *Anecdotal Class Grid*

WRITING CONFERENCE RECORDING FORM   Name: _____

DATE	GENRE	MEANING CONTENT	CONVENTIONS	TEACHING OPPORTUNITIES	NEXT STEPS

APPENDIX A8-2 *Writing Conference Recording Form*

WRITING ASSESSMENT FORM

STUDENT: _____   DATE: _____

	Present Observation	Future Focus
Writing		
Content		
Writes more than one sentence		
Picture		
Detail		
Conventions		
Spaces between words		
Appropriate spacing in words		
Capitals and periods		
Handwriting and legibility		
Uses some lower case letters		
Formation of letters		
Size of letters		
Effort		
Spelling		
Spelling		
Standard spelling		
Standard spelling patterns		
Uses Have-a-go paper		
Teacher comments		
Student comments		
Parent comments		

APPENDIX A8–3 *Writing Assessment Form*

SPELLING AND WRITING SKILLS EVALUATION

NAME: _____ **DATE:** _____

Capitals and periods _____

Lower case letters _____

Spaces between words _____

Approximate number of words written _____

Approximate number of correct spellings _____

Percent of correct spellings _____

Have-a-go words _____

List of correct spellings	Observations

APPENDIX A8–4 *Spelling and Writing Skills Evaluation*

MY WRITING IN SEPTEMBER

NAME: _____ DATE: _____

1. What I have drawn and written about.

2. What we notice about my drawings.

3. What we notice about my writing.

4. Some of the letters, sounds and "ear spellings" that I use in my writing.

5. In September I recognized:
   _____ upper case letters and _____ lower case letters.

6. Some of the words I spell in my writing.

7. What I plan to work on in October.

APPENDIX A8-5 *My Writing in September Form*

MY WRITING IN OCTOBER

NAME: _____ **DATE:** _____

_____

What I have drawn and written about.

_____

What we notice about my drawings.

_____

What we notice about my writing.

- Am I writing sentences?

- Am I leaving spaces between words?

_____

What we notice about my spelling.

_____

Words I know.

_____

What I plan to work on in November.

APPENDIX A8–6 *My Writing in October*

NOVEMBER WORK

During the past week the children and I have looked over all the work in their November file. They have put their most important pieces in a portfolio, which will be brought home at the end of the school year.

This envelope contains the rest of this month's work. It includes drafts, notes, and final copies of writing and topic reports.

I also talked with each child about his/her work, and have recorded some of the conversation below.

1. What is important about your writing?

2. What is important about your topic reports?

3. What is important about your reading?

4. What is important about your math?

5. When do you do your best learning in school right now?

If you can attend Visitor's Day on Wednesday, December 22nd from 11:45–12:45, your child will show you his/her portfolio and some of the other things that we have been doing in class. We also will give a short presentation of what we have learned about ancestors, immigration and settlement in this country.

APPENDIX A8–7 *November Work*

JANUARY WRITING CONFERENCE

GENERAL INTERVIEW

1. What have you learned about writing this year?

2. What do you like about writing?

3. What don't you like about writing?

4. Is writing time long enough? too long? too short?

5. Is quiet writing time too long? too short? just about right?

LOOKING AT A CURRENT CHILD-SELECTED PIECE

1. Why did you pick this piece?

2. What does it show that you can do?

3. Do you think that you are writing enough each day?

LOOKING AT A PIECE OF WRITING SINCE THE BEGINNING OF THE YEAR

1. What do you notice that you have learned?

2. What surprises you about your writing this year?

WRITING GOALS AND PLANS FOR THE REST OF THE YEAR

1. Writing conventions

2. Content

APPENDIX A8–8 *January Writing Conference Form*

MY WRITING IN FEBRUARY

NAME: _____ DATE: _____

What I have drawn and written about.

_____

What I notice about my drawings.

_____

What I notice about my writing.

- I am writing sentences. _____

- I am leaving spaces between words. _____

- I am using a capital letter at the beginning of the sentence. ___

- I am putting a period at the end of the sentence. _____

- I am using some lower case letters. _____

_____

Words I can spell.

_____

What I plan to work on in March.

APPENDIX A8–9 *My Writing in February Form*

MARCH PORTFOLIO ASSESSMENT

NAME: _____ **DATE:** _____

	Sept.	Now
I can think of topics.		
I write a lot.		
I write more than one sentence.		
I leave spaces between words.		
I use lower case letters.		
I use capitals and periods.		
I can spell words.		
My goals for the rest of the year.		

APPENDIX A8–10 *March Portfolio Assessment*

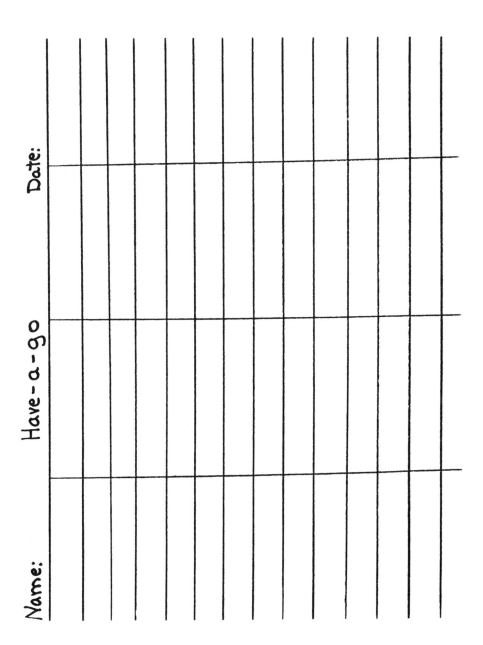

APPENDIX A9–1 *Have-A-Go Form*

NAME: _____ DATE: _____

SMALL GROUP SPELLING PRACTICE
("ear" and "eye" spelling)

	Practice	Practice	Word
1.			
2.			
3.			
4.			
5.			
6.			
7.			
8.			
9.			
10.			

APPENDIX A9-2 *Small Group Spelling Practice Form*

NAME: _____   DATE: _____

SPELLING PRACTICE

	Word	Practice	Word
1.			
2.			
3.			
4.			
5.			
6.			
7.			
8.			
9.			
10.			

Words 1-5, teacher choice
Words 6-10, student choice

Signed: _____
Parent comments.

APPENDIX A9–3 *Spelling Practice*

	Interest in spelling	Phonetic	Consonants	Vowels	Phonic to semantic	Correct vowels	Conventional patterns	Conventional spellings	Spelling stage						

APPENDIX A9–4 *Spelling Assessment Profile*

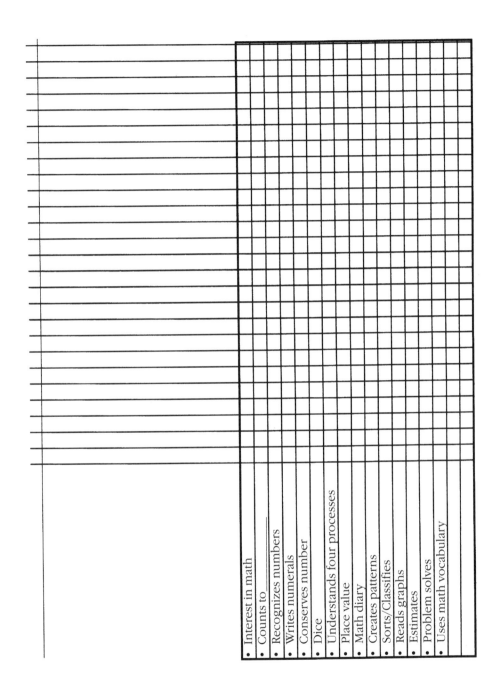

- Interest in math
- Counts to
- Recognizes numbers
- Writes numerals
- Conserves number
- Dice
- Understands four processes
- Place value
- Math diary
- Creates patterns
- Sorts/Classifies
- Reads graphs
- Estimates
- Problem solves
- Uses math vocabulary

APPENDIX A10–1 *Class Evaluation Form*

NAME _____ TEACHER _____ GRADE _____

Key: 1 = Most of the time   2 = Some of the time   3 = Not noticed yet
        * = Has full command   + = In control   o = Needs time

MATH ASSESSMENT   Date

• Interest in math				
• Counts to _____				
• Recognizes numbers				
• Writes numbers				
• Conserves number				
• Dice				
• Understands four processes				
• Place value				
• Math diary				
• Creates patterns				
• Sorts/classifies				
• Reads graphs				
• Estimates				
• Problem solving				
• Uses math vocabulary				

APPENDIX A10-2 *Individual Math Evaluation Profile*

OBSERVATION RECORDING FORM

SCIENTIST   DATE

OBJECT OBSERVED

MY PICTURE

PROPERTIES

APPENDIX A11–1 *Observation Recording Form*

OBSERVATION FORM

SCIENTISTS: _____

_____

DATE: _____

ITEM: _____

PICTURE: _____

_____

PROPERTIES:

Color: _____

Shape: _____

Size: _____

Texture: _____

Weight: _____

APPENDIX A11–2 *Observation Form Listing Each of the Properties*

OBSERVATION RECORDING FORM

SCIENTIST: _____ DATE: _____

OBJECT OBSERVED: _____

MY PICTURE: _____

_____

PROPERTIES:

1. Color: _____

2. Shape: _____

3. Texture: _____

4. Size: _____

5. Weight: _____

What I noticed: _____

_____

_____

_____

_____

APPENDIX A11–3 *Observation Form with Space for Children to Write What They Notice*

OBSERVATION RECORDING FORM

SCIENTIST: _____ DATE: _____

OBJECT OBSERVED: _____

MY PICTURE: _____

Material: Animal _____ Plant _____ Mineral _____

PROPERTIES:

1. Color _____

2. Shape _____

3. Texture _____

4. Size _____

5. Weight _____

What I noticed: _____

_____

_____

_____

_____

APPENDIX A11–4 *Observation Form with Place to Check Off Material of Object*

OBSERVATION RECORDING FORM

SCIENTIST: _____ DATE: _____

OBJECT OBSERVED: _____

MY PICTURE: _____

Material: Animal _____ Plant _____ Mineral _____

PROPERTIES:	ITEM ONE	ITEM TWO
1. Color		
2. Shape		
3. Texture		
4. Size		
5. Weight		

What we noticed: _____

_____

_____

_____

_____

APPENDIX A11–5 *Observation Form Recording Two Like Objects*

OBSERVATION OF CHANGES

SCIENTISTS: _____ _____

DATE STARTED: _____

ITEM: _____

How will it change? _____

_____

PROPERTIES:	WEEK 1	WEEK 2	WEEK 3	WEEK 4
1. Color				
2. Shape				
3. Texture				
4. Size				
5. Weight				
PICTURE				

APPENDIX A11–6 *Observations of Changes: Observing One Item for a Week*

OBSERVATION OF CHANGES

SCIENTIST: _____

DATE STARTED: _____

ITEM: _____

How will it change? _____

_____

_____

PROPERTIES:				
1. Color				
2. Shape				
3. Texture				
4. Size				
5. Weight				
PICTURE				

APPENDIX A11–7 *Observations of Changes over a Four-Week Period*

EXPERIMENT RECORDING FORM

SCIENTIST: _____ DATE: _____

My question: _____

_____

_____

Materials:

1. _____

2. _____

3. _____

4. _____

5. _____

What we will do: _____

_____

_____

What we will learn: _____

_____

_____

Picture of my experiment: _____

APPENDIX A11–8 *Experiment Recording Form*

WESTWARD HO!

HOME SURVEY

1. How many rooms are in your house? _____

2. How many children are in your family? _____

3. What chores do you have to do at home? _____

   _____

4. What animals do you have at home? _____

   _____

5. Where do you get your food? _____

6. Do you have a garden? _____

7. What do you grow? _____

   _____

8. Where do you get your clothes? _____

9. How do you get to school? _____

10. Why did you or your ancestors leave your homeland and come to
    this country? _____

APPENDIX A12–1 *Home Questionnaire*

MY FAMILY NOW AND LONG AGO

NAME: _____

ADDRESS: _____

THE PEOPLE WHO LIVE AT MY HOUSE:

_____

_____

HOLIDAYS WE CELEBRATE:

_____

WHAT WE LIKE TO DO TOGETHER:

_____

LANGUAGES WE SPEAK AT HOME:

_____

WHERE I WAS BORN: _____

WHERE MY MOM WAS BORN: _____

WHERE MY DAD WAS BORN: _____

WHEN MY ANCESTORS CAME TO THIS COUNTRY,
THEY CAME FROM _____

_____

APPENDIX A12–2 *My Family Now and Long Ago Questionnaire*

INTERVIEW:

MY IMMIGRANT ANCESTORS

1. Who were my ancestors who immigrated into this country?

2. Where did they come from?

3. When did they come?

4. How did they get here?

5. Where did they enter this country?

6. Where did they settle?

7. What did they do to make a living?

8. Why did they immigrate?

Name of person interviewed:

Interviewer: Date:

APPENDIX A12–3 *Interview: My Immigrant Ancestors*

Fisher

PARENT INFORMATION

Name: Telephone:

	Strengths	Areas for Growth	Parent Goal
Social			
Intellectual			

Work Schedule

Special ways you would like to help in the classroom.

APPENDIX A13–1 *Parent Information Form*

FIRST GRADE NEWS

MRS. FISHER'S CLASS   HAYNES SCHOOL   Week of

READING	WRITING	LITERATURE
MATH	SCIENCE	SOCIAL STUDIES

OTHER HAPPENINGS

NOTICES

APPENDIX A13–2 *First Grade News*

SOCIAL/EMOTIONAL: _____
_____
_____
_____

ACADEMIC: _____

    Reading: _____
_____
_____

    Writing: _____
_____
_____

    Math: _____
_____
_____

STRENGTHS: _____
_____

CONCERNS: _____
_____
_____

SUGGESTIONS: _____
_____
_____

PARENT COMMENTS: _____
_____
_____

Participants' Signatures: _____

APPENDIX A13-3 *Social/Emotional Form*

Name

Date:

The story I read to Mr. Bear was

_____

It had _____ pages.

I read to him in _____

He (liked) (didn't like) the story.

This is a picture of our favorite part.

APPENDIX A13-4 *Mr. Bear's Story Form*

Name: _____ Date _____

Project Time

Mr. Bear and I did a project together.

We _____

We did it _____

We learned that _____

Here is our Picture.

APPENDIX A13–5 *Mr. Bear's Project Time Form*

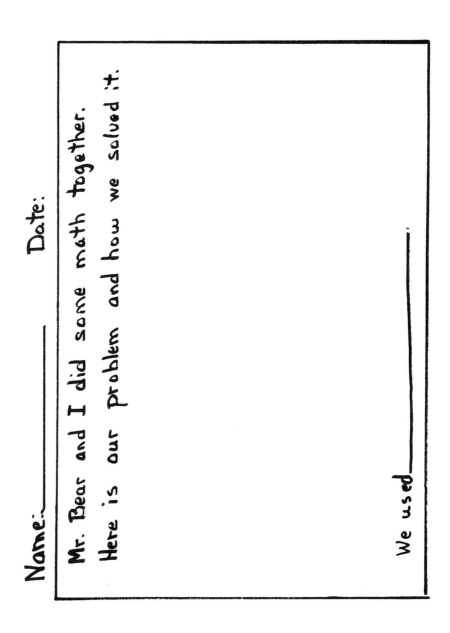

Name: _____   Date: _____

Mr. Bear and I did some math together.
Here is our problem and how we solved it.

We used _____

APPENDIX A13–6 *Mr. Bear's Math Project Form*

Appendix B
Letters and Charts

THE FISHER CLASSROOM NEWSPAPER

VOLUME 3 NUMBER 1   *August*

WELCOME LETTER

Dear First Graders,

School will be starting soon and I hope you are as excited about our year together as I am. I thought I would use our first newspaper of the year to welcome you, and tell you and your parents some things about the first day of school. We will write the next newspaper together.

Love,

Mrs. Fisher

A FAVORITE BOOK

On the first day of school, please bring in one of your favorite picture books to share with the class. Be sure to put your name in it, and plan to leave it in school for a week or so.

SNACK AND LUNCH

If you think you will get hungry in the morning, pack a nutritious snack that is easy to eat. You can buy lunch, or bring it from home.

THE FIRST DAY OF SCHOOL

When you arrive in the classroom on the first day of school, I will be waiting for you. Mrs. Schreiner, my assistant, and Mr. Berardi, a student teacher from Wheelock College, will also be there.

These are some things that you should do when you come in:

1. Find the coat hook with your name on it, and hang up your jacket and school bag.

2. Sign in on the piece paper on the table near the door.

3. Find your name on your writing folder at your place at one of the tables.

4. Take your favorite book to Mr. Berardi at the reading (rug) area.

5. In your mailbox, find the note I have written you. Put it in your school bag to take home. In the next week, write me back and put the answer in my mailbox.

6. Look around the room until I start singing, which is the signal to come to the rug area.

FOR PARENTS

1. Please label your child's clothing and lunch box.

2. If your child is going to be picked up, be sure to send me a note. It helps if the note is dated.

APPENDIX B1–1 *The Fisher Classroom Newsletter*

CLASSROOM RULE

Be kind to each other!

DATES TO REMEMBER

1. Back to school night will be Tuesday, September 21, 1993.
2. No school, Thursday, September 16th.
3. First early release day (no lunch is served) Wednesday, September 22nd.

COMPUTERS

I plan to give the children many opportunities to use our classroom computer (Mac SE) this year, but will need some assistance. If you are interested in helping, please let me know. I am open to possibilities and suggestions. More information will follow.

PUPPETS

I am looking for a parent or grandparent to sew a puppet for each child in the class, following a simple form. We will use them during the year, and in June, decorate them and take them home. If can help in this way, please drop me a note.

LOOKING AHEAD!

The year will be filled with:
- Africa
- Animals
- Art
- Blocks
- Books
- Building
- Caring
- Computers
- Creating
- Drawing
- Gym
- Hopi Indians
- Islands
- Japan
- Laughter
- Maps
- Math equations
- Music
- Note taking
- Painting
- Poems
- Problem solving
- Puppets
- Reading
- Science observations
- Science experiments
- Sharing
- Singing
- Stories
- Surveys
- Writing

What would you like to add to the list?

APPENDIX B1–1 (continued) *The Fisher Classroom Newsletter*

READING GROWTH CONTINUUM

Introduction to Books

1. Book awareness
   <u>Reading</u>
   - Displays interest in books
   - Likes to point out and name objects recognized in the picture
   - May look at books upside down and back to front
   - May mishandle them (e.g. rip them, color in them)
   - Doesn't see meaning as connected to print

   <u>Writing</u>
   - Drawing and writing indistinguishable
   - Scribble-like writing and a few letters may appear in drawings

2. I Am a Reader!: Emphasis on meaning of the story and the sound of language
   (semantic and syntactic cueing systems)
   <u>Reading</u>
   - Loves to listen to stories
   - Acts like a reader and writer
   - When looking at a new book, makes up a story from the pictures and uses book language such as "once upon a time" and other phrases from stories previously heard
   - When reading a familiar story, applies much of the book language in the retelling the story from memory
   - Reads story fluently and with a great deal of expression
   - Looks at pictures while reading
   - May pick a chapter book for silent reading and pretend to read it
   - Often reads alone or to stuffed animals
   - Recognizes more and more letters
   - Recognizes own name
   - Recognizes environmental print
   - Rhymes words
   - Give words that begin with same sound

   <u>Writing</u>
   - Drawings are central
   - Letters, and letter-like marks appear in writing
   - Strings lots of letters together
   - Reads writing by talking

© 1995 by Bobbi Fisher. For classroom use only.

APPENDIX B6–1 *Reading Growth Continuum*

Print Ranges

3. Print One: Close attention to print
   <u>Reading</u>
   - Moves back and forth from telling the story fluently (I am a reader stage) to trying to match the words to the print (Print Range One) and reading slowly, word for word
   - Points word for word with some accuracy to short texts that are familiar
   - Points accurately to the first and last words in a simple text, but not to the words in the middle
   - Uses beginning consonants to predict and confirm an unfamiliar word
   - Recognizes most letters
   - Gives words that begin with most consonants
   - Watches the print when being read to

   <u>Writing</u>
   - Draws more representationally
   - Labels drawings phonetically with beginning consonants
   - Strings letters together (some match phonetically and some are used as place holders)

4. Print Two: Intense attention to print
   <u>Reading</u>
   - Continued focus on and control of visual cueing system
   - Points word for word with accuracy with texts that are familiar
   - Can read some simple unfamiliar texts
   - Sometimes recognizes the same word in different texts
   - Develops strategies to help with meaning: looks at the pictures, starts at the beginning and reads again
   - Self-corrects
   - Uses the text and illustrations to sample, predict, and confirm
   - Semantic and syntactic cues are sometimes ignored because of intense focus on the print
   - Reads word for word.
   - Reads very slow, often in a monotone
   - Likes to practice familiar books
   - Watches the print when reading

APPENDIX B6–1 (continued) *Reading Growth Continuum*

Writing

- Includes more and more details in drawings
- Spells phonetically with beginning, middle, and ending consonants and some vowels
- Indicates spaces between words
- Begins some orthographic spelling
- Less labeling and more attempts at strings of words in writing
- Reads back own writing
- Writes on a single piece of paper

Independent Ranges

5. Becoming an Independent Reader

   ### Reading

   - Can read simple unfamiliar texts word for word
   - Strategies are uneven depending on the text
   - Fluency returns with familiar texts
   - Sorts out the use of all cueing systems—semantic, syntactic, and graphophonemic
   - Begins to integrate reading strategies
   - Often is aware when something doesn't make sense or sound right when reading
   - Wants to read to an adult often

   ### Writing

   - Drawings tell a story
   - Likes to writes books
   - Spelling shows more orthographic cues: sequence of letters, distribution, and word patterns
   - Writes sentences and leaves spaces between words
   - Begins to use punctuation

6. Independent Reader

   ### Reading

   - Reads a variety of genre
   - Begins to read from response, critical, curriculum, and writing perspectives
   - Brings own experiences to the text
   - Retells a story read independently
   - Can read longer and more complicated texts

APPENDIX B6–1 (continued) *Reading Growth Continuum*

- Uses semantic, syntactic, and graphophonemic cues in harmony
- Oral reading is fluent
- Reads orally with expression
- Adjusts reading strategies to fit the specific text
- Less attention to print
- Reads silently

Writing

- Writing is often more important than drawings
- Drawing supports written text
- Writes in a variety of genre
- Developing own voice and style
- Gaining control of writing conventions such as punctuation and paragraphs
- Many conventional spellings

7. Mature Range

Reading

- Uses semantic, syntactic, and graphophonemic cues automatically
- Adjusts reading strategies automatically
- Reads from response, critical, curriculum, and writing perspectives
- Reads a variety of genre
- Oral reading slows down the process
- Silent reading is more efficient than oral reading
- Adjusts reading rate to purpose and to text

Writing

- Text can stand alone without drawing
- Shows preference for particular genre
- Experiments with new genre
- Displays unique voice and style
- Reads like a writer and writes like a reader
- Adjusts writing to particular audience
- Has control of conventions
- Spells conventionally

APPENDIX B6–1 (continued) *Reading Growth Continuum*

INSTRUCTIONAL BOOKS

Print Range One

Book Levels 1-1 to 1-6

- Familiar subject matter
- Oral language text
- Repetitive
- Illustrations support text
- Text on one line
- Large print with sizable spaces between words
- 8 Pages

Book Level 1-7

- Same but text may be on two lines

Print Range Two

Book Levels 2 and 3
- Familiar subject matter
- Oral and written language text
- Repetitive text but with more variation
- Illustrations support text
- Text on one, two or three lines
- 8 or 16 pages

Becoming an Independent Reader

Levels 4-6, I Can Read Books
- Familiar subject matter
- Oral and written language text
- Repetitive text but with more variations
- Illustrations support text less specifically
- Text on one, two or three lines
- 8, 16 or 24 pages

Independent Reader,

Levels 7-8, I Can Read Books, short chapter books, trade books

- Varied genre—story books, information books, information story books, biographies, fairy tales, plays
- Written language texts
- More varied and complicated story structures
- More varied and specialized vocabulary, metaphor and symbolism
- Texts stands alone—illustrations enhance text but aren't essential
- Text on many lines and in smaller print
- 16 or 24 pages

Fluent Reader

All genre—for example, chapter books, non-fiction, newspapers, magazines,

APPENDIX B6-2 *Instructional Books: Ranges and Levels*

September

Dear Parents,

Throughout the year, as part of the first-grade reading program, your child will be bringing home an envelope containing one or more books (an envelope book) on which to practice her/his reading. Although I have selected the level of difficulty of the books for instructional purpose, it takes a while to reach an optimal level for each child. Initially, the books your child brings home may be too easy or too hard.

Please help your child read the books. On the accompanying form write the title and date, read, and fill in the column indicating the practice level. Also, your written comments from time to time will help us communicate throughout the year.

When the envelope is brought back to school, I will listen to your child read, assist in developing appropriate reading strategies, and help in selecting new books to bring home. I don't expect the envelope books to be returned every day, but try to have them back at least once a week.

Please keep in mind that reading is a strategic process. Predicting, making mistakes, self-correcting, and confirming are part of the process. Particularly with emergent and beginning readers, familiarity, repetition, and rhyme help children become successful readers.

Here are a few ideas to use in supporting your child's reading.

- You may need to read the book to your child first or read along with her or him.
- Encourage your child to point to the words and use the beginning letter and pictures when reading.
- Talk about the story. Ask your child to predict what the story might be about and what might happen next.
- When your child comes to a word he or she doesn't know, suggest rereading the first part of the sentence, looking at the picture and/or using the beginning sounds.
- Ask the questions: "Does it make sense?", "Does it sound right?", "Does the beginning sound of the word match the word you think it is?"
- It is all right to tell your child a word when he or she is stuck.
- Some children want their parents to spend a lot of time with them. Others want to work more independently. Follow your child's lead.
- Always keep this special reading time positive.

The purpose of this program is to help your child practice reading consistently in order to develop independence in reading. However, please don't let "envelope" book time take the place of your usual reading to your child.

I'll be happy to answer any questions you have throughout the year.

Sincerely,

APPENDIX B6–3 *Letter to Parents about Envelope Book Program*

GETTING PARENTS INVOLVED

*The following article by Laurel Stevick may be copied
and sent home to parents.*

HOME SUPPORT PROGRAM: SUGGESTIONS FOR PARENTS

The support of everyone important to children is needed to get a success cycle going in learning to read and write. A good general guide is to think back to when your child was learning to walk and talk. Remember how much you enjoyed and praised the first stumbling attempts. You understood naturally that learning begins in clumsiness and mistakes, yet moves slowly toward mastery.

When your child learned to speak, s/he was constantly surrounded by the sounds of people talking and was encouraged to try it him/herself. You probably didn't have any trouble responding when s/he said "baa" because you knew s/he meant, "May I have my bottle please, Dad?"

This is the spirit that is needed to support learning to read and write. The following suggestions will help you to experience that feeling again in supporting your child's efforts to master reading and writing:

1. Read aloud regularly from books your child would like to read but as yet cannot. With an older child who would consider such a situation babyish, prepare tape recordings of such readings and allow him or her to enjoy reading privately while following the text. This is called a "Read-along" situation, and it has proved very helpful in soundly researched programs. For an older child, include reading from some of the school subject texts which s/he finds difficult.

2. Invite your child to read along with you in a low-risk way that supports his/her attempts.
   - Assisted Reading. (I often refer to this as Whisper or Mumble Reading.) Your child chooses a book. You read through it first, discussing and enjoying the story together. Then invite your child to whisper or mumble along as you read it a second time. While your child is "getting the hang of it," keep your voice loud and steady. When it is clear that your child is feeling confident, lower your voice or even stop for a word or refrain that is very predictable.
   - Echo Reading. You read a bit (a phrase, sentence, a line or two of a poem) and suggest that your child read it back to you like an echo.

3. Now the really difficult part. When your child volunteers, listen to him or her read to you. Some suggestions for this risky situation:
   - Encourage practice before oral reading to you, or allow the child to make a tape recording for you to hear later.
   - Bite your tongue! Children might meet unknown words or substitute a word that doesn't make sense or sound like language. They often can correct

APPENDIX B6–4 *Article: Getting Parents Involved Sent With Letter to Parents* themselves if you exercise patience and show the confidence that they can work out some problems for themselves.

- If your child seems about to become frustrated, provide ready help. For instance, simply provide a difficult word or give hints related to meaning. Offer no criticism or attempts to teach or give advice.
- If the child becomes tangled in a sentence or loses the drift of what is being read, encourage a rereading of the tangled portion.
- Never correct or call attention to error in the middle of a sentence. Wait until the end and then gently question:

"Did that make sense to you?"

"You read _____ (repeating exactly what was read). Are you happy with that?"

- Gently throw correction back to the child wherever possible. Read the sentence correctly yourself and ask, "How does that sound?"
- Encourage and praise self-correction.
- Spend just a short time on hearing reading. Stop before the child tires.

4. A special technique that proves very helpful in many cases is to read an interesting book while the child follows the text. Leave out one in every 10th to 15th word for the child to read. This can be a very enjoyable sharing activity in which the child remains fresh and interested while learning. (The technique of leaving out portions of text is called the "cloze procedure.")

5. A variation of this technique is for you to read a sentence and then for the child to read a sentence. This allows for spaced relaxation during the period when reading is still exhausting for the child.

6. Be positive! Don't display anxiety or frustration about reading and writing. Be a cheerleader and a listener. Talk about the books with your child as you would with a friend.

Some portions adapted from Don Holdaway, Cambridge/Lesley Literacy Project.

From the Fall 1991 Newsletter of the Whole Language Teachers Association.

APPENDIX B6–4 (continued) *Article: Getting Parents Involved Sent With Letter to Parents*

THE LEARNING CLASS
MRS. FISHER'S FIRST GRADE
JOSIAH HAYNES SCHOOL

March

Dear Parents,

During vacation I looked at the writing the children have done since the beginning of school, and this week I talked with each child about his or her particular work. Enclosed is a recent piece of your child's writing, as well as one or more past pieces, so you can see the growth that has occurred during the year.

On the Writing Assessment Form I have briefly commented on some of the important areas of writing and indicated by a check or comment which areas I particularly want each child to focus on during the last four months of school. Everyone will be concentrating on neatness and legibility.

Please go over these papers with your child, add your comments in the space provided, and return them to school. You will get them back at the end of the year.

I'm impressed with the children's progress in story and picture content, and in writing conventions, handwriting, and spelling. This class continues to prove that it is The Learning Class.

Sincerely,

APPENDIX B8–1 *Letter to Parents to Accompany Writing Assessment Form*

January

Dear Parents,

The first of the year seems like a good time for all of us, teachers, children, and parents, to take a renewed look at spelling, especially for first graders. Research tells us that spelling is developmental and that children go through various stages as they become conventional spellers. Part of my job is to help each child in this developmental process.

Writing this year has included a lot of the children's own spelling, often referred to as "invented", "temporary" or "functional" spelling. This has enabled the children to be free to write with ease about what is interesting, meaningful and authentic to them. However, you may have noticed that your child's spelling has become more conventional during the year. This has occurred due to several reasons: the children's progress as readers, focus on spelling during shared reading, and exposure to explicit instruction and practice of the correct spelling of high frequency words.

"Invented" spelling as part of the developmental process will continue. As a class we will maintain our focus on vowels, blends, word endings and high frequency words. However, in order to support the children in their development toward standard spelling, I will be helping them individually to focus on words to spell conventionally. I will take into consideration their developmental stage, varying interests in spelling, and individual approaches to spelling as they write.

In order to do this, I will be focusing on three procedures which address these individual needs. The first is the have-a-go paper, which I introduced earlier in the year and described briefly in the Parent Newsletter of November 12th. It works like this: in the first two columns the child has-a-go at spelling a word he/she needs. In the next column, as I spell the word conventionally, we discuss what the child knew, what spelling patterns are in the word and other

APPENDIX B8–2 *Letter to Parents to Accompany Spelling and Writing Skills Evaluation* aspects of spelling that I think will be useful to that individual child. Then, in the last column the child writes the word conventionally. I will now be requiring that the children have their have-a-go paper (sample included) available for daily use in their writing folders.

Second, the children will be making their own have-a-go dictionaries in an alphabetized composition book. These will include high-frequency words that we learn as a class, as well as words that individual children want to spell conventionally.

Finally, I would like each child to bring from home two small (3" × 5" or a little bigger) spiral notebooks, one to list words that he/she wants to learn to spell, and the other to record ideas for writing. I'd appreciate it if the notebooks could be brought in by next Monday.

Thank you for your support. Please let me know if you have any questions.

Sincerely,

Bobbi Fisher

APPENDIX B8–2 (continued) *Letter to Parents to Accompany Spelling and Writing Skills Evaluation*

June

Dear Parents,

At back to school night in September I told to you that my goal for the year was to help your children become engaged as independent, self-motivated learners. Well, they have surpassed my highest expectations. All of the children in the class love to read, write and explore mathematics, and they take their work very seriously.

Visitors to the class, including the two video production teams, were impressed with the way the children went about their work, the extent and depth of their involvement, and their willingness to help and work with each other.

This folder includes a variety of school related papers and momentos for you. The children also have several books and portfolios that represent their journey as learners in first grade.

In the past week they have spent time getting together a folder that they can use as they continue to read, write and do math over the summer. Please let them tell you about its contents. Since they are ready to continue to be responsible for their learning, I suggest that you follow their leads.

I am grateful to the parent community in Sudbury. Thank you for your support and partnership.

Sincerely,

Bobbi Fisher

APPENDIX B8–3 *Letter to Parents: End of Year*

GETTING PARENTS INVOLVED

*The following letter may be copied or paraphrased
to help parents better understand the writing process.*

Dear Parents,

Some parents have been wondering why children in early primary grades are bringing home papers with temporary spellings that haven't been corrected.

Do you remember when your child learned to talk? S/he probably made many "mistakes," or approximations, in speech, and they didn't bother you much. You may have corrected a few, now and then, but mostly you included the child in the events of everyday life, encouraged the child to talk, and enjoyed the conversations. You probably knew, as parents do, that children learn to talk the way they learn to sit up and crawl and walk—they learn to talk by talking.

Learning to write works the same way. For example, early in the year, one child wrote:

Now this doesn't look like your writing any more than a child's early words sound like your speech, but it's a tremendous piece of work! First of all, and most important, this child knows that written language is supposed to mean something, and he knows exactly what it means:

I was seeing TV at my house. Then I saw a little mouse.

Just about every letter stands for one word in the story:

I y s tv a m H D is al m

I was seeing TV at my house. Then I saw a little mouse.

Some developmental stages in writing come before this one, and others come after. From this sample we see that the child knows the following:

- print proceeds in a straight line from left to right across a page
- print is made up of letters
- letters come in upper and lower case
- letters stand for sounds in the words he wants to write.

Later on the child wrote the following response to a story about two friends playing together.

APPENDIX B9-1 *Getting Parents Involved*

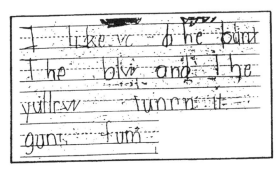

I like the part (where)
the blue and the
yellow turn into
green. from (author's name)

The writing still doesn't look like yours, but its closer.

Since writing the earlier sample, this child has learned that:

- written language is made up of words separated by spaces
- each word between spaces stands for one word in speech
- written words are made up of a number of different letters
- there are a number of letter/sound combinations in each word (both beginning and ending sounds are included here)
- when you "know" a word (The), you spell it the same way every time
- if you don't "know a word," you can use what you do know about letters and sounds to say what you mean until you learn the dictionary spelling
- you self-correct your own writing when it doesn't look right to you, just as children self-correct their own speech
- punctuation is a part of written language.

That's a lot to have learned, and the child has doubtless learned more that cannot be documented by looking at this one sample alone.

Teachers help children learn to write the way parents and families help them learn to talk. If we put all our energy into correcting temporary spellings, children get discouraged and lose a natural desire to write. What they learn from heavy correction is that meaning is less important than spelling the words right.

If we invite them to use their oral language in their writing, even though they can't spell all the words correctly, we free them to say what they mean. And, in fact, as the examples show, they learn a lot about writing in general, and spelling in particular, from the risks they take along the way. Children learn to write by writing, and we are most helpful to them when we appreciate and encourage their "best attempts."

Is there a time for teaching particular points of spelling, grammar, punctuation, and handwriting? Yes. Full group and individual conferences address such points as the need is noted in the children's own writing.

Is there a time when children correct their work and turn out finished copy? Yes—when publishing or "going public." In very early grades the children do the hard work—writing the stories—and we make the corrections. As children become more experienced, they begin to take responsibility for this work, too.

I hope this letter helps you to share some of your child's joy in writing, much as you share his/her pleasure in speaking.

Sincerely,

From the Fall 1988 Newsletter of the Whole Language Teachers Association Newsletter

APPENDIX B9–1 (continued) *Getting Parents Involved*

March

Dear Parents,

Last week I asked the children to write on lined paper and to use words to tell what they have previously been describing through drawings and pictures. My intention was to encourage them to write more, focus on their audience, and pay closer attention to writing and spelling conventions. (There will still be times for art work.)

During writing time the children had opportunities to ask for have-a-go- words. At the end of the period I asked them to proofread their writing and fill out the enclosed form. I have looked over the papers with them and selected a few misspelled words that I think they can practice and learn. The children are bringing home their papers and at least five words to practice. If they want to add more, please help them add them to the list and return the signed paper by Friday.

Lucy Calkins, in *The Art of Teaching Writing* helps us understand these developing writers as they look ahead to second grade:

"In kindergarten and first grade, many children convey their meaning more easily through drawing than through print. Drawing, therefore, can provide a supportive scaffolding for the writing. Because more information is embedded in the pictures than in the print, drawing provides a horizon and leads the child deeper into the writing. In a sense, our goal is to help children's writing catch up with their drawings.

"By second grade, writing has often surpassed drawing. Although these children may still find it easier to draw than to write, most find it easier to embed meaning into a written text than into a drawing. When second graders draw before each new page of writing, the pictures often hold back the written text."

I am so impressed with the challenges that this class meets. Thanks for your continued support.

Sincerely,

APPENDIX B9–2 *Letter to Parents: Spelling Practice*

June

Dear Parents,

This packet includes some of the end-of-the year spelling evaluation that I have conducted. In September, January and May I asked the children to spell the words listed on the attached assessment list so I could evaluate their progress throughout the year. We didn't study the words and I didn't help them in any way. Attached are your child's three assessments with some specific comments concerning her/his growth and progress

The development of spelling skills usually proceeds in the following general sequence: from scribble writing, to letter-like forms, to random letters, to beginning consonant, to adding ending and middle consonants, to including vowels, to conventional patterns, and finally to conventional spelling. You will probably notice that your child has progressed through several of these stages as he or she has learned to take control of his/her spelling during the year. The important thing to notice is growing command of spelling patterns. Also you may notice that a word previously spelled correctly, is misspelled in June. This may be due to the fact that your child has gained more knowledge of the variety of potential spelling patterns and is trying out different possibilities.

I have also included a list of words that most first graders should be able to spell, along with your child's final spelling evaluation of those words.

Please encourage your child to write during the summer. The best way to do this is to provide paper, markers, notebooks and other writing supplies, and to show an interest when your child wants to share her/his work.

Sincerely,

Bobbi Fisher

APPENDIX B9–3 *Letter to Parents: Spelling Evaluation*

THE FISHER CLASSROOM NEWSPAPER

VOLUME 2 NUMBER 2

April

HAMSTERS BORN

by Greg

Hello everybody. March 6, 1993 the hamster in Mrs. Fisher's room had eleven babies. In three weeks you can touch them.

picture by Greg

HAMSTER OBSERVATIONS

by Amanda
1. The babies are feeding.
2. The mom got up.
3. The babies are crying.

by Alex
1. The mother is nursing her young.
2. She sniffs around. 3. She sniffs her young.
4. The mother got off! 5. She got back on.

by Lindsay

The mom got off of the hamsters. They look happy to me. I took a close look at them.

by Chuck

I saw a few of the hamsters get off the mom, and the mom got off of the baby hamsters.

by Lauren

The mom nurses a lot. The mom licks them. The mom sleeps but gets up sometimes.

The babies have blue ears and fur. It looks like they kick.

by Amy

The hamsters are being nursed. The mom likes them. I hope I can have one.

by Jennifer

The babies are beginning to drink water. They have pink feet and go under the wheel.

by Danielle

The baby hamsters are going on the equipment. And the mother is not feeding them. One of the hamsters is squished. But it was just sleeping.

by Erica

The baby hamsters are eating food and they are going through the tunnel. They are still drinking from the mom hamster. And they are growing fur.

by Danielle

Two hamsters have their eyes open. They are 18 days old and they are cute.

APPENDIX B11–1 *The Fisher Classroom Newsletter: Hamsters*

by Chris
The babies look very happy with their mother.

by Luke
The hamsters' cheeks are puffing up and the mother is not feeding all the babies.

by Amanda
The hamsters are puffing their cheeks.

by Kevin
I noticed that they fight over food and they are saved. They climb the water bottle.

by Kathryn
Some are sleeping and some are eating and most are curled up with each other. Some are scratching.

by Billy
The hamsters are moving. They are playing in a pile. One is scratching.

by Christian
They stopped nursing. Almost everybody took them. Only one is left. I feel sad because I cannot get a hamster.

by Ryan
I took one home. He runs fast around his wheel.

by Vanessa
The mother hamster is sleeping. The hamster is scratching. The hamster is eating.

by Daniel
They are all gone. I feel pretty sad because there are no more baby hamsters, and I wish I could touch one.

by Jennifer

by Lindsay

INVITATION REMINDER

You are invited to visit the classroom on April 14 from 11:45–12:45 to see what we have been learning. The format will be similar to the December visit, with the formal group sharing starting at 12:00. Parents, grandparents and younger siblings are welcome.

APPENDIX B11–1 (continued) *The Fisher Classroom Newsletter: Hamsters*

THE LEARNING CLASS
MRS. FISHER'S FIRST GRADE
JOSIAH HAYNES SCHOOL

February

Dear Parents,

Since the first day of school The Learning Class has been very enthusiastic about science. So far our focus has been primarily on animals, but many children have expressed interest in physical science, particularly in performing experiments. In order to encourage this interest, I am setting up the following procedure.

With your help at home, I would like the children to plan an experiment. As scientist for the day, they will work with small groups in the science area during workshop time (usually on Monday, Tuesday, Wednesday or Friday) demonstrating and helping their friends with the experiment. It should be simple enough so they can set up the materials, perform the experiment, and clean up with minimal help from an adult.

Included is a recording sheet to help plan and describe the experiment. The children should bring this to school, along with the supplies they will need. Please keep in mind that we will be working on this project until April vacation, so the experiment doesn't need to be brought in right away.

Today the school launched a school-wide theme about water. Although many of the children may want to focus on that topic, they do not need to limit their experiment to the theme.

Thanks for your help.

Sincerely,

Bobbi Fisher

APPENDIX B11–2 *Letter to Parents Explaining Science Procedure*

December

Dear Parents,

Please help your child fill out the form, *My Family Now and Long Ago,* and collect some pictures, books and artifacts to bring to school over the next two weeks. The items should come in a bag or box marked with your child's name. We would like to keep them in school until the week of December 16 when you will be invited to *Our Families Now and Long Ago Museum.* An invitation will be coming to you soon.

The children will have the opportunity to tell about their family and ancestors and share what they bring in. Please help them locate one of their ancestors' countries and plan something to show and tell about it (for example, climate, geography, animals, customs, clothing, occupations).

Here are some suggestions of things the children might bring to school for our museum.

- A family picture.
- Some things from the country of their ancestors.
- Some pictures and books from the country of their ancestors.
- Some clothing from the country of their ancestors.
- Some food from the country of their ancestors. (If you would like to come in and cook with the class, please let me know. This could also be arranged for after the holidays.)
- A song or poem

Sincerely,

Bobbi Fisher

APPENDIX B12–1 *Letter to Parents about Museum*

November

Dear Parents,

Today your children have brought home two forms to use to interview you about their immigrant ancestors. The two forms will enable them to get information about both sides of their family.

If your ancestors came from more than one country, please pick the country about which you have the most information. Also, the children realize that you may not have all of the information. If you can't get it within the next week, just tell them you don't know.

For clarification, question three, "Where did they enter this country?" is included because we have been reading about Ellis Island and the port of New York. It will be interesting if any of your ancestors came through there.

As part of the Open Circle program we have been discussing the qualities of a good interview, and this is the children's first official attempt at it. They know that it is important to speak so the other person can hear, look at the person, and ask questions that require more than a yes or no answer. (We've been focusing on questions that start with *what, where, when, who, why and how.*) They also know that good listeners look at the person, perhaps nod their head and smile, and respond to what the person has said.

If possible, we'd like these back by November 19th.

Sincerely,

Bobbi Fisher

APPENDIX B12–2 *Letter to Parents: Immigration Study*

January

Dear Parents,

For the next six weeks we will be studying Africa as part of Sudbury's first grade social studies curriculum. Before the holiday vacation the children and I talked about what we would like to learn, and I have summarized our list into the following six topics: **animals, clothing, food, houses, languages and the arts**. Our study will concentrate on the similarities and differences between our culture and the cultures of Africa..

We are now in the process of forming study committees. Each committee will research its topic, arrange activities and plan ways to present information to the rest of the class. Although we have talked about each topic in class, I am asking that the children make their final committee choice after discussing the project with you. Please help them write their first and second choice on the form below and bring it to school tomorrow.

If you can help in any of the following ways, please let me know:

- Loan artifacts, pictures, books etc.
- Help with a cooking project.
- Help with an art project.
- Help make adrinka cloths at the craft center.

Sincerely,

Bobbi Fisher

NAME

First Choice _____

Second Choice _____

APPENDIX B12–3 *Letter to Parents: Africa Study*

September

Dear Parents,

The first day of school is always exciting for me, and this year is no exception. I hope your children are anticipating a wonderful year too.

First grade is different from kindergarten. The day is longer, lunch is part of the program, and as the children will tell you, they have two recesses. For all of us, making the adjustment to a full day takes time. Usually the children do fine in school, but are instantly exhausted when they walk in the door at home at the end of the day.

During the year your children will be developing as independent readers and writers. As part of the first grade science curriculum, we will be studying the senses and properties (Physical Science), organisms (Life Science), and weather and seasons (Earth Science). These will be integrated with social studies, as we learn about Hopi Indians, Africa and Japan. Literature studies focus on fables, folktales, legends, and myths, primarily through picture books and poetry. In math we will be gaining understandings of the four basic processes (addition, subtraction, multiplication and division) using Cuisinaire Rods and other manipulatives. We will also explore place value, patterns, estimation, fractions, geometry and measurement.

Aside from this required curriculum, I am planning many topics that we will study together, For example, we'll be starting the year studying about islands. As I read stories to the class, we will discuss reading strategies, our personal response, and different literary structures.

I am also interested in topics of inquiry that generate from the interests of the children, so it will be helpful to know about your children's particular interests. As a start, please be sure that the letter, which I've asked them to write to me (you may be their scribe and write it for them), includes some of these special areas of pursuit.

Several forms are included with this letter. Please return them as soon as possible. The parent information form is optional. I have

APPENDIX B13–1 *Letter to Parents: First Day*

used a similar form for many years and have found that it helps me to get to know you and your children better. Also, let me know if you are interested in helping with the computer.

Three important items:

- Please send a note if your child is not taking the bus home.
- Have your child come to school each day with a bag or backpack big enough to carry a book and papers.
- If you need to get in touch with me, send a note with your child. I will try to get back to you as soon as possible.

Liz Schreiner, our classroom assistant, Paul Berardi, a Wheelock College graduate student teacher and I are looking forward to meeting and talking with you at Parent's Night, Tuesday, September 21st. See you then.

Sincerely,

Bobbi Fisher

APPENDIX B13–1 (continued) *Letter to Parents: First Day*

THE FISHER CLASSROOM PARENT NEWSLETTER

VOLUME 3 NUMBER 1   *September*

THE CLASS

This class is going to be another great one. I can tell by the way the children care for each other, by their curiosity and by their sense of humor–three important ingredients for a successful year.

There are so many things to learn during the first week, and everyone has done a super job with the new routines.

I look forward to meeting you on Tuesday, September 21st at Back to School Night.

Writing

The children write every day, which means writing and drawing about a topic of their own choice. They are learning where to file their work and are beginning to create a portfolio of important pieces. The portfolio will help all of us see progress over time.

Please enjoy the pieces that your child brings home, and celebrate what he/she can do. Keep in mind that writing is a process which takes time.

I have enclosed an article about invented (also called temporary or functional) spelling, and will be happy to answer any questions during the year.

READING

Every day after lunch we have silent reading. We started with five minutes on the first day and are already up to ten. By the end of the month I know that this group will be able to sit quietly and read or look at books for half an hour. During this time I read with individual children.

MATH

During math time the children are exploring a variety of manipulatives that we will be using throughout the year. I am getting to know them as I play the "banking game" with small groups.

CHILDREN'S INTERESTS

As the children write me the letter from home telling what countries they would like to "visit" and what they are interested in learning, I put their responses on the bulletin board. Already we are noticing some common interests and beginning to generate curriculum connections through literature and projects.

Topics of inquiry so far are magnets and the solar system. Many children have drawn flowers with cray-pas and several worked together to make a mural of Humpty Dumpty.

BOOKS HOME

The children may borrow my books to take home. I ask that they take only one book at a time and return it the next day.

APPENDIX B13–2 *Parent Newsletter: September*

THE FISHER CLASSROOM PARENT NEWSLETTER

VOLUME 3 NUMBER 2   *November*

THE CLASS

The class is really coming together as a learning and caring community. I am especially pleased with the way the children participate in group and are engaged during reading, writing and math.

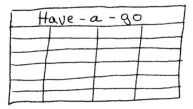

We are also focusing on short and long vowel patterns and word families (for example *ake* and *ack*).

READING

The children read silently for 15 minutes after lunch, and we are ready to extend that time to 20 minutes. This give uninterrupted time for the grownups to read individually with children.

About twice a week the children (and grownups) write in response journals. In a special notebook they write the title of a book they have read, what they liked or noticed about it, and perhaps include an illustration. After school I write a response.

WRITING

The children are writing more and more, and easily come up with a topic. Sometimes they write books, and other times they write what we call a "single piece".

I have introduced a "Have-a-go" paper to help them develop toward conventional spelling. The paper, which is kept in their writing folders, has four columns. During writing, when they come to a word they want to spell correctly, they "have-a-go" writing it in the first two columns. Next, I discuss their spelling of the word as I write it correctly in the third column. Then the children copy the word in the fourth column, as well as on their paper. This procedure enables me to help children with spelling by acknowledging what they do know and extending their learning.

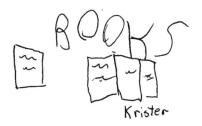

APPENDIX B13–3 *Parent Newsletter: November*

MATH

The children have become very adept at making their own addition equations with the rods, and we are

just starting to make the connection of addition to multiplication. For example: r + r = p is the same as 2 × r = p

From there we will move to division and subtraction, and in January we will transfer to number equivalents.

Rods are only one part of our math work. We continue to have many experiences with numbers, especially with the banking game.

TOPICS

About twice a week, during workshop time, the children learn about a topic they have chosen. I've enclosed a copy of the topic planning form that they use. Ask your child to tell you about it.

The children fill in the form, pursue a project relating to their topic, and choose something new they have learned to teach the class. Their project must include some form of writing.

A lot of reading, writing, use of study skills, discussion, collaboration and decision making goes on during this time. For example, some children are still working on their original topic, while others have completed several topic studies. Some work alone, and others work in teams. Some present in front of the whole group and others choose to display their work so their classmates can informally look at what they have done.

SOCIAL COMPETENCY CURRICULUM

We participate in the Open Circle program about twice a week.

Last week's lesson was about the difference between tattling and responsible reporting to grownups. We decided that a tattling is telling a grownup some things that the children could take care of themselves. A Double D, on the other hand is something that is Dangerous or Destructive and therefore should be reported to grownups. This has been a constructive way for us to respond to (and consequently eliminate) tattling. We just ask, "Is that a Double D?"

I've also told the children that if someone continues to bother them, but it's not a Double D, they can write me a note or ask to talk with me if they need my help.

DEMOCRACY IN THE CLASSROOM

My communications with you about the post card and immigrant projects have described some of the ways that I am trying to help the children develop as democratic citizens.

APPENDIX B13–3 (continued) *Parent Newsletter: November*

The class is divided into five committees: math, reading, science, trips (social studies) and writing. The committees sit together, and are responsible for some of the planning preparation, and organization of their discipline for the rest of the class.

The leader for the day, called the "moderator", is responsible for dismissing the group for certain classroom activities, specialists, recess, lunch and dismissal. They are learning what it is like to be the teacher in certain situations.

COMPUTER

Mark Thompson, the school systems media specialist, is up-grading my computer so that the children can record their attendance on a spread sheet each day and work on some writing, spelling and math programs.

If anyone is interested volunteering some time to help the children with the new programs, please let me know. I will be available after school on November 30 and December 1 to introduce them to you.

REMINDERS

- Names tags and hanging hooks on jackets.
- Please check your child's bag for notices.

FOOD PANTRY

The next Haynes School Food Pantry day is December 1st, the Wednesday after Thanksgiving. We are hoping that everyone will contribute this time. Contributions can be brought in anytime.

UP-COMING DATES

Nov. 17, 24	Early release
Nov. 18–19	Thanksgiving
Dec. 1	Food Pantry
Dec. 1, 15	Early release
Dec. 17	Mr. Berardi's last day
Dec. 24	Holiday break
December Visitors' Day–to be announced.	

APPENDIX B13–3 (continued) *Parent Newsletter: November*

THE FISHER CLASSROOM PARENT NEWSLETTER

VOLUME 2 NUMBER 3   *May*

READING

• Silent reading often lasts 30 minutes and most of that time the children are practicing their reading. They are delighted when they realize that they can really read the book.
• During that time I read individually with children and I find that I can read with each one about twice a week. They either read their envelope books or a book they choose from the classroom library.

WRITING

• Each year Sudbury teachers are asked to collect a writing sample from each child. The prompt for first graders: "Write about a time you had fun." The children did a great job.
• The following list tells one thing that they said they noticed about their writing since the beginning of the year.
Alex: I use lower case letters.
Amanda: I hold my pencil better.
Amanda: I write smaller.
Amy: I do more lower case letters.
Billy: I do more writing.
Carolyn: I write words.
Chuckie: I spell words better.
Chris: I use periods.
Christian: I get ideas from other people.
Daniel: I leave spaces between words.
Danielle: My writing is neater.
Danielle: My writing is smaller and not squished.
Erica: I write a lot.
Greg: I learned a lot of letters.

Greg: I write lots of words.
Jennifer: I spell a lot of words.
Kathryn: I write words.
Kevin: I spell more words.
Lauren: I write more words from the Have-a-go paper.
Lindsay: I learned lots of words.
Luke: I learned to get ideas from books.
Ryan: I write a lot more.
Vanessa: I learned letters and some words.

LITERATURE

• We are going to be comparing different stories of *The Three Little Pigs* and *Little Red Riding Hood*.
• The children worked in groups to draw pictures of houses made of straw, sticks and bricks.
• Some of the children used the puppets Chuckie's mom made for us to tell the story of *The Three Little Pigs*.
• We have read over 200 different books this year.

MATH

• We are writing equations for numbers 10–20 in math journals. I am impressed with the children's understanding of number and their flexibility in using numbers. Those backward numerals are getting much better.
• Each child wrote an equation for the box math for next week.

APPENDIX B13–4 *Parent Newsletter: May*

• Mr. Gross gave us a candy bar problem. Ask you child to explain it.

SCIENCE

• Observation of forcythia.
• Alex's lizard visited on Tuesday.
• Jennifer's bunny visited on Wednesday.

WHAT DO YOU WANT TO LEARN ABOUT.

• For the remainder of the school year (6 1/2 weeks) we are going to research topics that interest us. So far we have generated lists of topics, talked about possibilities and picked one to start. We wrote why we are interested in the topic and on Friday we went to the library to get books. I envision a combination of group work and individual projects. Some children may study several topics, while others may stick to one for the entire time. We will invite you come to see the projects and celebrate the year during the week of June 14. I'll set the date as soon as possible.

LEARNING TOPICS

Alex: Animal families
Amanda: Japan and Japanese
Amanda: Spirits, Gods, Myths

Amy: Claws
Billy: Night animals
Carolyn: Cats
Chuckie: Reptiles
Chris: Snakes
Christian: Archery
Daniel: Vampire bats
Danielle: Human body
Danielle: Japan and Japanese
Erica: Japan and Japanese
Greg: Plants
Greg: Habitats
Jennifer: Animals
Kathryn: Nature
Kevin: Sharks
Lauren: Japan and Japanese
Lindsay: Out of doors
Luke: Sharks
Ryan: Bugs
Vanessa: Cows
Mrs. Fisher: Seals
Mrs. Schreiner: Plants

NOTICES

• The editors from Teaching K/8 Magazine are sending me copies of the magazine in which our classroom and Haynes School was featured. I'll send them home with the children as soon as I get it.
• Japan Day is June 9th. If you did not receive the notice about it, which was send home yesterday, please let me know.
• Drumlin Farm–May 28.

APPENDIX B13–4 (continued) *Parent Newsletter: May*

373

December

Dear Parents,

For the past two years the children in my classes have donated books to a homeless shelter in the Boston area. I would like to continue the project this year.

In class we have talked about the fact that some children don't have books available for a "bedtime" story. The children have suggested that they could contribute a new book, a favorite from home, or one that they write themselves.

We have a box ready in the classroom. If your child wants to participate, please have him or her bring a book (unwrapped) by Monday, December 21st. I'd like to thank Kathy's mom for offering to help distribute them.

Also, every month, Haynes School participates in a food drive for needy families in the area. Canned food, and soap and paper products are appreciated.

Sincerely,

APPENDIX B13–5 *Letter to Parents: Outreach Projects*

October

Dear Parents,

In past years, parents and I have communicated with each other using home/school journals, and I would like to continue them again this year, as one more way for us to keep in touch.

This year I am giving them to you at our parent conference. Please feel free to write to me as often as you want. Give the journal to your child, who will put it in the basket in the classroom, and I will respond as soon as possible. In this way, you will be keeping the journal until you have something to write.

The journal can be used to :

• Ask a specific question about your child's progress in school
• Share what your child is enjoying in school
• Share what you child is concerned about in school
• Tell me about something important that has happened at home
• Share a learning experience from home
• Request a phone call or conference
• Schedule to help in the classroom

I will return the journal to you at the end of the year so you can keep it as a snapshot of your child's first grade year.

Sincerely,

Bobbi Fisher

APPENDIX B13–6 *Letter to Parents: Home/School Journals*

September

Dear Boys and Girls,

I am so glad that school has started because Mrs. Fisher has
suggested that I take turns spending the night with you. I've been
living at her house since she bought me in Oregon at the beginning
of the summer while she was visiting her brother.

I like living at the Fisher's house, but there isn't a lot of action.
Mrs. Fisher's husband, Jim, their dog, Bow, and cat, Boots live there.
But her two children, Tim and Emily, only come home to visit once
in a while. Tim writes for a theater company in San Francisco, and
Emily works in Indiana.

I will take turns visiting you, so be sure to bring me back to
school each day. The first time you take me home, please help me
tell about your family. Also, I love bedtime stories. I hope you will
read one to me.

Your pal, Mr. Bear

APPENDIX B13–7 *Mr. Bear's Letter*

THE FISHER CLASSROOM PARENT NEWSLETTER

VOLUME 3 NUMBER 7   *June*

SINGING IN GROUP

by Marina

Every morning when I go to school I hang up my bag and sign in.

When Mrs. Fisher starts singing that means we have to go to the rug and start singing, too. We sing songs like "Water," "There Was a Frog," "This Pretty Planet," and "Together Tomorrow," and many more. We always sing when we go to group. Mrs. Fisher makes our day better when we sing.

We start the day by putting on a smile.

MR. BEAR

by Kate

Mr. Bear was a part of Mrs. Fisher's class. We all miss Mr. Bear. Mr. Bear is special because he is a puppet. Mr. Bear has a brown face and black eyes. We love sleeping with Mr. Bear because he is so cozy. Mr. Bear was almost part of the family.

Mr. Bear gets to do lots of good stuff. Mr. Bear really gets to see soccer. Sometimes Mr. Bear plays games with the kids. People like writing in Mr. Bear's journal!!!

THE MODERATOR

by Alex

The moderator sits in a chair. Each day a moderator sits in a chair and Mrs. Fisher asks you to get stuff for her and she asks you to get a crayon to fill in the words. You also get to wear a special kimono, and you get to be the leader every time you go somewhere, and you get to take the attendance down.

CLASS MEETING AND OPEN CIRCLE

by Elizabeth

Sometimes we have class meeting. Mrs. Fisher talks about news stories. If the kids have any questions, they raise their hands. The leader will choose which one will ask the question. We each take turns being the leader. We learn a lot.

At Open Circle everybody in the class must get their chairs except the leader. The leader sits in the moderator's chair.

We have a can in our classroom that kids drop notes in. The kids write about something that has happened in class on the notes. Then we talk about what is on the notes. We talk about good and bad things.

IT'S FUN TO BE ON A COMMITTEE

by Julie

In our classroom we have 5 committees. Each committee works on a special topic. The science committee works on plants and seeds. The reading committee is working on insects. The trips committee learns about bones. The math committee

APPENDIX B13–8 *Parent Newsletter: End of Year*

works on birds. The writing committee is studying about the senses. Our committees help us learn.

COMMITTEES

by Laura

These are some of the things that the committees do.

For the writing committee: they change the date. For the trips committee: they hand out the passports. The math committee reads what the groups do in math. The reading committee brings books back to the library. The science committee planted seeds.

COMMITTEES

by Kristen

Committees used information books and studied bones, birds, insects, seeds and the senses.

HOW POMPERAUG AND HAYNES SCHOOLS ARE DIFFERENT AND ALIKE

by Ben

I moved to Sudbury on May 31st and so I have been in two schools this year. How they are different is there are moderators instead of special days. In gym we have squads and in my old school we did not have squads. In my new school we have outside lunch.

What is alike is school meeting. But math is different. We have two school libraries. We had parties for birthdays in my old school, too.

OUR NEW FRIENDS

by Daniel

Our class is writing to penpals in Texas. Each penpal likes a different color. Some like red, some like orange, some like yellow, some like green, some like blue and some like purple.

My penpals name is Keshav and he has a big brother and a little brother.

READING FOR 35 MINUTES

by Elizabeth

First we read for 5 minutes. And some people read one book. In a few weeks we could read for 10 minutes. In a couple of more weeks we could read for 20 minutes. In a couple of more weeks we could read for 25 minutes. When the new year 1994 came, then we could read for 30 minutes. In a couple of more weeks we could read for 35 minutes. And now we can read for 45 minutes.

DIFFERENT KINDS OF BOOKS

by Curtis

I liked the books we read. Mrs. Fisher read some to us at group and I read some myself. We have read 237 books this year, and still going!

An information book is like a book about snakes, a story book is like *The Tub Grandfather,* and information story book like a story about wolves that gives information, and a biography like *Teammates.*

APPENDIX B13-8 (continued) *Parent Newsletter: End of Year*

VOWELS

by Tyler

Vowels are letters. There are six vowels in the alphabet. They are a, e, i, o, u and sometimes y. If we didn't have vowels we couldn't write words.

Vowels make sounds. Vowels make sounds no other letters can make. Vowels work together with other letters to help us read.

WRITING

by Danielle Dorey

We wrote every day. In the beginning of the year Mrs. Fisher made us tell her ideas and she wrote them down for us on a piece of paper.

Everyone published one story. Mrs. Fisher printed it on a computer. We made the cover and illustrated it.

DIGIT AND PLACE GAME

by Brandon

There is a number game we sometimes play in our class called Digit and Place. Someone will pick a number and we try to guess it. If there is a check mark, that means that one digit is right. If there is a line, that means one digit or place is wrong. Two checks are one digit and one place are right. If there are two lines, that means that both digit and place are wrong. If there are two check marks, the number is right.

MATH DIARIES

by Jacob Baldassini

Math diaries are small books that each person makes during math. We write one page per math day. Each page has a number with 15 or more equations with the number. We think of the equations ourselves. The equations can have addition, subtraction, multiplication, division, and parentheses. Math diaries are my absolute favorite activity–even more favorite than recess.

100'S CHART

by Carolyn

In my class we made a book with counting by 2's, 5's, and 10's. We could make another counting paper if we wanted to. The counting paper looked like a board that goes to 100. If you count by 5's you go 1,2,3,4,5, and color in 5.

HOW WE DO THE COUNTING CHART

by Chris

I like when we made an answer sheet and giving sheets. I like when the people came to you and you showed the answer to them. Next, you took it to Mrs. Fisher. Mrs. Fisher checked the paper. After being checked we put the paper in our bag. Then we are done. I feel GREAT when I'm done.

Appendix B13–8 (continued) *Parent Newsletter: End of Year*

BOX MATH

by Sarah

What: Box math is a way to learn the answers to an equation.

When: The equations are put on the board twice a month.

Where: Mrs. Fisher writes 25 equations on the chalkboard, but instead of an answer, she puts a box. The members of our class put the answer in the box and sign our work.

How: We use our heads, not calculators.

BANKING GAMES

by Jake Bloom

We used to bank with blocks. Now we bank with money: 1 block, one penny; 5 blocks, one nickle; 10 blocks, one dime; 25 blocks, one quarter; 100 blocks, one dollar. We also use dice.

A DAY AT DRUMLIN FARM

by Michael

We had two trips to Drumlin Farm and I will tell you about one. I bet you want to know how we got there. We took a bus, sat in groups and got ready to see the animals.

We would see baby animals like billy goats, piglets, hens and lots of yellow baby chicks. A big fat sow walked lazily while the baby pigs ran around looking for food.

A hay ride at the end of the day was the best part. I got to sit in the front and had a horse's view of the farm.

If you go to Drumlin Farm on a nice sunny day, you too can see all the fun of animals.

APPLE ORCHARD

by Eric

We went to the apple orchard. It was a rainy day, but we had fun. We picked apples, and then we squished them to make apple cider.

THE SUN AND THE EARTH

by Paul

The hottest star in the world is the sun. The thing that brightens the moon is the sun. It is weird that the sun comes up every day to bring the earth light. Now if you go to the universe, all you can see are stars.

The earth has air and water and plants and food for everybody to live.

PETS VISIT SCHOOL

by Ashley

This year my dog Rocky came to school for a little while. Danielle's bunny came to the classroom for our observation, but it was moving around a lot. A humongous lot! Kristen's bunnies came in but they were very, very fragile.

APPENDIX B13–8 (continued) *Parent Newsletter: End of Year*

JAPAN

by Andrew

Today we are going to Japan. So fasten your seatbelts, it's going to be a bumpy ride. We have landed.

In school we are studying Japan. We are making books on Japan. We are also learning stuff about Japan. One thing I find interesting about Japan is that the Japanese mostly eat a fish called carp, which is found in the sea surrounding Japan.

CRAFT CENTER

by Caroline

The craft center is in front of the music room. The room mothers tell the kids what to do. The kids make things like Adinkra cloth from Africa, and paper dogs, cats and boat from Japan. I even made a paper turtle! I like the craft center. It is great!

A BUSTLING COMMUNITY

by Mrs. Schreiner

This is a bustling community of learners! Well, not just learners, but highly motivated learners. Day by day, in an atmosphere of trust, the children have become the masters of their own fate. They are guided in the process of learning about those things of the greated interest to them. I guess it's called, "learning how to learn," and addresses that mystery called "motivation."

Books are heaped into the room and some young voices ask, "Can I go to the library for my research?"

It is also a caring, sharing community that has grown and developed like a symphony, with each instrument making its unique sound. At this moment in time, I believe that these children stand strong and well-prepared for life's adventures. Let the journey continue and have a Great Summer.

27. AN AMAZING CLASS

by Mrs. Fisher

When I tell people that the first graders I teach can read silently for 35 minutes without talking or getting out of their seats, they are amazed. That's what happens in this class every day after lunch.

The two video crews that came to our class this year captured on film a group of children engaged in learning, responsible for managing their work and classroom routines, and willing to help each other in the process. The tapes show a group of children that loved to read, write and investigate math, and also are fully interested in the world around them.

APPENDIX B13–8 (continued) *Parent Newsletter: End of Year*

381

LITERATURE RESOURCES

SUPPORTIVE TEXTS

Random House, New York
- 10-Word Readers, by Patty Wolcott

Rigby, Crystal Lake, IL
- Literacy 2000 (includes Big Books)
- Supplemental Literature (includes Big Books)

The Wright Group, Bothell, WA
- The Book Bank
- The Story Box (includes Big Books)
- Sunshine (includes Big Books)
- Twig Books (includes Big Books)

SUGGESTED SCIENCE SERIES FOR BEGINNING READERS

Alfred A. Knopf, New York
- Eyewitness
- Eyewitness Juniors
- My First Book Series, by Angela Wilks

Children's Press, Chicago, IL
- Rookie Read-About Science
- New True Books

Franklin Watts, New York
- Keeping Minibeasts
- Science Starters

Gloucester Press, New York
- Junior Science

Harcourt Brace, New York
- The Science Book of . . .

HarperCollins, New York
- Let's Read and Find Out Books

Kingfisher Books, New York
- I Wonder Why . . .

Macmillan, New York
- Eye Openers

Raintree Children's Books, Milwaukee, WI
- Read About Series

Rigby, Crystal Lake, IL
- Literacy 2000
- Science series

Schoolhouse Press, Lexington, MA
- The Animal Kingdom
- The Face of the Earth

Steck-Vaughn, Austin, TX
- My World Books

Thomas Y. Crowell, New York
- Let's-Read-and-Find-Out Science Series

The Wright Group, Bothell, WA
- Content Area Science (includes Big Books)
- Sunshine Science (includes Big Books)

Books by Gail Gibbons
- Various publishers

FAVORITE TAPES

Amidon, Peter and Mary Alice. *This Pretty Planet: Songs for the Earth.* 8 Willow Street, Brattleboro, VT 05301.

Chapin, Tom. *Family Tree.* Sundance Music, Inc. Distributed by A & M Records, Inc.

Charette, Rick. *Where Do My Sneakers Go at Night.* Pine Point Records, North Windham, ME 04062.

Daniels, Alan and Lee. *Once an Austrian Went Yodeling.* Bothell, WA: The Wright Group. (Tape and Big Book)

Gentner, Norma. *Bear Facts. Dig a Dinosaur. Gravity. Munch, Munch, Munch.* Bothell, WA: The Wright Group. (Tapes and Big Books)

Grammer, Red and Cathy. *Teaching Peace.* Smilin'Atcha Music.

Ippolito, Paul. *Together Again.* RFD 2, Box 128, North Street, Chester, VT 05143.

Valley, Jim. *Friendship Train.* Rainbow Planet, P.O. Box 735, Edmonds, WA 98020.

Valley, Jim. *Rain Forest.* Bothell, WA: The Wright Group. (Tape and Big Book)

Van Brammer, Joan. *Whale Rap.* Crystal Lake, IL: Rigby. (Tape and Big Book)

PROFESSIONAL ORGANIZATIONS, JOURNALS, AND NEWSLETTERS

THE ARITHMETIC TEACHER
NATIONAL COUNCIL OF TEACHERS OF MATHEMATICS (NCTM)
1906 ASSOCIATION DRIVE
RESTON, VA 22091

BOOK LINKS
434 W. DOWNER
AURORA, IL 60506

THE HORN BOOK MAGAZINE
14 BEACON STREET
BOSTON, MA 02108

LANGUAGE ARTS
PRIMARY VOICES
NATIONAL COUNCIL OF TEACHERS OF ENGLISH (NCTE)
1111 W. KENYON ROAD
URBANA, IL 61801

THE NEW ADVOCATE
P.O. BOX 809
NEEDHAM HEIGHTS, MA 02194

THE READING TEACHER
INTERNATIONAL READING ASSOCIATION (IRA)
800 BARKSDALE ROAD
P.O. BOX 8139
NEWARK, DE 19714

RETHINKING SCHOOLS: AN URBAN EDUCATIONAL JOURNAL
1001 E. KEEFE AVE.
MILWAUKEE, WI 53212

SCIENCE AND CHILDREN
NATIONAL COUNCIL OF TEACHERS OF SCIENCE (NCTS)
1742 CONNECTICUT AVE. N.W.
WASHINGTON, DC 20009

TALKING POINTS
WHOLE LANGUAGE UMBRELLA
P.O. BOX 2029
BLOOMINGTON, IN 47402

TEACHER RESEARCH: THE JOURNAL OF CLASSROOM INQUIRY
JOHNSON PRESS
49 SHERIDAN AVE.
ALBANY, NY 12210

TEACHERS NETWORKING: THE WHOLE LANGUAGE NEWSLETTER
RICHARD C. OWEN PUBLISHERS, INC.
135 KATONAH AVENUE
KATONAH, NY 10536

TEACHING K-8
40 RICHARDS AVENUE
NORWALK, CT 06854

THE WHOLE IDEA
THE WRIGHT GROUP
19201 120TH AVE. NE
BOTHELL, WA 98011

WHOLE LANGUAGE TEACHERS ASSOCIATION NEWSLETTER
P.O. BOX 216
SOUTHBORO, MA 01772

YOUNG CHILDREN
NATIONAL ASSOCIATION OF THE EDUCATION OF YOUNG CHILDREN (NAEYC)
1834 CONNECTICUT AVENUE, N.W.
WASHINGTON, DC 20009

CHILDREN'S LITERATURE

AARDEMA, VERNA. 1977. *WHO'S IN RABBIT'S HOUSE?* NEW YORK: DIAL.

——. 1981. *BRINGING THE RAIN TO KAPITI PLAIN.* NEW YORK: SCHOLASTIC.

——. 1992. *ANANSI FINDS A FOOL.* NEW YORK: DIAL.

ADLER, DAVID. 1989. *A PICTURE BOOK OF MARTIN LUTHER KING.* NEW YORK: HOLIDAY HOUSE.

——. 1992. *A PICTURE BOOK OF HARRIET TUBMAN.* NEW YORK: HOLIDAY HOUSE.

AGARD, JOHN. 1989. *THE CALYPSO ALPHABET.* LITTLETON, MA: SUNDANCE.

AHLBERG, JANET AND ALLAN. 1978. *EACH PEACH PEAR PLUM.* NEW YORK: SCHOLASTIC.

AKER, SUZANNE. 1990. *WHAT COMES IN 2'S, 3'S, & 4'S.* NEW YORK: SIMON & SCHUSTER.

ALIKI. 1968. *HUSH LITTLE BABY.* NEW YORK: SIMON & SCHUSTER.

——. 1974. *GO TELL AUNT RHODY.* NEW YORK: MACMILLAN.

——. 1979. *MUMMIES MADE IN EGYPT.* NEW YORK: HARPER.

ALLEN, MARJORIE N. 1991. *CHANGES.* NEW YORK: MACMILLAN.

ANGELOU, MAYA. 1993. *LIFE DOESN'T FRIGHTEN ME.* NEW YORK: STEWART, TABORI & CHANG.

ANNO, MITSUMASA. 1977. *ANNO'S COUNTING BOOK.* NEW YORK: THOMAS Y. CROWELL.

——. 1986. *ALL IN A DAY.* NEW YORK: PHILOMEL.

——. 1991. *ANNO'S MATH GAMES III.* NEW YORK: PHILOMEL.

ARCHAMBAULT, JOHN. 1989. *COUNTING SHEEP.* NEW YORK: HENRY HOLT.

ARGENT, KERRY. 1989. *ANIMAL CAPERS.* NEW YORK: DIAL.

ARNOLD, KATYA. 1994. *BABA YAGA & THE LITTLE GIRL.* NEW YORK: NORTH-SOUTH BOOKS.

ARNOLD, TEDD. 1987. *NO MORE JUMPING ON THE BED!* NEW YORK: DIAL.

——. 1992. *THE SIGNMAKER'S ASSISTANT.* NEW YORK: DIAL

AVISON, BRIGID. 1993. *I WONDER WHY I BLINK AND OTHER QUESTIONS ABOUT MY BODY.* NEW YORK: KINGFISHER BOOKS.

AYLESWORTH, JIM. 1992A. *THE FOLKS IN THE VALLEY.* NEW YORK: HARPER.

——. 1992B. *OLD BLACK FLY.* NEW YORK: HENRY HOLT.

AZARIAN, MARY. 1981. *A FARMER'S ALPHABET.* BOSTON, MA: DAVID R. GODINE.

BAER, EDITH. 1990. *THIS IS THE WAY WE GO TO SCHOOL.* NEW YORK: SCHOLASTIC.

BAER, GENE. 1989. *THUMP, THUMP, RAT-A-TAT-TAT.* NEW YORK: HARPER & ROW.

BAKER, JEANNIE. 1987. *WHERE THE FOREST MEETS THE SEA.* NEW YORK: SCHOLASTIC.

BANGS, EDWARD. 1976. *STEPHEN KELLOGG'S YANKEE DOODLE.* NEW YORK: PARENTS' MAGAZINE PRESS.

BARCUS, SARAH. 1975. *I WAS WALKING DOWN THE ROAD.* NEW YORK: SCHOLASTIC.

BARRETT, JUDI. 1983. *A Snake is Totally Tail.* New York: Macmillan.

BARTON, BYRON. 1987. *Machines at Work.* New York: Thomas Y. Crowell.

——. 1989. *Dinosaurs, Dinosaurs.* New York: Thomas Y. Crowell.

BASH, BARBARA. 1989. *Tree of Life: The World of the African Baobab.* Boston, MA: Little, Brown.

BASKWILL, JANE. 1989. *Pass the Poems Please.* Halifax, Nova Scotia: Wild Things Press.

BAUER, CAROLINE. 1984. *Too Many Books.* New York: Viking.

BAYER, JANE. 1984. *A My Name is Alice.* New York: Dial.

BAYLOR, BYRD. 1986. *I'm in Charge of Celebrations.* New York: Scribner.

BEDARD, MICHAEL. 1992. *Emily.* New York: Doubleday.

BELANGER, CLAUDE. 1988. *I Like the Rain.* Bothell, WA: The Wright Group.

BENNETT, JILL. 1986. *Teeny Tiny Woman.* New York: G. P. Putnam.

BERENSTAIN, STAN AND JAN. 1969. *Bears on Wheels.* New York: Random House.

BERNARD, EMERY. 1992. *Ladybug.* New York: Holiday House.

BERRY, JOY. 1986. *Every Kid's Guide to Understanding Human Rights.* Sebastopol, CA: Living Skills Press.

BIDDULPH, FRED AND JEANNE. 1992. *Earth and Moon.* Bothell, WA: The Wright Group.

BONSALL, CROSBY. 1990. *Who's A Pest?* New York: Clarion.

BOTTING, TOM. 1975. *The Mitten.* Moscow: Malysh Publishing.

BRAND, OSCAR. 1974. *When I First Came to This Land.* New York: G. P. Putnam.

BRANLEY, FRANKLYN M. AND ELEANOR K. VAUGHN. 1956. *Mickey's Magnet.* New York: Thomas Y. Crowell.

BRETT, JAN. 1989. *The Mitten.* New York: G. P. Putnam.

——. 1990. *The Wild Christmas Reindeer.* New York: G. P. Putnam.

——. 1991A. *Berlioz the Bear.* New York: G. P. Putnam.

——. 1991B. *The Owl and the Pussycat.* New York: G. P. Putnam.

——. 1992. *The Trouble with Trolls.* New York: G. P. Putnam.

BRETT, JAN, AND EDWARD LEAR. 1991. *The Owl and the Pussycat.* New York: G. P. Putnam.

BROWNE, ANTHONY. 1989. *The Tunnel.* New York: Knopf.

BUCKNALL, CAROLINE. 1988. *One Bear in the Picture.* New York: Dial.

BUNTING, EVE. 1991. *Fly Away Home.* New York: Clarion.

BURNINGHAM, JOHN. 1985. *John Burningham's 1 2 3.* New York: Crown.

BURTON, VIRGINIA LEE. 1942. *The Little House.* Boston, MA: Houghton Mifflin.

——. 1976. *Mike Mulligan and His Steam Shovel.* Boston, MA: Houghton Mifflin.

BUSTARD, ANNE. 1989. *T is for Texas.* New York: Voyageur Press.

BUTTERWORTH, CHRISTINE. 1990. *INSIDE A BEEHIVE.* NEW YORK: NATIONAL EDUCATION CORP.

CAMERON, POLLY. 1961. *"I CAN'T," SAID THE ANT.* NEW YORK: SCHOLASTIC.

CANNON, JANNELL. 1993. *STELLALUNA.* NEW YORK: HARCOURT BRACE.

CARLE, ERIC. 1990. *THE VERY QUIET CRICKET.* NEW YORK: PHILOMEL.

——. 1993. *TODAY IS MONDAY.* NEW YORK: PHILOMEL.

CASELEY, JUDITH. 1991. *DEAR ANNIE.* NEW YORK: GREENWILLOW.

CAZET, DENYSE. 1993. *BORN IN THE GRAVEY.* NEW YORK: ORCHARD BOOKS.

CHAISSON, JOHN. 1987. *AFRICAN JOURNEY.* NEW YORK: BRADBURY.

CHERRY, LYNNE. 1992. *THE RIVER RAN WILD.* NEW YORK: HARCOURT BRACE.

CHMIELARZ, SHARON. 1994. *DOWN AT ANGEL'S.* NEW YORK: TICKNOR & FIELDS.

CHRISTENSEN, BONNIE. 1994. *AN EDIBLE ALPHABET.* NEW YORK: DIAL.

CLEMENTS, ANDREW. 1988. *BIG AL.* NEW YORK: PICTURE BOOK STUDIO.

CLIMO, SHIRLEY. 1989. *THE EGYPTIAN CINDERELLA.* NEW YORK: HARPERCOLLINS.

COERR, ELEANOR. 1986. *THE JOSEFINA STORY QUILT.* NEW YORK: HARPER.

COHEN, MIRIAM. 1967. *WHO WILL BE MY FRIEND?* NEW YORK: MACMILLAN.

COLE, JOANNA. 1986. *THE MAGIC SCHOOL BUS AT THE WATERWORKS.* NEW YORK: SCHOLASTIC.

——. 1992. *THE MAGIC SCHOOL BUS ON THE OCEAN FLOOR.* NEW YORK: SCHOLASTIC.

CONRAD, PAM. 1989. *THE TUB PEOPLE.* NEW YORK: SCHOLASTIC.

——. 1993. *THE TUB GRANDFATHER.* NEW YORK: HARPERCOLLINS.

COONEY, BARBARA. 1988. *ISLAND BOY.* NEW YORK: VIKING.

——. 1994. *ONLY OPAL: THE DIARY OF A YOUNG GIRL.* NEW YORK: PHILOMEL.

COWCHER, HELEN. 1988. *RAIN FOREST.* NEW YORK: FARRAR, STRAUS & GIROUX.

COWLEY, JOY. 1984. *I'M THE KING OF THE MOUNTAIN.* KATONAH, NY: RICHARD C. OWEN.

——. 1987A. *NUMBER ONE.* KATONAH, NY: RICHARD C. OWEN.

——. 1987B. *THE TINY WOMAN'S COAT.* BOTHELL, WA: THE WRIGHT GROUP.

——. 1988A. *ALONG COMES JAKE.* BOTHELL, WA: THE WRIGHT GROUP.

——. 1988B. *GREEDY CAT.* BOTHELL, WA: THE WRIGHT GROUP.

——. 1988C. *THE LITTLE YELLOW CHICKEN.* BOTHELL, WA: THE WRIGHT GROUP.

——. 1988D. *MRS. MUDDLE MUD-PUDDLE.* BOTHELL, WA: THE WRIGHT GROUP.

——. 1993. *MRS. WISHY-WASHY DAY.* BOTHELL, WA: THE WRIGHT GROUP.

CUMMINGS, PAT. 1992. *TALKING WITH ARTISTS.* NEW YORK: BRADBURY.

CUTTING, BRIAN AND JILIAN. 1992. *ANTS, ANTS, ANTS.* BOTHELL, WA: THE WRIGHT GROUP.

DABCOVICH, LYDIA. 1982. *SLEEPY BEAR.* NEW YORK: DUTTON

DANIEL, ALAN, AND LEA DANIEL. 1992. *THE ANTS GO MARCHING.* BOTHELL, WA: THE WRIGHT GROUP.

——. 1994. *ONCE AN AUSTRIAN WENT YODELING.* BOTHELL, WA: THE WRIGHT GROUP.

DAVIDSON, AVELYN. 1991. *CREEPY CRAWLIES.* CRYSTAL LAKE, IL: RIGBY.

DINEEN, JACQUELINE. 1986. *THE FACE OF THE EARTH: RIVERS AND LAKES.* LEXINGTON, MA: SCHOOLHOUSE PRESS.

DORROS, ARTHUR. 1991. *FOLLOW THE WATER FROM BROOK TO OCEAN.* NEW YORK: HARPER & ROW.

———. 1992. *THIS IS MY HOUSE.* NEW YORK: SCHOLASTIC.

DRAGONWAGON, CRESCENT. 1989. *THIS IS THE BREAD I BAKED FOR NED.* NEW YORK: MACMILLAN.

———. 1990. *HOME PLACE.* NEW YORK: MACMILLAN.

DREW, DAVID. 1988A. *CREATURE FEATURES.* CRYSTAL LAKE, IL: RIGBY.

———. 1988B. *SOMEWHERE IN THE UNIVERSE.* CRYSTAL LAKE, IL: RIGBY.

———. 1990. *I SPY.* CRYSTAL LAKE, IL: RIGBY.

DUNBAR, JOYCE. 1990. *TEN LITTLE MICE.* NEW YORK: METHUEN BOOKS.

DUNREA, OLIVER. 1985. *MOGWOGS ON THE MARCH!* NEW YORK: HOLIDAY HOUSE.

———. 1989. *DEEP DOWN UNDERGROUND.* NEW YORK: MACMILLAN.

DUVOISIN, ROGER. 1950. *PETUNIA.* NEW YORK: KNOPF.

———. 1953A. *PETUNIA TAKES A TRIP.* NEW YORK: KNOPF.

———. 1953B. *VERONICA AND THE BIRTHDAY PRESENT.* NEW YORK: KNOPF.

———. 1961. *VERONICA.* NEW YORK: KNOPF.

———. 1962. *OUR VERONICA GOES TO PETUNIA'S FARM.* NEW YORK: KNOPF.

EASTMAN, P. D. 1960. *ARE YOU MY MOTHER?* NEW YORK: RANDOM HOUSE.

———. 1961. *GO DOG GO.* NEW YORK: RANDOM HOUSE

EGGLETON, JILL. 1986. *THE OLD OAK TREE.* BOTHELL, WA: THE WRIGHT GROUP.

———. 1988. *THE WICKED PIRATES.* BOTHELL, WA: THE WRIGHT GROUP.

EHLERT, LOIS. 1988. *PLANTING A RAINBOW.* NEW YORK: HARCOURT BRACE.

———. 1991. *RED LEAF, YELLOW LEAF.* NEW YORK: HARCOURT BRACE.

EHRLICH, AMY. 1993. *PARENTS IN THE PIGPEN, PIGS IN THE TUB.* NEW YORK: DIAL.

ELTING, MARY, AND MICHAEL FOLSOM. 1980. *Q IS FOR DUCK.* NEW YORK: CLARION.

EOVALSI, MARYANN. 1987. *THE WHEELS ON THE BUS.* BOSTON, MA: LITTLE, BROWN.

EPSTEIN, SAM AND BERYL. 1968. *HARRIET TUBMAN: GUIDE TO FREEDOM.* NEW YORK: DELL.

ERNST, LISA. 1986. *UP TO TEN AND DOWN AGAIN.* NEW YORK: LOTHROP, LEE & SHEPARD.

FARMER, PENELOPE. 1971. *DAEDALUS AND ICARUS.* NEW YORK: HARCOURT.

FEELINGS, MURIEL. 1974. *JAMBO MEANS HELLO.* NEW YORK: DIAL.

FIELD, RACHEL. 1988. *GENERAL STORE.* BOSTON, MA: LITTLE, BROWN.

FISHER, LEONARD EVERETT. 1986. *ELLIS ISLAND: GATEWAY TO THE NEW WORLD.* NEW YORK: HOLIDAY HOUSE.

———. 1988. *THESEUS AND THE MINITOR.* NEW YORK: HOLIDAY HOUSE.

———. 1989. *THE GREAT WALL OF CHINA.* NEW YORK: MACMILLAN.

———. 1990. *JASON AND THE GOLDEN FLEECE.* NEW YORK: HOLIDAY HOUSE.

FLACK, MARJORIE, AND KURT WIESE. 1933. *THE STORY ABOUT PING.* NEW YORK: VIKING.

FLOURNOY, VALERIE. 1985. *THE PATCHWORK QUILT.* NEW YORK: DIAL.

FOX, DAN, ED. 1987. *GO IN AND OUT THE WINDOW.* NEW YORK: HENRY HOLT.

FOX, MEM. 1988. *KOALA LOU.* NEW YORK: GULLIVER.

——. 1989. *NIGHT NOISES.* NEW YORK: HARCOURT.

——. 1994. *TIME FOR BED.* NEW YORK: HARCOURT BRACE.

——. 1995. *TOUGH BORIS.* NEW YORK: HARCOURT BRACE.

FRASIER, DEBRA. 1991. *ON THE DAY YOU WERE BORN.* NEW YORK: HARCOURT BRACE.

——. 1994. *WE GOT HERE TOGETHER.* NEW YORK: HARCOURT BRACE.

FREEDMAN, RUSSELL. 1980. *IMMIGRANT KIDS.* NEW YORK: E. P. DUTTON.

FROST, ROBERT. 1978. *STOPPING BY WOODS ON A SNOWY EVENING.* NEW YORK: E. P. DUTTON.

GAMMELL, STEPHEN. 1991. *WAKE UP, BEAR . . . IT'S CHRISTMAS.* NEW YORK: LOTHROP, LEE & SHEPARD.

GENTNER, NORMA. 1993A. *BEAR FACTS.* BOTHELL, WA: THE WRIGHT GROUP.

——. 1993B. *DIG A DINOSAUR.* BOTHELL, WA: THE WRIGHT GROUP.

——. 1993C. *GRAVITY.* BOTHELL, WA: THE WRIGHT GROUP.

——. 1993D. *MUNCH, MUNCH, MUNCH.* BOTHELL, WA: THE WRIGHT GROUP.

GEORGE, WILLIAM T. AND LINDSAY. 1988. *BEAVER AT LONG POND.* NEW YORK: GREENWILLOW.

GEORGES, D. V. 1991. *A NEW TRUE BOOK: AFRICA.* CHICAGO, IL: CHILDREN'S PRESS.

GERSON, MARY-JOAN. 1992. *WHY THE SKY IS FAR AWAY.* BOSTON, MA: LITTLE, BROWN.

GERSTEIN, MORDICAI. 1984. *ROLL OVER.* NEW YORK: CROWN.

GIBBONS, GAIL. 1985. *THE MILK MAKERS.* NEW YORK: MACMILLAN.

——. 1986. *CHECK IT OUT! THE BOOK ABOUT LIBRARIES.* NEW YORK: HARCOURT BRACE.

——. 1988. *SUNKEN TREASURE.* NEW YORK: THOMAS Y. CROWELL.

GIGANTI, PAUL JR. 1992. *EACH ORANGE HAD 8 SLICES.* NEW YORK: GREENWILLOW.

GILE, JOHN. 1989. *THE FIRST FOREST.* STEVENS POINT, WI: WORZALLA.

GILMAN, ALEX. 1990. *TAKE ME OUT TO THE BALL GAME.* NEW YORK: FOUR WINDS.

GOLDENBOCH, PETER. 1990. *TEAMMATES.* NEW YORK: HARCOURT BRACE.

GORSLINE, DOUGLAS. 1978. *THE PIONEERS.* NEW YORK: RANDOM HOUSE.

GRATER, MICHAEL. 1988A. *ON FRIDAY THE GIANT . . .* BOTHELL, WA: THE WRIGHT GROUP.

——. 1988B. *ON MONDAY THE GIANT. . .* BOTHELL, WA: THE WRIGHT GROUP.

——. 1988C. *ON SUNDAY THE GIANT . . .* BOTHELL, WA: THE WRIGHT GROUP.

——. 1988D. *ON THURSDAY THE GIANT . . .* BOTHELL, WA: THE WRIGHT GROUP.

——. 1988E. *ON TUESDAY THE GIANT . . .* BOTHELL, WA: THE WRIGHT GROUP.

——. 1988F. *ON WEDNESDAY THE GIANT . . .* BOTHELL, WA: THE WRIGHT GROUP.

GREENFIELD, ELOISE. 1972. *HONEY, I LOVE.* NEW YORK: THOMAS Y. CROWELL.

——. 1973. *ROSA PARKS.* NEW YORK: THOMAS Y. CROWELL.

———. 1988. *Nathan Talking*. New York: Black Butterfly Children's Books.

———. 1991. *First Pink Light*. New York: Black Butterfly Children's Books.

Grifalconi, Ann. 1986. *The Village of Round and Square Houses*. Boston, MA: Little, Brown.

———. 1990. *Osa's Pride*. Boston, MA: Little, Brown.

Gross, Ruth Belov. 1978. *A Book about Your Skeleton*. New York: Scholastic.

Grossman, Virginia, and Sylvia Long. 1991. *Ten Little Rabbits*. Littleton, MA: Sundance.

Guthrie, Donna, N. Bentley, and K. Arnsteen. 1994. *The Young Author's Do-It-Yourself Book*. Brookfield, CT: Millbrook Press.

Hague, Michael. 1992. *Twinkle, Twinkle, Little Star*. New York: Morrow.

Hale, Sarah. 1990. *Mary Had a Little Lamb*. New York: Scholastic.

Haley, Gail. 1970. *A Story A Story*. New York: Atheneum.

Hall, Donald. 1979. *Ox-Cart Man*. New York: Viking.

Hayes, Sarah. 1990. *Nine Ducks Nine*. New York: Lothrop.

Heide, Florence, and Judith Gilliland. 1990. *The Day of Ahmed's Secret*. New York: Lothrop.

Heller, Ruth. 1987. *Kites Sail High and Other Collective Nouns*. New York: Grosset & Dunlap.

———. 1988. *Kites Sail High: A Book about Verbs*. New York: Grosset & Dunlap.

Henkes, Kevin. 1991. *Chrysanthemum*. New York: Greenwillow.

Henry, Joanne Landers. 1988. *Log Cabin in the Woods: A True Story about a Pioneer Boy*. New York: Macmillan.

Hill, Eric. 1981. *Spot's First Walk*. New York: G. P. Putnam.

———. 1982. *Spot's Birthday Party*. New York: G. P. Putnam.

———. 1985. *Spot Goes to the Beach*. New York: G. P. Putnam.

Hirschi, Ron. 1986. *One Day on Pika's Peak*. New York: Dodd Mead.

Hoban, Tana. 1971. *Look Again!* New York: Greenwillow.

———. 1974. *Circles, Triangles and Squares*. New York: Macmillan.

———. 1983. *Round & Round & Round*. New York: Greenwillow.

———. 1984a. *Is it Rough? Is it Smooth? Is it Shiny?* New York: Greenwillow.

———. 1984b. *I Walk and Read*. New York: Greenwillow.

———. 1986. *Shapes, Shapes, Shapes*. New York: Greenwillow.

———. 1987. *26 Letters and 99 Cents*. New York: Greenwillow.

———. 1988. *Look! Look! Look!* New York: Greenwillow.

———. 1989. *Of Colors and Things*. New York: Greenwillow.

———. 1990. *Exactly the Opposite*. New York: Greenwillow.

Hoberman, Mary Ann. 1994. *My Song is Beautiful*. Boston, MA: Little, Brown.

Hoffman, Mary. 1991. *Amazing Grace*. New York: Dial.

HOPKINS, LEE BENNETT, COLLECTED BY. 1988. *SIDE BY SIDE: POEMS TO READ TOGETHER.* NEW YORK: SIMON & SCHUSTER.

HOPKINSON, DEBORAH. 1993. *SWEET CLARA AND THE FREEDOM QUILT.* NEW YORK: KNOPF.

HOUSTON, GLORIA. 1992. *MY GREAT AUNT ARIZONA.* NEW YORK: HARPER.

HUTCHINS, PAT. 1971. *CHANGES, CHANGES.* NEW YORK: MACMILLAN.

———. 1972. *GOODNIGHT OWL.* NEW YORK: MACMILLAN.

———. 1983. *YOU'LL GROW INTO THEM, TITCH.* NEW YORK: GREENWILLOW.

———. 1986. *THE DOORBELL RANG.* NEW YORK: GREENWILLOW.

HUTTON, WARWICK. 1989. *THESEUS AND THE MINITOR.* NEW YORK: MARGARET K. MCELDERRY.

JASPERSOHN, WILLIAM. 1994. *MY HOMETOWN LIBRARY.* NEW YORK: HOUGHTON MIFFLIN.

JENKINS, HEATHER. 1993. *THE SURVIVAL OF FISH.* BOTHELL, WA: THE WRIGHT GROUP.

JOHNSON, ANGELA. 1989. *TELL ME A STORY, MAMA.* NEW YORK: ORCHARD.

JOHNSTON, TOM. 1988. *SCIENCE IN ACTION: WATER! WATER!* MILWAUKEE, WI: GARETH STEVENS.

JOHNSTON, TONY. 1985. *THE QUILT STORY.* NEW YORK: G. P. PUTNAM.

———. 1988. *YONDER.* NEW YORK: DIAL.

JONAS, ANN. 1984. *THE QUILT.* NEW YORK: GREENWILLOW.

———. 1987. *REFLECTIONS.* NEW YORK: GREENWILLOW.

———. 1989. *COLOR DANCE.* NEW YORK: GREENWILLOW.

JONES, CAROL. 1990. *THIS OLD MAN.* BOSTON, MA: HOUGHTON MIFFLIN.

JONES, DIANA. 1992. *YES, DEAR.* NEW YORK: GREENWILLOW.

KANDOIAN, ELLEN. 1989. *IS ANYBODY UP?* NEW YORK: G. P. PUTNAM.

KAUFMANN, JOHN. 1970. *ROBINS FLY NORTH, ROBINS FLY SOUTH.* NEW YORK: THOMAS Y. CROWELL.

KEEGAN, MARCIA. 1991. *PUEBLO BOY.* NEW YORK: COBBLEHILL.

KELLOGG, STEVEN. 1974. *THE MYSTERY OF THE MISSING RED MITTEN.* NEW YORK: DIAL.

———. 1988. *JOHNNY APPLESEED.* NEW YORK: MORROW.

KLINSEY-WARNOCK, NATALIE. 1994. *WILDERNESS CAT.* NEW YORK: COBBLEHILL.

KILLILEA, MARIE. 1992. *NEWF.* NEW YORK: PHILOMEL.

KITAMURA, SATOSHI. 1985. *WHAT'S INSIDE?* NEW YORK: FARRAR, STRAUS & GIROUX.

KLINTING, LARS. 1987. *PEARL'S ADVENTURE.* NEW YORK: RAND S. BOOKS.

KNIGHT, AMELIA S. 1993. *THE WAY WEST: JOURNAL OF A PIONEER WOMAN.* NEW YORK: SIMON & SCHUSTER.

KNIGHT, JAMES E. 1982. *THE FARM: LIFE IN COLONIAL PENNSYLVANIA.* MAHWAH, NJ: TROLL.

KNIGHT, MARGY BURNS. 1992. *TALKING WALLS.* GARDINER, ME: TILLBURY HOUSE.

KNOWLTON, JACK. 1988. *GEOGRAPHY FROM A TO Z.* NEW YORK: HARPERCOLLINS.

KNUTSON, BARBARA. 1990. *HOW THE GUINEA FOWL GOT HER SPOTS.* MINNEAPOLIS: CAROLRHODA BOOKS.

KOMAIKO, LEAH. 1990. *My Perfect Neighborhood*. New York: Harper & Row.

KOVALSKI, MARYANN. 1987. *The Wheels on the Bus*. Boston, MA: Little, Brown.

KRAUS, ROBERT. 1967. *Come Out and Play Little Mouse*. New York: Greenwillow.

——. 1970. *Whose Mouse Are You?* New York: Macmillan.

——. 1986. *Where Are You Going Little Mouse?* New York: Greenwillow.

——. 1989. *Phil the Ventriloquist*. New York: Greenwillow.

KRAUSS, RUTH. 1945. *The Carrot Seed*. New York: Harper & Row.

——. 1948. *Bears*. New York: Harper.

KROLL, VIRGINA. 1992. *Masai and I*. New York: Four Winds.

——. 1993A. *African Brothers and Sisters*. New York: Four Winds.

——. 1993B. *A Carp for Kimiko*. New York: Charlesbridge.

KURELEK, WILLIAM. 1985. *They Sought a New World*. Plattsburgh, NY: Tundra Books.

LATHAM, ROSS. 1985. *The Bulldozer Cleared the Way*. Crystal Lake, IL: Rigby.

LAWRENCE, LUCY. 1990. *Fly Fly Witchy*. Crystal Lake, IL: Rigby.

LEAF, MUNRO. 1988. *Wee Gillis*. New York: Viking.

LEEDY, LOREEN. 1994. *Fraction Action*. New York: Holiday House.

LEGUIN, URSULA K. 1989. *Fire and Stone*. New York: Macmillan.

LEHER, LORE. 1970. *A Letter Goes to Sea*. Irvington-on-Hudson, NY: Harvey House.

LENSKI, LOIS. 1987. *Sing a Song of People*. Boston, MA: Little, Brown.

LESIEG, THEO. 1961. *Ten Apples Up On Top*. New York: Random House.

LEVINE, ELLEN. 1989. *I Hate English!* New York: Scholastic.

——. 1993. *. . . If Your Name was Changed*. New York: Scholastic.

LINDBERGH, REEVE. 1990. *Johnny Appleseed*. Boston, MA: Little, Brown.

LOCKER, THOMAS. 1984. *Where the River Begins*. New York: Dial.

——. 1986. *Sailing with the Wind*. New York: Dial.

——. 1991. *The Boy Who Held Back the Sea*. New York: Dial.

LYE, FRANKLIN. 1983. *Nigeria*. New York: Franklin Watts.

LYON, GEORGE ELLA. 1992. *Who Came Down that Road?* New York: Orchard.

——. 1993. *Dreamplace*. New York: Orchard Books.

MACDONALD, AMY. 1990. *Little Beaver and the Echo*. New York: G. P. Putnam.

MACDONALD, SUE, AND BILL OAKES. 1990. *Once Upon Another*. New York: Dial.

MANSON, CHRISTOPHER. 1993. *The Tree in the Woods*. New York: North-South Books.

MANUSHKIN, FRAN. 1990. *Latkes and Applesauce*. New York: Scholastic.

MARSHALL, JAMES. 1989. *The Three Little Pigs*. New York: Dial.

MARTIN, RAFE. 1992. *The Rough-Face Girl*. New York: G. P. Putnam.

——. 1993. *The Boy Who Lived with the Seals*. New York: G. P. Putnam.

MARTIN, BILL JR., AND JOHN ARCHAMBAULT. 1985. *Here Are My Hands*. New York: Holt.

———. 1986. *Barn Dance.* New York: Henry Holt.

———. 1988. *Listen to the Rain.* New York: Holt.

———. 1990. *Sounds of an Owly Night.* New York: DLM.

Mayers, Florence C. 1986. *ABC: Museum of Fine Arts, Boston.* New York: Harry N. Abrams.

McCord, David. 1974. *One at a Time.* Boston, MA: Little, Brown.

McCurdy, Michael. 1988. *Hannah's Farm.* New York: Holiday House.

McDermott, Gerald. 1972. *Anansi the Spider.* New York: Holt.

———. 1974. *Arrow to the Sun.* New York: Viking.

———. 1975. *The Stone Cutter.* New York: Viking.

———. 1992. *Zomo the Rabbit.* New York: Harcourt Brace.

———. 1993. *Raven.* New York: Harcourt Brace.

McDonald, Mary. 1988. *Debra's Dog.* Crystal Lake, IL: Rigby.

Merriam, Eve. 1985. *The Christmas Box.* New York: William Morrow.

———. 1991. *The Wise Woman and Her Secret.* New York: Simon & Schuster.

———. 1993. *12 Ways to Get to Eleven.* New York: Simon and Schuster.

Mitchell, Rita Phillips. 1993. *Hue Boy.* New York: Dial.

Mochizuki, Ken. 1993. *Baseball Saved Us.* New York: Lee & Low.

Modesitt, Jeanne. 1990. *The Story of Z.* Saxonville, MA: Picture Book Studio.

Montague, Bill. 1993. *Little Mouse.* Concord, MA: Concord Mouse Trap.

Morris, Dean. 1988. *Underwater Life: the Oceans.* Milwaukee, WI: Raintree Children's Books.

Munsch, Robert. *Below Zero.* Toronto, Canada: Amick Press.

Murrow, Liza Ketchum. 1989. *Good-Bye, Sammy.* New York: Holiday House.

Naden, C. J. 1981. *Theseus and the Minitor.* New York: Troll.

Owens, Mary Beth. 1988. *A Caribou Alphabet.* New York: Farrar, Straus & Giroux.

Pallotta, Jerry. 1986. *The Icky Bug Alphabet Book.* Watertown, MA: Charlesbridge.

———. 1991. *The Underwater Alphabet Book.* Watertown, MA: Charlesbridge.

Parker, Nancy, and Joan Wright. 1987. *Bugs.* New York: William Morrow.

Parnell, Peter. 1988. *Feet.* New York: Macmillan.

Patterson, Katherine. 1990. *Tale of the Mandarin Duck.* New York: Dutton.

Peek, Merle. 1969. *Roll Over! A Counting Book.* New York: Clarion.

———. 1985. *Mary Wore Her Red Dress.* New York: Clarion.

———. 1987. *The Balancing Act.* New York: Clarion.

Perkin, Rex. 1948. *The Red Carpet.* New York: Macmillan.

Perrault, Charles. 1979. *Puss in Boots.* New York: Troll.

Pfister, Marcus. 1992. *The Rainbow Fish.* New York: North-South Books.

Polacco, Patricia. 1988. *The Keeping Quilt.* New York: Simon & Schuster.

POLLOCK, YEVONNE. 1986. *The Old Man's Mitten.* New York: Scholastic.

PORTER, KEITH. 1986. *The Insect World.* Lexington, MA: Schoolhouse Press.

POTTER, BEATRIX. 1988. *Peter Rabbit.* New York: Viking Penguin.

PRELUTSKY, JACK, SELECTED BY. 1983. *The Random House Book of Poetry for Children.* New York: Random House.

PRICEMAN, MARJORIE. 1994. *How to Make an Apple Pie.* New York: Knopf.

PROVENSEN, ALICE AND MARTIN. 1987. *Shaker Lane.* New York: Viking.

PRYOR, BONNIE. 1987. *The House on Maple Street.* New York: William Morrow.

QUACKENBUSH, ROBERT. 1973. *Go Tell Aunt Rhody.* New York: Lippincott.

RAUZON, MARK, AND CYNTHIA BIX. 1994. *Water, Water Everywhere.* San Francisco: Sierra Club Books for Children.

RENDALL, JENNY. 1986. *When Goldilocks Went to the House of the Bears.* New York: Scholastic.

RICE, EVE. 1980. *Goodnight, Goodnight.* New York: Greenwillow.

RINGGOLD, FAITH. 1991. *Tar Beach.* New York: Crown.

ROSE, GERALD. 1975. *Trouble in the Ark.* New York: Scholastic.

ROSEN, MICHAEL. 1989. *We're Going on a Bear Hunt.* New York: Margaret K. McElderry Books.

ROSENBERG, MAXINE B. 1986. *Making a New Home in America.* New York: Lothrop, Lee & Shepard.

ROUNDS, GLEN. 1990. *I Know an Old Lady Who Swallowed A Fly.* New York: Holiday House.

ROYSTON, ANGELA. 1992. *Eye Openers: Sea Animals.* New York: Macmillan.

RYDER, JOANNE. 1988. *The Snail's Spell.* New York: Viking.

RYLANT, CYNTHIA. 1982. *When I Was Young in the Mountains.* New York: E. P. Dutton.

——. 1985. *The Relatives Came.* New York: Bradbury Press.

——. 1988. *All I See.* New York: Orchard Books.

SABUDA, ROBERT. 1994. *Tutankhamen's Gift.* New York: Atheneum.

SALMON, MICHAEL. 1990. *Who's Behind the Door?* New York: Steck-Vaughn.

SAN SOUCI, ROBERT D. 1992. *Sukey and the Mermaid.* New York: G. P. Putnam.

SANDERS, SCOTT R. 1989. *Aurora Means Dawn.* New York: Macmillan.

SANDIN, JOAN. 1981. *The Long Way to a New Land.* New York: Harper.

——. 1989. *The Long Way Westward.* New York: Harper.

SAY, ALAN. 1974. *Once Under the Cherry Blossom Tree.* New York: Harper & Row.

——. 1982. *The Bicycle Man.* New York: Scholastic.

——. 1991. *Tree of Cranes.* Boston, MA: Houghton Mifflin.

——. 1993. *Grandfather's Journey.* Boston, MA: Houghton Mifflin.

SCHERTLE, ALICE. 1990. *That's What I Thought.* New York: Harper & Row.

SCIESZKA, JON. 1989. *THE TRUE STORY OF THE THREE LITTLE PIGS!* NEW YORK: VIKING.

SELWAY, MARTINA. 1994. *I HATE ROLAND ROBERTS.* NASHVILLE, TN: IDEALS CHILDREN'S BOOKS.

SEULING, BARBARA. 1976. *THE TEENY TINY WOMAN.* NEW YORK: PUFFIN BOOKS.

SEUSS, DR. 1957. *THE CAT IN THE HAT.* NEW YORK: RANDOM HOUSE.

SHEFELMAN, JANICE. 1988. *VICTORIA HOUSE.* ORLANDO, FL: HARCOURT BRACE.

SHELBY, ANNE. 1991. *POTLUCK.* NEW YORK: ORCHARD.

SHERIDAN, JOHN. 1992. *ANTS, ANTS, ANTS.* BOTHELL, WA: THE WRIGHT GROUP.

SINGER, MARILYN. 1991. *NINE O'CLOCK LULLABY.* NEW YORK: HARPERCOLLINS.

SIS, PETER. 1989. *GOING UP.* NEW YORK: GREENWILLOW.

SLOAT, TERI. 1989. *FROM LETTER TO LETTER.* NEW YORK: E. P. DUTTON.

———. 1991. *FROM ONE TO ONE HUNDRED.* NEW YORK: E. P. DUTTON.

SMITH, JUDITH. 1986. *THE THREE BILLY GOATS GRUFF.* CRYSTAL LAKE, IL: RIGBY.

SMITH, TREVOR. 1990. *AMAZING LIZARDS.* NEW YORK: KNOPF.

SNYDER, DIANNE. 1988. *THE BOY OF THE THREE-YEAR NAP.* BOSTON, MA: HOUGHTON MIFFLIN.

STEIG, WILLIAM. 1971. *AMOS AND BORIS.* NEW YORK: FARRAR, STRAUS & GIROUX.

STEVENSON, ROBERT LOUIS. 1990. *MY SHADOW.* NEW YORK: G. P. PUTNAM.

SWANSON, JUNE. 1990. *I PLEDGE ALLEGIANCE.* MINNEAPOLIS: CAROLRHODA.

TAFURI, NANCY. 1989. *THE BALL BOUNCED.* NEW YORK: GREENWILLOW.

TASHJIAN, VIRGINIA. 1969. *JUBA THIS AND JUBA THAT.* NEW YORK: SCHOLASTIC.

TOMPERT, ANN. 1990. *GRANDFATHER TANG'S STORY.* NEW YORK: CROWN.

TRESSELT, ALVIN. 1964. *THE MITTEN.* NEW YORK: LOTHROP.

TURNER, DOROTHY. 1988. *POTATOES.* MINNEAPOLIS: CAROLRHODA.

VAGIN, VAGIN, AND FRANK ASCH. 1989. *HERE COMES THE CAT.* NEW YORK: SCHOLASTIC.

VALLEY, JIM. 1993. *RAIN FOREST.* BOTHELL, WA: THE WRIGHT GROUP.

VAN BRAMER, JOAN. 1992. *WHALE RAP.* CRYSTAL LAKE, IL: RIGBY.

VAN ALLSBURG, CHRIS. 1988. *TWO BAD ANTS.* NEW YORK: HOUGHTON MIFFLIN.

VAUGHN, MARCIA. 1989. *THE SANDWICH THAT MAX MADE.* CRYSTAL LAKE, IL: RIGBY.

WADDELL, MARTIN. 1992. *OWL BABIES.* NEW YORK: CANDLEWICK PRESS.

WALKER, COLINS. 1992. *PLANTS AND SEEDS.* BOTHELL, WA: THE WRIGHT GROUP.

WALSH, ELLEN STOLL. 1989. *MOUSE PAINT.* NEW YORK: HARCOURT.

WARD, CINDY. 1988. *COOKIE'S WEEK.* NEW YORK: G. P. PUTNAM.

WATERS, JOHN. 1973. *SEAL HARBOR: THE LIFE OF THE HARBOR SEAL.* NEW YORK: FREDERICK WARNE.

WATTS, BARRIE. 1990. *KEEPING MINIBEASTS: ANTS.* NEW YORK: FRANKLIN WATTS.

WEISNER, DAVID. 1991. *TUESDAY.* NEW YORK: CLARION.

WEISS, NICKI. 1989. *WHERE DOES THE BROWN BEAR GO?* NEW YORK: GREENWILLOW.

WESCOTT, NADINE. 1980. *I Know an Old Lady Who Swallowed a Fly.* BOSTON, MA: LITTLE, BROWN.

——. 1988. *The Lady with the Alligator Purse.* BOSTON, MA: LITTLE, BROWN.

——. 1990. *There's a Hole in the Bucket.* NEW YORK: HARPER.

WHEATLEY, NADIA, AND DONNA RAWLINS. 1992. *My Place.* BROOKLYN, NY: KANE/MILLER.

WICKSTROM, SYLVIE. 1988. *The Wheels on the Bus.* NEW YORK: CROWN.

WILLIAM-ELLIS, ANNABEL. 1987. *Tales from the Enchanted World.* BOSTON, MA: LITTLE, BROWN.

WILLIAMS, KAREN LYNN. 1990. *Galimoto.* NEW YORK: MULLBURY BOOKS.

WILLIAMS, LAWRENCE. 1990. *Last Frontiers for Mankind: Oceans.* NEW YORK: MARSHALL CAVENDISH.

WILLIAMS, MARGERY. 1922. *The Velveteen Rabbit.* NEW YORK: DOUBLEDAY.

WILLIAMS, SHERLEY ANN. 1992. *Working Cotton.* NEW YORK: HARCOURT BRACE.

WILLIAMS, SUE. 1989. *I Went Walking.* NEW YORK: HARCOURT BRACE.

WILLIAMS, VERA B. 1984. *Music, Music for Everyone.* NEW YORK: GREENWILLOW.

WILLIAMSON, FRASER. 1993. *Why Frog and Snake Can't Be Friends.* CRYSTAL LAKE, IL: RIGBY.

WILLOW, DIANE. 1991. *At Home in the Rain Forest.* WATERTOWN, MA: CHARLESBRIDGE.

WOLCOTT, PATTY. 1991. *Where Did that Naughty Little Hamster Go?* NEW YORK: RANDOM HOUSE.

WOOD, AUDREY. 1982. *Quick as a Cricket.* WEST ORANGE, NJ: CHILD'S PLAY

——. 1984. *The Napping House.* NEW YORK: HARCOURT BRACE.

YASHIMA, TARO. 1983. *Crow Boy.* NEW YORK: PUFFIN BOOKS.

YEE, PAUL. 1991. *Roses Sing on New Snow.* NEW YORK: MACMILLAN.

YOLEN, JANE. 1987. *Owl Moon.* NEW YORK: PHILOMEL.

——. 1992. *Letting Swift River Go.* BOSTON, MA: LITTLE, BROWN.

YORINKS, ARTHUR. 1989. *Oh, Brother.* NEW YORK: FARRAR, STRAUS & GIROUX.

YOUNG, ED. 1992. *Seven Blind Mice.* NEW YORK: PHILOMEL.

YOUNG, JIM. 1974. *When the Whale Came to My Town.* NEW YORK: KNOPF.

YOUNG, MARGARET. 1968. *The Picture Life of Martin Luther King.* NEW YORK: FRANKLIN WATTS.

ZEMACH, MARGOT. 1976. *Hush Little Baby.* NEW YORK: E. P. DUTTON.

——. 1989. *The Three Little Pigs.* NEW YORK: FARRAR, STRAUS & GIROUX.

PROFESSIONAL LITERATURE

ARMSTRONG, MICHAEL. 1980. *CLOSELY OBSERVED CHILDREN: THE DIARY OF A PRIMARY CLASSROOM.* LONDON: WRITERS AND READERS.

ATWELL, NANCIE. 1987. *IN THE MIDDLE.* PORTSMOUTH, NH: BOYNTON/COOK.

AVERY, CAROL. 1993. *. . .AND WITH A LIGHT TOUCH: LEARNING ABOUT READING, WRITING, AND TEACHING WITH FIRST GRADERS.* PORTSMOUTH, NH: HEINEMANN.

BAKER, ANN, AND JOHN BAKER. 1990. *MATHEMATICS IN PROCESS.* PORTSMOUTH, NH: HEINEMANN.

BAKER, DAVE, CHERYL SEMPLE, AND TONY STEAD. 1990. *HOW BIG IS THE MOON? WHOLE MATHS IN ACTION.* PORTSMOUTH, NH: HEINEMANN.

BARATTA-LORTON, MARY. 1976. *MATHEMATICS THEIR WAY.* READING, MA: ADDISON-WESLEY.

BERMAN, SHELDON, AND PHYLLIS LA FARGE. 1993. *PROMISING PRACTICES IN TEACHING SOCIAL RESPONSIBILITY.* ALBANY, NY: STATE UNIVERSITY OF NEW YORK PRESS.

BISSEX, GLENDA, AND RICHARD H. BULLOCK. 1987. *SEEING FOR OURSELVES: CASE-STUDY RESEARCH BY TEACHERS OF WRITING.* PORTSMOUTH, NH: HEINEMANN.

BOLTON, FAYE, AND DIANE SNOWBALL. 1993A. *IDEAS FOR SPELLING.* PORTSMOUTH, NH: HEINEMANN.

——. 1993B. *TEACHING SPELLING: A PRACTICAL RESOURCE.* PORTSMOUTH, NH: HEINEMANN.

BROWN, REXFORD G. 1991. *SCHOOLS OF THOUGHT: HOW THE POLITICS OF LITERACY SHAPE THINKING IN THE CLASSROOM.* SAN FRANCISCO: JOSSEY-BASS.

BUCHANAN, ETHEL. 1989. *SPELLING FOR WHOLE LANGUAGE CLASSROOMS.* KATONAH, NY: RICHARD C. OWEN.

——. 1994. "SPELLING FOR THE WHOLE LANGUAGE CLASSROOM." IN *UNDER THE WHOLE LANGUAGE UMBRELLA: MANY CULTURES, MANY VOICES,* EDITED BY ALAN D. FLURKEY AND RICHARD J. MEYER. URBANA, IL: NATIONAL COUNCIL OF TEACHERS OF ENGLISH.

BURK, DONNA, ALLYN SNIDER, AND PAULA SYMONDS. 1988. *BOX IT OR BAG IT: TEACHERS RESOURCE GUIDE: MATHEMATICS, FIRST-SECOND.* SALEM, OR: THE MATH LEARNING CENTER.

——. 1991. *MATH EXCURSIONS 2: PROJECT-BASED MATHEMATICS FOR SECOND GRADERS.* PORTSMOUTH, NH: HEINEMANN.

——. 1992. *MATH EXCURSIONS 1: PROJECT-BASED MATHEMATICS FOR FIRST GRADERS.* PORTSMOUTH, NH: HEINEMANN.

BURNS, MARILYN. 1992. *ABOUT TEACHING MATHEMATICS: A K-8 RESOURCE.* SAUSALITO, CA: MARILYN BURNS EDUCATION ASSOCIATES.

BURNS, MARILYN, CATHY HUMPHREYS, AND BONNIE TANK. 1988. *A COLLECTION OF MATH LESSONS: FROM GRADES 1 THROUGH 3.* NEW YORK: CUISENAIRE COMPANY.

BUTZOW, CAROL M. AND JOHN W. 1989. *SCIENCE THROUGH CHILDREN'S LITERATURE: AN INTEGRATED APPROACH.* ENGLEWOOD, CO: TEACHER IDEAS PRESS.

CALKINS, LUCY M. 1994. *THE ART OF TEACHING WRITING.* NEW EDITION. PORTSMOUTH, NH: HEINEMANN.

CAMBOURNE, BRIAN. 1988. *THE WHOLE STORY: NATURAL LEARNING AND THE ACQUISITION OF LITERACY IN THE CLASSROOM.* NEW YORK: ASHTON SCHOLASTIC.

CAMBOURNE, BRIAN, AND JAN TURBILL, EDS. 1994. *RESPONSIVE EVALUATION: MAKING VALID JUDGEMENTS ABOUT STUDENT LITERACY.* PORTSMOUTH, NH: HEINEMANN.

CHOMSKY, CAROL. 1971. "INVENTED SPELLING IN THE OPEN CLASSROOM." *WORD* 27: 499–518.

CLAY, MARIE. 1985. *THE EARLY DETECTION OF READING DIFFICULTIES.* PORTSMOUTH, NH: HEINEMANN.

——. 1991. *BECOMING LITERATE: THE CONSTRUCTION OF INNER CONTROL.* PORTSMOUTH, NH: HEINEMANN.

——. 1993. *AN OBSERVATION SURVEY OF EARLY LITERACY ACHIEVEMENT.* PORTSMOUTH, NH: HEINEMANN.

CLEMMONS, JOAN, LOIS LAASE, DONNALYNN COOPER, NANCY AREGLADO, AND MARY DILL. 1993. *PORTFOLIOS IN THE CLASSROOM: A TEACHER'S SOURCEBOOK.* NEW YORK: SCHOLASTIC.

COCHRANE, ORIN, DONNA COCHRANE, SHAREN SCALENA, AND ETHEL BUCHANAN. 1984. *READING, WRITING, AND CARING.* KATONAH, NY: RICHARD C. OWEN.

COPELAND, JEFFREY S. 1993. *SPEAKING OF POETS: INTERVIEWS WITH POETS WHO WRITE FOR CHILDREN AND YOUNG ADULTS.* URBANA, IL: NATIONAL COUNCIL OF TEACHERS OF ENGLISH.

CORDERIO, PAT. 1992A. *WHOLE LEARNING: WHOLE LANGUAGE AND CONTENT IN THE UPPER ELEMENTARY GRADES.* KATONAH, NY: RICHARD C. OWEN.

——. 1992B. "BECOMING A LEARNER WHO TEACHERS." *TEACHING NETWORKING* 12(1): 1–5.

——, ED. 1995. *ENDLESS POSSIBILITIES: GENERATING CURRICULUM IN SOCIAL STUDIES AND LITERACY.* PORTSMOUTH, NH: HEINEMANN.

COWLEY, JOY. 1994. *WHOLE LEARNING: WHOLE CHILD.* BOTHELL, WA: THE WRIGHT GROUP.

CUISENAIRE RODS: CUISENAIRE COMPANY OF AMERICA, MT. VERNON, NY 10550.

DAHL, KARIN L. 1992. *TEACHER AS WRITER: ENTERING THE PROFESSIONAL CONVERSATION.* URBANA, IL: NATIONAL COUNCIL OF TEACHERS OF ENGLISH.

DEFORD, DIANE E., CAROL A. LYONS, AND GAY SU PINNELL. 1991. *BRIDGES TO LITERACY: LEARNING FROM READING RECOVERY.* PORTSMOUTH, NH: HEINEMANN.

DEPARTMENT OF EDUCATION, WELLINGTON (NEW ZEALAND). 1985. *READING IN JUNIOR CLASSES.* KATONAH, NY: RICHARD C. OWEN.

DEPREE, HELEN, AND SANDRA IVERSEN. 1994. *EARLY LITERACY IN THE CLASSROOM: A NEW STANDARD FOR YOUNG READERS*. BOTHELL, WA: THE WRIGHT GROUP.

DERMAN-SPARKS, LOUISE, AND THE A.B.C. TASK FORCE. 1989. *ANTI-BIAS CURRICULUM: TOOLS FOR EMPOWERING YOUNG CHILDREN*. WASHINGTON, DC: NATIONAL ASSOCIATION FOR THE EDUCATION OF YOUNG CHILDREN.

DONALDSON, MARGARET. 1978. *CHILDREN'S MINDS*. NEW YORK: W. W. NORTON.

DORIS, ELLEN. 1991. *DOING WHAT SCIENTISTS DO: CHILDREN LEARN TO INVESTIGATE THEIR WORLD*. PORTSMOUTH, NH: HEINEMANN.

DRIVER, TOM. 1991. *THE MAGIC OF RITUAL*. SAN FRANCISCO, CA: HARPER

DURST, SUSAN S. 1988. "OSCAR'S JOURNAL." IN *UNDERSTANDING WRITING: WAYS OF OBSERVING, LEARNING, AND TEACHING*, EDITED BY TOM NEWKIRK AND NANCIE ATWELL. PORTSMOUTH, NH: HEINEMANN.

DYSON, ANNE HAAS. 1989. *MULTIPLE WORLDS OF CHILD WRITERS: FRIENDS LEARNING TO WRITE*. NEW YORK: TEACHERS COLLEGE PRESS.

EARLY LITERACY IN-SERVICE COURSE. CRYSTAL LAKE, IL: RIGBY.

EDELSKY, CAROL, BESS ALTWERGER, AND BARBARA FLORES. 1990. *WHOLE LANGUAGE: WHAT'S THE DIFFERENCE?* PORTSMOUTH, NH: HEINEMANN.

ELLEMAN, BARBARA. 1992. "WATER AND WATERWAYS." *BOOK LINKS* (NOVEMBER): 7–15.

FISHER, BOBBI. 1991. *JOYFUL LEARNING: A WHOLE LANGUAGE KINDERGARTEN*. PORTSMOUTH, NH: HEINEMANN.

——. 1993. "PLANNING FOR THE FIRST DAY OF SCHOOL." *TEACHING K/8* (SEPTEMBER): 66–68.

——. 1994. *CLASSROOM CLOSE-UP. BOBBI FISHER: ORGANIZATION AND MANAGEMENT*. BOTHELL, WA: THE WRIGHT GROUP. VIDEOTAPE.

——. 1995. "THINGS TAKE OFF." IN *ENDLESS POSSIBILITIES: GENERATING CURRICULUM IN SOCIAL STUDIES AND LITERACY*, EDITED BY PAT CORDEIRO. PORTSMOUTH, NH: HEINEMANN.

FISHER, BOBBI, AND PAT CORDEIRO, EDS. 1994. "GENERATING CURRICULUM: BUILDING A SHARED CURRICULUM." *PRIMARY VOICES K-6* 2(3).

FLURKEY, ALAN D., AND RICHARD J. MEYER. 1994. *UNDER THE WHOLE LANGUAGE UMBRELLA: MANY CULTURES, MANY VOICES*. URBANA, IL: NATIONAL COUNCIL OF TEACHERS OF ENGLISH.

GARDNER, HOWARD. 1991. *THE UNSCHOOLED MIND: HOW CHILDREN THINK; AND HOW SCHOOLS SHOULD TEACH*. NEW YORK: BASIC BOOKS.

——. 1993. *CREATING MINDS*. NEW YORK: BASIC BOOKS.

GENTRY, RICHARD. 1985. "YOU CAN ANALYZE DEVELOPMENTAL-SPELLING—AND HERE'S HOW TO DO IT!" *EARLY YEARS* MAY.

GENTRY, RICHARD, AND JEAN WALLACE GILLET. 1992. *TEACHING KIDS TO SPELL*. PORTSMOUTH, NH: HEINEMANN.

GIACOBBE, MARY ELLEN. 1992. TALK GIVEN AT MASSACHUSETTS WHOLE LANGUAGE TEACHERS ASSOCIATION MEETING. WESTWOOD, MA.

GIROUX, HENRY A. 1988. *TEACHERS AS INTELLECTUALS: TOWARD A CRITICAL PEDAGOGY OF LEARNING.* NEW YORK: BERGIN AND GARVEY.

GOODMAN, KENNETH. 1986. *WHAT'S WHOLE IN WHOLE LANGUAGE.* PORTSMOUTH, NH: HEINEMANN.

———. 1992. "I DIDN'T FOUND WHOLE LANGUAGE." *THE READING TEACHER* 46: 188–99.

———. 1993. *PHONICS PHACTS.* PORTSMOUTH, NH: HEINEMANN.

GOODMAN, YETTA. 1985. "KIDWATCHING: OBSERVING CHILDREN IN THE CLASSROOM." IN *OBSERVING THE LANGUAGE LEARNER,* EDITED BY ANGELA JAGUAR AND M. TRINKA SMITH-BURKE. NEWARK, DE: INTERNATIONAL READING ASSOCIATION.

GOODMAN, YETTA, WENDY J. HOOD, AND KENNETH GOODMAN, EDS. 1991. *ORGANIZING FOR WHOLE LANGUAGE.* PORTSMOUTH, NH: HEINEMANN.

GOODMAN, YETTA, DOROTHY WATSON, AND CAROLYN BURKE. 1987. *READING MISCUE INVENTORY: ALTERNATIVE PROCEDURES.* KATONAH, NY: RICHARD C. OWEN.

GRAVES, DONALD. 1983. *WRITING: TEACHERS AND CHILDREN AT WORK.* PORTSMOUTH, NH: HEINEMANN.

———. 1989. *DISCOVER YOUR OWN LITERACY.* PORTSMOUTH, NH: HEINEMANN.

———. 1991A. *BUILD A LITERATE CLASSROOM.* PORTSMOUTH, NH: HEINEMANN.

———. 1991B. TALK GIVEN AT THE WHOLE LANGUAGE TEACHERS ASSOCIATION MEETING. WESTON, MA. APRIL.

———. 1994. *A FRESH LOOK AT WRITING.* PORTSMOUTH, NH: HEINEMANN.

GRAVES, DONALD, AND BONNIE SUNSTEIN. 1992. *PORTFOLIO PORTRAITS.* PORTSMOUTH, NH: HEINEMANN.

HANSEN, JANE, AND DONALD GRAVES. 1983. "THE AUTHOR'S CHAIR." *LANGUAGE ARTS* 60: 176–83.

HARP, BILL, ED. 1991. *ASSESSMENT AND EVALUATION IN WHOLE LANGUAGE PROGRAMS.* NORWOOD: MA: CHRISTOPHER-GORDON.

———. 1993. *BRINGING CHILDREN TO LITERACY: CLASSROOMS AT WORK.* NORWOOD, MA: CHRISTOPHER-GORDON.

HARRIS, VIOLET, ED. 1992. *TEACHING MULTICULTURAL LITERATURE IN GRADES K-8.* NORWOOD, MA: CHRISTOPHER-GORDON.

HARSTE, JEROME. 1993. "INQUIRY-BASED INSTRUCTION." *PRIMARY VOICES K-6,* PREMIER ISSUE.

HARSTE, JEROME, AND KATHY SHORT, WITH CAROLYN BURKE. 1988. *CREATING CLASSROOMS FOR AUTHORS.* PORTSMOUTH, NH: HEINEMANN.

HART-HEWINS, LINDA, AND JAN WELLS. 1990. *REAL BOOKS FOR READING: LEARNING TO READ WITH CHILDREN'S LITERATURE.* PORTSMOUTH, NH: HEINEMANN.

HARWAYNE, SHELLEY. 1992. *LASTING IMPRESSIONS: WEAVING LITERATURE INTO THE WRITING WORKSHOP.* PORTSMOUTH, NH: HEINEMANN.

HEALY, JANE. 1990. *ENDANGERED MINDS: WHY CHILDREN DON'T THINK AND WHAT WE CAN DO ABOUT IT.* NEW YORK: SIMON & SCHUSTER.

HICKMAN, JANET, AND BERNICE E. CULLINAN, EDS. 1989. *CHILDREN'S LITERATURE IN THE CLASSROOM: WEAVING CHARLOTTE'S WEB.* NORWOOD, MA: CHRISTOPHER-GORDON.

HOLDAWAY, DON. 1979. *THE FOUNDATIONS OF LITERACY.* PORTSMOUTH, NH: HEINEMANN.

———. 1980. *INDEPENDENCE IN READING.* PORTSMOUTH, NH: HEINEMANN.

———. 1986. "THE STRUCTURE OF NATURAL LEARNING AS A BASIS FOR LITERACY INSTRUCTION." IN *THE PURSUIT OF LITERACY: EARLY READING AND WRITING,* EDITED BY MICHAEL SAMPSON. DUBUQUE, IA: KENDALL/HUNT.

HUBBARD, RUTH S. 1989. *AUTHORS OF PICTURES, DRAUGHTSMEN OF WORDS.* PORTSMOUTH, NH: HEINEMANN.

HUBBARD, RUTH S., AND BRENDA M. POWER. 1993. *THE ART OF CLASSROOM INQUIRY: A HANDBOOK FOR TEACHER-RESEARCHERS.* PORTSMOUTH, NH: HEINEMANN.

JOHNSTON, PETER H. 1991. *CONSTRUCTIVE EVALUATION OF LITERATE ACTIVITY.* NEW YORK: LONGMAN.

JORGENSEN, KAREN. 1993. *HISTORY WORKSHOP: RECONSTRUCTING THE PAST WITH ELEMENTARY STUDENTS.* PORTSMOUTH, NH: HEINEMANN.

KATZ, LILLIAN, AND SYLVIA CHARD. 1989. *ENGAGING CHILDREN'S MINDS: THE PROJECT APPROACH.* NORWOOD, NJ: ABLEX PUBLISHING CORPORATION.

KIERAN, EGAN. 1986. *TEACHING AS STORY TELLING: AN ALTERNATIVE APPROACH TO TEACHING AND CURRICULUM IN THE ELEMENTARY SCHOOL.* CHICAGO, IL: THE UNIVERSITY OF CHICAGO PRESS.

KOHN, ALFIE. 1993. *PUNISHED BY REWARDS: THE TROUBLE WITH GOLD STARS, INCENTIVE PLANS, A'S, PRAISE, AND OTHER BRIBES.* NEW YORK: HOUGHTON MIFFLIN.

LEAL, DOROTHY. 1993. "STORYBOOKS, INFORMATION BOOKS, AND INFORMATIONAL STORYBOOKS: AN EXPLICATION OF THE AMBIGUOUS GRAY GENRE." *THE NEW ADVOCATE* 6(1): 61–70.

LEIVA, M. 1991. *CURRICULUM AND EVALUATION STANDARDS FOR SCHOOL MATHEMATICS: ADDENDA SERIES, FIRST GRADE BOOK.* RESTON, VA: NATIONAL COUNCIL OF TEACHERS OF MATHEMATICS, INC.

MANNING, GARY, MARYANN MANNING, AND ROBERTA LONG. 1994. *THEME IMMERSION: INQUIRY-BASED CURRICULUM IN ELEMENTARY AND MIDDLE SCHOOLS.* PORTSMOUTH, NH: HEINEMANN.

MARTIN, BILL, JR. 1972. *SOUNDS OF LAUGHTER.* TEACHER'S EDITION. NEW YORK: HOLT.

MCCLURE, AMY, AND JANICE V. KRISTO, EDS. 1994. *INVITING CHILDREN'S RESPONSE TO LITERATURE.* URBANA, IL: NATIONAL COUNCIL OF TEACHERS OF ENGLISH.

MCGRUDER, SHERYL. 1993. "BRINGING CHILDREN TO LITERACY THROUGH DRAMA." IN *BRINGING CHILDREN TO LITERACY,* EDITED BY BILL HARP. NORWOOD, MA: CHRISTOPHER-GORDON.

MILLS, HEIDI, AND JEAN ANN CLYDE, EDS. 1990. *PORTRAITS OF WHOLE LANGUAGE CLASSROOMS: LEARNING FOR ALL AGES.* PORTSMOUTH, NH: HEINEMANN.

MILLS, HEIDI, TIMOTHY O'KEEFE, AND DIANE STEPHENS. 1992. *LOOKING CLOSELY: EXPLORING THE ROLE OF PHONICS IN ONE WHOLE LANGUAGE CLASSROOM.* URBANA, IL: NATIONAL COUNCIL OF TEACHERS OF ENGLISH.

MOFFETT, JAMES. 1994. *THE UNIVERSAL SCHOOLHOUSE: SPIRITUAL AWAKENING THROUGH EDUCATION*. SAN FRANCISCO: JOSSEY-BASS.

MOSS, JOY F. 1990. *FOCUS ON LITERATURE: A CONTEXT FOR LITERACY LEARNING*. KATONAH, NY: RICHARD C. OWEN.

NATIONAL COUNCIL OF TEACHERS OF MATHEMATICS. 1989. *CURRICULUM AND EVALUATION STANDARDS FOR SCHOOL MATHEMATICS*. RESTON, VA: NCTM.

NEWMAN, JUDITH M. 1991. *INTERWOVEN CONVERSATIONS: LEARNING AND TEACHING THROUGH CRITICAL REFLECTION*. PORTSMOUTH, NH: HEINEMANN.

NODDINGS, NEL. 1992. *THE CHALLENGE TO CARE IN SCHOOLS*. NEW YORK: TEACHERS COLLEGE PRESS.

OHANIAN, SUSAN. 1992. *GARBAGE PIZZA, PATCHWORK QUILTS, AND MATH MAGIC*. PORTSMOUTH, NH: HEINEMANN.

OLSON, JANET L. 1992. *ENVISIONING WRITING: TOWARD AN INTEGRATION OF DRAWING AND WRITING*. PORTSMOUTH, NH: HEINEMANN.

PARRY, JAN, AND DAVID HORNSBY. 1985. *WRITE ON: A CONFERENCE APPROACH TO WRITING*. PORTSMOUTH, NH: HEINEMANN.

PERRONI, VITO. 1991. *A LETTER TO TEACHERS: REFLECTIONS ON SCHOOLING AND THE ART OF TEACHING*. SAN FRANCISCO: JOSSEY-BASS.

PETERSON, BARBARA. 1991. "SELECTING BOOKS FOR BEGINNING READERS." IN *BRIDGES TO LITERACY: LEARNING FROM READING RECOVERY*, EDITED BY DIANE E. DEFORD, CAROL A. LYONS, AND GAY SU PINNELL. PORTSMOUTH, NH: HEINEMANN.

PETERSON, RALPH. 1992. *LIFE IN A CROWDED PLACE*. PORTSMOUTH, NH: HEINEMANN.

PETERSON, RALPH, AND MARYANN EEDS. 1990. *GRAND CONVERSATIONS*. NEW YORK: SCHOLASTIC.

PHELAN, CAROLYN. 1994. "JOANNA COLE AND BRUCE DEGEN'S MAGIC SCHOOL BUS." *BOOK LINKS* (SEPTEMBER): 44–47.

PHINNEY, MARGARET Y. 1988. *READING WITH THE TROUBLED READER*. PORTSMOUTH, NH: HEINEMANN.

POWELL, DEBBIE, AND DAVID HORNSBY. 1993. *LEARNING PHONICS AND SPELLING IN A WHOLE LANGUAGE CLASSROOM*. NEW YORK: SCHOLASTIC.

REED, CHARLES. 1971. "PRE-SCHOOL CHILDREN'S KNOWLEDGE OF ENGLISH PHONOLOGY." *HARVARD EDUCATIONAL REVIEW* 41: 1–34.

RHODES, LYNN K., ED. 1993. *LITERACY ASSESSMENT: A HANDBOOK OF INSTRUMENTS*. PORTSMOUTH, NH: HEINEMANN.

ROSENBLATT, LOUISE. 1978. *THE READER, THE TEXT, THE POEM: THE TRANSACTIONAL THEORY OF THE LITERARY WORK*. CARBONDALE, IL: SOUTHERN ILLINOIS UNIVERSITY PRESS.

ROUTMAN, REGIE. 1991. *INVITATIONS*. PORTSMOUTH, NH: HEINEMANN.

SAUL, WENDY, ET AL. 1993. *SCIENCE WORKSHOP: A WHOLE LANGUAGE APPROACH*. PORTSMOUTH, NH: HEINEMANN.

SAUL, WENDY, AND SYBILLE A. JAGUSCH, EDS. 1991. *VITAL CONNECTIONS: CHILDREN, SCIENCE, AND BOOKS*. PORTSMOUTH, NH: HEINEMANN.

SCHON, DONALD A. 1983. *THE REFLECTIVE PRACTITIONER.* NEW YORK: BASIC BOOKS.

SEIGLE, PAMELA, AND GAYLE MACKLEM. 1993. "REACH OUT TO SCHOOLS: SOCIAL COMPETENCY PROGRAM." THE STONE CENTER, WELLESLEY COLLEGE, 106 CENTRAL STREET, WELLESLEY, MA, 02181.

SHANNON, KATHLEEN. 1995. *AT HOME AT SCHOOL: A CHILD'S TRANSITION.* BOTHELL, WA: THE WRIGHT GROUP.

SHANNON, PATRICK, AND KENNETH GOODMAN. 1994. *BASAL READERS: A SECOND LOOK.* KATONAH, NY: RICHARD C. OWEN.

SHORT, KATHY, AND CAROLYN BURKE. 1991. *CREATING CURRICULUM: TEACHERS AND STUDENTS AS A COMMUNITY OF LEARNERS.* PORTSMOUTH, NH: HEINEMANN.

SHORT, KATHY, AND KATHY MITCHELL PIERCE, EDS. 1990. *TALKING ABOUT BOOKS: CREATING LITERATE COMMUNITIES.* PORTSMOUTH, NH: HEINEMANN.

SLOAN, GLENNA D. 1984. *THE CHILD AS CRITIC: TEACHING LITERATURE IN ELEMENTARY AND MIDDLE SCHOOLS.* NEW YORK: TEACHERS COLLEGE PRESS.

SMITH, FRANK. 1982. *WRITING AND THE WRITER.* NEW YORK: HOLT, RINEHART AND WINSTON.

———. 1983. *ESSAYS INTO LITERATURE.* PORTSMOUTH, NH: HEINEMANN.

———. 1988A. *UNDERSTANDING READING: A PSYCHOLINGUISTIC ANALYSIS OF READING AND LEARNING TO READ.* 4TH ED. HILLSDALE, NJ: LAWRENCE ERLBAUM.

———. 1988B. *JOINING THE LITERACY CLUB: FURTHER ESSAYS INTO EDUCATION.* PORTSMOUTH, NH: HEINEMANN.

———. 1990. *TO THINK.* NEW YORK: TEACHERS COLLEGE PRESS.

TAKAKI, RONALD. 1993. *A DIFFERENT MIRROR: A HISTORY OF MULTICULTURAL AMERICA.* BOSTON, MA: LITTLE, BROWN.

TOMPKINS, GAIL E., AND LEA M. MCGEE. 1993. *TEACHING READING WITH LITERATURE: CASE STUDIES TO ACTION PLANS.* NEW YORK: MACMILLAN.

TOUSDALE, ANN M., SUE A. WOESTEHOFF, AND MARNI SCHWARTZ, EDS. 1994. *GIVE A LISTEN: STORIES OF STORYTELLING IN SCHOOL.* URBANA, IL: NATIONAL COUNCIL OF TEACHERS OF ENGLISH.

TUNNELL, MICHAEL O., AND RICHARD AMMON. 1993. *THE STORY OF OURSELVES: TEACHING HISTORY THROUGH CHILDREN'S LITERATURE.* PORTSMOUTH, NH: HEINEMANN.

VYGOTSKY, LEV S. 1978. *MIND IN SOCIETY: THE DEVELOPMENT OF HIGHER PSYCHOLOGICAL PROCESSES.* CAMBRIDGE, MA: HARVARD UNIVERSITY PRESS.

WEAVER, CONSTANCE. 1994. *READING PROCESS AND PRACTICE: FROM SOCIO-PSYCHOLINGUISTICS TO WHOLE LANGUAGE.* 2D ED. PORTSMOUTH, NH: HEINEMANN.

WEAVER, CONSTANCE, JOEL CHASTON, AND SCOTT PETERSON. 1993. *THEME EXPLORATION: A VOYAGE OF DISCOVERY.* PORTSMOUTH, NH: HEINEMANN.

WHITIN, DAVID J., HEIDI MILLS, AND TIMOTHY O'KEEFE. 1990. *LIVING AND LEARNING MATHEMATICS: STORIES AND STRATEGIES FOR SUPPORTING MATHEMATICAL LITERACY.* PORTSMOUTH, NH: HEINEMANN.

WHITIN, DAVID J., AND SANDRA WILDE. 1992. *READ ANY GOOD MATH LATELY? CHILDREN'S BOOKS FOR MATHEMATICAL LEARNING, K-6.* PORTSMOUTH, NH: HEINEMANN.

WIGGINTON, ELLIOT. 1985. *SOMETIMES A SHINING MOMENT: THE FOXFIRE EXPERIENCE.* GARDEN CITY, NY: ANCHOR BOOKS.

WILDE, SANDRA. 1990. "A PROPOSAL FOR A NEW SPELLING CURRICULUM." *THE ELEMENTARY SCHOOL JOURNAL* 90: 275–89.

———. 1991. *YOU KAN RED THIS! SPELLING AND PUNCTUATION FOR WHOLE LANGUAGE CLASSROOMS, K-6.* PORTSMOUTH, NH: HEINEMANN.

WORTMAN, BOB. 1994. TALK GIVEN AT THE NORTHEAST WHOLE LANGUAGE CONFERENCE. JOHNSON, VT. AUGUST.

YOLEN, JANE. 1992. "ON WRITING AND ILLUSTRATING *LETTING SWIFT RIVER GO.*" *BOOK LINKS: CONNECTING BOOKS, LIBRARIES, AND CLASSROOMS* 2(1), SEPTEMBER.